SKYLINES

A JOURNEY THROUGH 50 SKYLINES OF THE WORLD'S GREATEST CITIES

Yolanda Zappaterra
and Jan Fuscoe
Illustrations by Jenny Seddon

Aurum
Press

First published in Great Britain
2015 by Aurum Press Ltd
74–77 White Lion Street
Islington
London N1 9PF
www.aurumpress.co.uk

A catalogue record for this book is available from the British Library.

ISBN 978 1 78131 451 7

1 3 5 7 9 10 8 6 4 2
2015 2017 2019 2018 2016

Printed in China

Typeset in Trade Gothic and Odette. Design by Tim Peters (www.timpeters.co.uk)

This book is dedicated to our dads, Egidio and Frank, who inspired us to explore the world, and to learn from what we found.

With thanks to...

We're indebted to all those people who've shared their knowledge and passion for the cities and their attractions. For helping us develop the book's ideas, and keeping us going, our thanks go in particular to Steve Miller, Chris Collins, Anna Norman and Paul Murphy, and to our editor Melissa Smith. Finally, Jenny Seddon's beautiful illustrations were always an inspiration and a delight; thank you Jenny for making this book what it is.

Contents

Introduction

How do we understand our first impressions of a city? What is it we encounter that helps us make sense of where we are and what it means? We read a city from the first few glances of the shapes and structures we see. From the air as we fly in, or the road as we approach it from afar, or the sea as it looms up on the horizon, a city's shapes and structures are the things that tell us something about its age, its unique history and the personal stories that make it. They go to the very heart of a city, which is why they were our starting point for each of the 50 cities included in *Skylines*, and for each of those city's illustrated skylines.

What do we learn from a city's skyline and indeed, what does the perfect city skyline look like? Is it one that is immediately identifiable through a city's iconic structures? Is it one made up of a balance of old and new, tall and small, functional and aesthetic? Or is it something less tangible or definable? Within these pages, we explore this last idea, choosing what we believe to be the iconic buildings of a city, the ones that define it, and collating them into an imagined skyline that can act as a metaphor for each place.

Often spanning centuries, many of the structures we've chosen are not necessarily ones you would see now on the skyline, but they are those that have played – or in some cases, are likely to play – an important role in its physical development. Looking back, they are also often linked to its social or political history. Others reflect the way a city has evolved in step with technological advances. And some stand as testament to failed ideologies as well as rampantly successful ones.

In essence, each of the buildings combines to create what we hope is a compelling cityscape for anyone who's ever flown over a city and marvelled at its component parts; walked out of a train station to be faced with the whole glorious mess of humanity at its most vibrant; stood at the top of a skyscraper and thrilled at the beauty of the urban sprawl below; or even dared to imagine themselves redesigning what they see to make it work better for the 21st century.

For those who love cities, *Skylines* strips away the noise, the ephemera and the distractions to get to each one's beating heart: the key buildings, monuments, bridges and historical sites that define and shape it, spreading across the globe and drawing inspiration from six continents.

But this constructed visual panorama of a city is only half its story. The other half goes to the heart of the book: why we chose the buildings and cities we did. A city's architecture is not shaped just by famous buildings, but by its location, its climate, its housing, its recreational spaces, its planning, its geographical position, its natural features and, above all, by its history. It's these things we've tried to illuminate through the text accompanying each city, creating a contextual overview of each entry from its founding to the 21st century and beyond.

By using illustrations and words in this way, *Skylines* creates a lively mix of insight and evaluation, meaning and context, delivering a city overview that sums it up not just visually, but also historically and socially. In this way, we hope the core and true shape of each city is revealed, and offers a rare and unusual in-depth view and feel for the place.

Finally, perhaps the most important thing to explain is why we chose the cities we did. This isn't a book about the world's most important cities, its biggest, the most well known, the highest number of visitors, or most architecturally spectacular. There are already many excellent books that focus on some or all of those. Instead, we drew up a longlist from our own personal experience and interests, and then chose the 50 that offered the most fascinating, compelling stories, told under the themes of seaside cities, skyscraper cities, cultural cities, fortress cities, sacred cities and visionary cities. And, believing it would offer the widest range of locations and skylines, we strived to include a broad global mix; we've been enthralled by what we've found; differences of course, but also unexpected similarities, and influences that have travelled thousands of miles.

We hope that once you've read some of the following entries you'll decide that, while our selection of cities may seem arbitrary, their stories are anything but, and that you find them as enjoyable to read as we found them to write. Perhaps providing you with the inspiration to explore some of the less familiar locations yourself.

Illustration key:

Within the illustration pages of the skylines, below each building, is an entry for the location (L), the architect (A) and a fast fact (FF). These provide extra information about the cities at a glance as well as the key aspects of the building.

Cultural Capitals

Istanbul *

Delhi *

Beijing *

Paris

'I ought to be jealous of the tower. She is more famous than I am.'
Gustave Eiffel

No structure better represents a city than the **Eiffel Tower** does Paris… but it was never meant to last. It was built to commemorate the World Exhibition of 1889 which, in turn, was held to celebrate the centenary of the French Revolution of 1789. At the time it was higher than any skyscraper in the world and semiotician Roland Barthes wrote that it was the purest and most vacant of signs, enabling a visitor to 'read the text' of the city by making its structures visible; effectively 'every visitor… was forced to make structuralism without knowing it'. Today, with its new glass floor 57m (187ft) above ground, it's possible to see directly below as well as above and 360 degrees around the iron structure. Not everybody was as enamoured of the Tower however… Guy de Maupassant famously ate in the Tower's restaurant precisely because it was the only place where he didn't have to look at it.

Paris has long understood the importance of making a statement. Long before President Mitterrand's *Grands Projets*, Henry IV was keen to create a series of public buildings that would make Paris the true capital of his kingdom. Among them was the 17th-century Place Royale, now the **Place des Vosges** – the oldest square in Paris and a great example of royal planning. The square is surrounded by a series of houses with identical fronts of red brick with strips of stone over vaulted arcades standing on stone pillars. Important inhabitants included Cardinal Richelieu (No. 21), Alphonse Daudet (No. 8), Madame de Sévigné (No. 1 bis) and Victor Hugo (No. 6), who appeared on the 1959 five-franc banknote against a backdrop of his house – today No. 6 is a museum devoted to his memory.

Jean-Baptiste Colbert, as Superintendent of Buildings, ensured that Louis XIV's reputation would endure by commissioning innumerable churches, squares and triumphal arches, as well as bringing Bernini, architect to the Pope, to Paris to design the new east facade of the Louvre. That didn't go as planned as the two fell out over designs, but Colbert did preside over the exhibition of great works of art and extensively added to the royal collection.

Beginning life as a royal castle in 1202, the Louvre Palace was the seat of French power until 1682, when Louis XIV moved to his new palace in Versailles. Pierre Lescot designed the Renaissance palace and it has evolved architecturally over the centuries right up to I. M. Pei's glass **Louvre Pyramid** and the €100 million Department of Islamic Art.

Hugo's most famous work *The Hunchbank of Notre Dame* was partly written to raise awareness of the importance of Gothic architecture at a time when much of it was being torn down to be replaced by more modern buildings. The novel is centred around one of the finest examples of French

Gothic in the world – the 12th-century **Notre Dame Cathedral** – which is also thought to have been one of the first to use flying buttresses. As a symbol of power and inevitably corruption, the cathedral was desecrated during the French Revolution when it was rededicated to the Cult of Reason, and later the Cult of the Supreme Being.

Another representation of royalty to get its comeuppance was the Bastille – a 14th-century fortress built to protect Paris from the English during the Hundred Years War – considered one of the most important fortifications in late medieval Paris. It was later used as a prison for upper-class members of French society who offended the King, and on 14 July 1789 it was stormed and set alight – an action thought of as the flashpoint for the start of the French Revolution. Today nothing remains except the **July Column**, a memorial in the Place de la Bastille, but its image is still a potent symbol of Republic ideals.

The 19th-century **Arc de Triomphe** is one of the best examples of the Empire style. The neoclassical triumphal arch, built following Napoleon's greatest victory at Austerlitz, is situated at the centre of 12 radiating avenues. In 1989 the **Grande Arche de la Défense** – another of Mitterrand's *Grands Projets* – was built at the westernmost point of the Historical Axis of Paris as the 20th-century version of the Arc. Shaped like a cube, it's made of pre-stressed concrete and covered with glass and Carrara marble.

Before the First World War, Auguste Perret and his one-time employer Le Corbusier were the modernist names on every architect's lips. Perret combined his love of classic lines with reinforced concrete, and his own **Rue Franklin apartments**, with their highly glazed facades and non-structural partition walls, are perfect examples of his ability to bring classical architecture bang up to date.

In keeping with the tradition of building to keep your name alive, President Georges Pompidou commissioned the **Pompidou Centre** – a high-tech postmodern construction, designed by Renzo Piano, Richard Rogers and Gianfranco Franchini, that houses the National Museum of Modern Art. Nothing like this had been seen before: primary colour-coded tubes and pipes housed electric cables, air conditioning, water and elevators; and this 'inside-out' design has been repeated many times since.

The latest celebrated building is Frank Gehry's **Louis Vuitton Foundation**. The sleek building resembles a ship with glass sails and, in spite of its modernity, Gehry admits to being inspired by the past, by Romanesque and Gothic churches: 'I always felt that putting sculpture on the outside is kind of a French thing.'

Jean Nouvel's **Arab World Institute** – one of Mitterrand's most popular *Grands Projets* – is a highly original building featuring a glass-clad curtain wall behind which a metallic screen unfolds. Moving geometric motifs on the screen contain 240 photosensitive apertures that open and close to control the amount of heat and light coming into the building, and so create visual changes within the building itself. Nouvel's Philharmonie de Paris at Parc de la Villette is well under way and hotly anticipated…

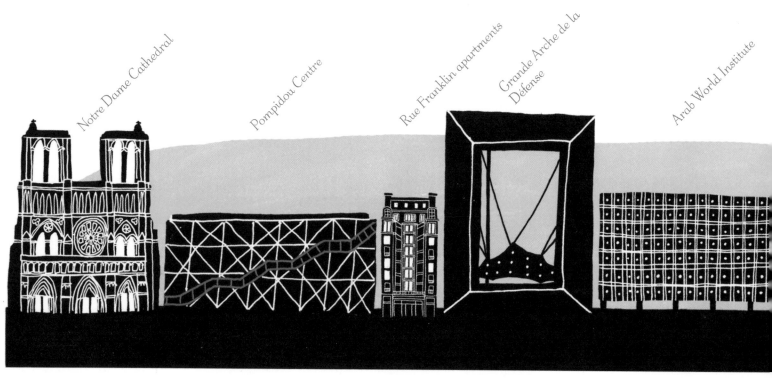

Notre Dame Cathedral

Pompidou Centre

Rue Franklin apartments

Grande Arche de la Défense

Arab World Institute

L: No. 6 Parvis Notre-Dame – Place Jean-Paul II, Place de la Bastille
A: Peter of Montereau, Jean-Baptiste-Antoine Lassus, Jean de Chelles, 1163–1345
FF: The Archaeological Crypt was created to protect historical ruins discovered during construction work. It contains detailed models of the architecture and under-floor heating installed during the Roman occupation.

L: Place Georges Pompidou
A: Renzo Piano, Richard Rogers and Gianfranco Franchini, 1971–7
FF: The pipes and ducts are colour-coded: blue for air, green for water, red for elevators and yellow for electricity.

L: No. 25 Rue Franklin
A: Auguste Perret, 1904
FF: Perret anticipated Le Corbusier's 'free plan' interior by making the partition walls non-structural so that their removal would create an open space.

L: 1 Parvis de la Défense
A: Johan Otto von Spreckelsen, 1989
FF: The roof houses a Computer Museum and a restaurant with views across Paris.

L: 1 Rue des Fosses
A: Jean Nouvel, 1987
FF: Big names in the Arab music world perform in the auditorium, and the roof terrace once offered fabulous views but closed in 2010 following elevator problems.

Louvre (including Pyramid)

Eiffel Tower

No. 6 Place des Vosges

July Column

Louis Vuitton Foundation

Arc de Triomphe

L: Rue Saint-Honoré
A: Pierre Lescot (Palace), 1546; I. M. Pei (Pyramid), 1989; Mario Bellini (Department of Islamic Art), 2012
FF: The museum continues to come under fire for refusing to return contested artwork stolen during the Nazis' sequestration.

L: Champ de Mars, 5 Avenue Anatole
A: Gustave Eiffel, 1889
FF: The addition of an aerial in 1957 means it is taller than the Chrysler Building by 5.2m (17ft).

L: No. 6 Place des Vosges
A: Baptiste Androuet du Cerceau, 1612
FF: The museum charts the life of Victor Hugo, one of France's best-loved writers.

L: Place de la Bastille
A: Jean-Antoine Alavoine and Joseph-Louis Duc, 1835–40
FF: The Bastille no longer exists but some of its stone foundation was relocated to the side of the Boulevard Henri IV.

L: Bois de Boulogne
A: Frank Gehry, 2006–14
FF: The 3,600 glass panels and 19,000 concrete panels that form the facade were moulded by robots.

L: Place Charles de Gaulle
A: Jean Chalgrin, Louis-Étienne Héricart de Thury, 1806–36
FF: Inside the monument, a permanent exhibition examines its symbolism over the past two centuries, oscillating between war and peace.

Mexico City

'Mexico is a country of architects. Architecture is one of the pillars of our culture and part of our daily life: every Mexican is an architect at heart.'

Ricardo Legorreta

If there is one adjective that sums up Mexico City, it is 'multi-layered'. Literally and metaphorically, this megametropolis of more than 21 million inhabitants is as deep as it is wide, with new civilisations piled on top of old ones and the whole lot piled shakily on a lake bed 2,250m (7,380ft) above sea level. At the city's core are some of the most arresting buildings in the Americas, giving way to some of its biggest shanty towns. It all combines to create a compelling mix featuring, thanks to the likes of homegrown talent such as architect Ricardo Legorreta, some world-class architecture and some clever town planning.

While Legorreta's comments may be an affectionate exaggeration, it is certainly true that the country has an unusual amount of architects – perhaps a centuries-old consequence of the influence of the Aztecs on the conquering Spanish in 1521. When Hernán Cortés arrived to find the astonishing pyramids and plazas of the Aztecs, built here from AD 1100, he promptly set about systematically demolishing their city of Tenochtitlan and building Christian edifices on top of it – literally, in the case of the area around the Plaza de la Constitución, commonly called the Zócalo. By building over things like the palace of Aztec king Montezuma, Cortés turned the buildings on and around the largest plaza in the pre-Conquest capital and the ceremonial and religious centre of Tenochtitlan into the centre of the new country, Nueva España.

Nowadays, the Zócalo is flanked by a range of historical structures, including the remains of the Aztec Templo Mayor pyramid, rediscovered by electricians laying cables in 1979, and the Zócalo's key attraction, the **Catedral Metropolitana**, sited atop the former sacred Aztec precinct and around the original church constructed by Cortés soon after the Spanish conquest of Tenochtitlan. Next door to it, the Sagrario Metropolitano is a fine example of mid-18th-century *churrigueresque* (Spanish Baroque) architecture, which is just one of the styles featured on the Cathedral.

Despite construction spanning 277 years, the cathedral's different styles combine to create a surprisingly harmonious blend, but it's a long way from being the city's most sacred site. That accolade goes to the **Basilica of Our Lady of Guadalupe**, the most important Catholic pilgrimage site on the continent and the home of the cloak of Juan Diego, which bears the image of the dark-skinned La Virgen Morena. The site is made up of two basilicas, an 18th-century Baroque church and, perpendicular to it, the far more arresting – and presumably unintentionally circus-like – circular building designed by Pedro Ramírez Vázquez, which houses the miraculous cloak. Vázquez's other claim to fame in the city is the equally arresting marble-clad Museum of Anthropology, whose iconic giant concrete canopy seems to defy engineering and gravity as it floats above the stately main courtyard on just one giant column.

As Legorreta's quote suggests, Mexicans accept – and even appreciate – buildings that would possibly be much more contentious elsewhere. One would expect them to feel proud of the beautiful **Palacio de Bellas Artes** opera house, with its spectacular murals by national heroes like Diego Rivera and Rufino Tamayo inside and its striking Art Nouveau facade that mixes Aztec motifs with winged angels and cherubs. But they're equally proud of the city's more challenging buildings, such as the gigantic concrete and glass Auditorio Nacional built in the 1950s and the determinedly modernist **Ciudad Universitaria (UNAM)**. Here the **Biblioteca Central**, with its monumental Juan O'Gorman mosaic depicting the country's scientific and cultural history, is the crowning glory of an impressive range of brutalist buildings and structures, including the 64 giant concrete triangles and lava bed that make up the striking Espacio Escultórico. What makes the collection so special is the pre-Hispanic influence visible in so many of the structures, and the use of innovative engineering and materials pioneered by the likes of Félix Candela, whose unusual **Church of la Medalla de la Virgen Milagrosa** (Church of the Miraculous Virgin) across the city in Navarte, offers a soaring yet airy take on traditional Gothic.

The church's bold geometry is a key theme of buildings in the city – as is the use of equally bold colour. Legorreta's five-star **Hotel Camino Real** in Polanco is a great case in point, its hot pinks, purples and copper orange contrasting with cool blues and bright yellow to create a lovely interplay that has made it popular with visiting celebrities for more than 40 years. Its fame is centred around its pink wall by sculptor Mathias Goeritz, who was also instrumental in developing – with Mexico's most celebrated architect, Luis Barragán, and painter Jesús Reyes Ferreira – the city's five

Torres de Satélite. This huge urban sculpture was conceived as a seven-piece set of coloured towers ranging in height from 30m to 200m (98ft to 656ft), but was eventually realised as five towers, to create an iconic structure that's undiminished by the rising number of tall competitors on the horizon. Of these, the 230m (755ft) Torre Mayor soars above the rest, but it's the two legs of the quirkier **Torre del Pantalón** (the 'Trousers Tower') that has won the hearts of city dwellers… although they're more bemused by its recent neighbour, two towers speared by a connecting bridge (together the towers are known as Conjunto Arcos Bosques). Still, neither is as loved as the **Torre Latinoamericana** downtown. Joining the long queue of Mexicans in the scraggy, deteriorating foyer of the scraggy, deteriorating communications tower waiting to be whisked up 183m (600ft) to the top, it's hard to imagine why it's so popular, until you learn that in its time the tower has successfully withstood two massive earthquakes that destroyed many buildings in Mexico City. Unsurprisingly, in a nation of architects, it's this fact that has made it a symbol of good luck and safety in a city built on very shaky ground. And there's nothing to suggest that the **Torre BBVA Bancomer**, due to be completed in 2015, will oust its popularity. What might though is a shiny newcomer that is truly enticing, both inside and out. The **Museo Soumaya** is an organically shaped delectable delight that houses the art collection of Carlos Slim Helú, the richest man in the world according to *Forbes* magazine. Its lead architect, Fernando Romero, has said its design reflects the organic forms growing out of the earth, and it certainly does that. Combined with its shimmering facade and the colours playing over the aluminium cladding, this is a building that must surely claim the heart of the architect in everyone – Mexican or not.

Basílica of Our Lady
of Guadalupe

Church of la Medalla de la
Virgen Milagrosa

Catedral Metropolitana

Museo Soumaya

Torre Latinoamericana

Torre BBVA
Bancomer

L: Plaza de les Américas
A: Pedro Ramírez Vázquez, 1987
FF: The basílica's circular design is meant
to symbolise the universality of God,
but has a more prosaic role too; it helps
distribute the building's weight evenly on
the very soft ground it's built on.

L: Ixcateopan y Matías Romero
A: Félix Candela, 1953–5
FF: The church committee responsible
for its building didn't realise the
church wasn't going to be a traditional
Gothic one until it was already under
construction.

L: Zócalo
A: Various, incl. Claudio de Arciniega and José Damián
Ortiz de Castro, 1525–1813
FF: De Arciniega drew inspiration for his original design
of the cathedral from Gothic cathedrals in Spain. It
includes 16 chapels each dedicated to a different saint
or saints, five naves and two bell towers.

L: Plaza Carso, Nuevo
Polanco
A: FR-EE/Fernando
Romero Enterprise,
2011
FF: The windowless
facade of the
museum is covered
with 16,000
hexagonal aluminum
panels, none of them
touching each other.

L: Eje Central Lázaro
Cardenas
A: Augusto H. Álvarez,
1956
FF: The tower stars
in a number of
films, including Baz
Luhrmann's *Romeo +
Juliet*, Alfonso Cuarón's
Sólo con tu pareja, and
Alejandro González
Iñárritu's *Amores Perros*.

L: Paseo de la Reforma
A: Legorogers (Rogers, Stirk
Harbour and Partners, and
Legorreta + Legorreta), 2015
FF: The 235m building
features 50 storeys above
ground and six below, with
sky gardens on every ninth
floor creating outdoor space.
At the time of writing, it
is the tallest building in
Mexico City.

Torre del Pantalón
(Conjunto Arcos
Bosques)

Biblioteca Central &
Ciudad Universitaria
(UNAM)

Torres de Satélite

Palacio de Bellas Artes

Hotel Camino Real

L: Paseo de Los Tamarindos, Santa Fe
A: Teodoro González de León, Francisco
Serrano, Carlos Tejeda, 1996–2008
FF: The heliport on top of the towers sits
at a lofty 2,560m (770ft) above sea level.

L: Av. Universidad 3000, Ciudad
Universitaria, Coyoacán
A: Juan O'Gorman (library) and
various others, inc. Gustavo
Saavedra and Juan Martínez de
Velasco, 1940s–1950s
FF: The 20+ buildings designed
by more than 60 architects that
make up the university campus
have provided the backdrop for a
range of surreal and sci-fi films,
including *Total Recall*.

L: Ciudad Satélite, Naucalpan
A: Luis Barragán and Mathias
Goeritz, 1958
FF: The towers were originally
meant to be painted in
different shades of orange,
but after some external
pressure were designed in red,
blue, yellow and white.

L: Av. Juárez, Centro Histórico
A: Adamo Boari and Federico Mariscal,
1934
FF: Conceived to mark the 1910
centenary of the Mexican War of
Independence, the Palacio was beset
by problems, including the Mexican
Revolution and subsidence, so wasn't
completed until 1934, explaining its Art
Nouveau exterior and Art Deco interior.

L: Calle Mariano Escobedo
A: Ricardo Legorreta, sculptural wall
by Matthias Goeritz, 1965
FF: Built for the Mexico City 1968
Olympics, the Camino Real's foyer
featured a sculpture by Alexander
Calder that was sold in 2003 by
Christie's New York for US $5,831,500.

Berlin

'Nobody had forgotten anything here. In Berlin, you had to wrestle with the past, you had to build on the ruins, inside them. It wasn't like America where we scraped the earth clean, thinking we could start again every time.'

Janet Fitch, *White Oleander*

All cities have their architectural ghosts. In Berlin, the ghosts still hold sway over the physical city, and resonate not just in the city's spirit of historic revival, but with millions of us around the world. The dark echoes of Germany's role in two world wars and its post-Second World War partition into democratic West and communist East exist in nearly all its 20th-century buildings and monuments, and perhaps no more so than one of its newest. The Denkmal für die Ermordeten Juden Europas (Memorial to the Murdered Jews of Europe), designed by architect Peter Eisenman and engineer Buro Happold as a memorial to the Jewish people killed during the Second World War, is best described as a vast sculpture made up of 2,711 concrete slabs and columns or 'stelae', arranged in a grid pattern on an uneven 19,000 sq m (62,336 sq ft) site. The stelae range in width, height and angle to create a disorientating effect that resembles nothing less than a medieval cemetery, with sunken and collapsed headstones and graves uprooted to a bleak sci-fi setting. In this, the memorial captures not just Berlin's more modern history but also aspects of its ancient one – such as the burning to death of 38 Jews in 1510.

But medieval Berlin was also an early site of some extraordinary architecture. The **Marienkirche**, built largely of granite in the 13th century and later clad in red brick, is one such rare example of medieval construction. And as with most sites in Berlin, it also has a place in more recent history, having been the site in 1989 of a civil rights sit-in by East Berlin citizens exploiting the fact that churches were some of the few buildings they could gather in without state permission from the Deutsche Demokratische Republik.

The Marienkirche is overlooked by Berlin's most iconic manifestation of the DDR – the **Berliner Fernsehturm**, or Berlin TV Tower. As the tallest structure in Germany, it's a spire of singular design inspired by a number of other designs (including Sputnik), and, as is often the case with towers, it divided opinion between those who loved or loathed it. Ranked among the latter group were those who saw it for what it was – a symbol of the DDR's strength, and something to be torn down as unceremoniously and joyfully as the Berlin Wall was in 1989. And yet, there it stands, and is likely to continue to stand, such is the warmth of feeling towards it 25 years after the fall of the DDR. Less controversial is the **Siegessäule Column**, the victory monument marking the last wars that Germany won; the Prussian campaigns against Denmark, Austria and France in the late 19th century. As designs go, the column nicknamed 'Goldelse' (Golden Lizzy) is as traditional as they come, and acts as a noble elder statesman counterpoint to the determinedly futuristic Fernsehturm, though had it not been for a strategic repositioning of it before the war and a British-American veto against destroying it after the war, it wouldn't be there at all.

The spot at which the Siegessäule stood, the Königsplatz (now the Platz der Republik), is dominated by another controversial Berlin icon – the **Reichstag**. From the very start, its 120-year history has been one of disagreement and turbulence, beginning with architect Paul Wallot's struggle to find a style that effectively symbolised the German national identity following the country's unification in 1884–94. Through fire damage and bombing it was barely used for most of the 20th century, but Norman Foster's post-reunification rebuilding has been a triumph, and the building is once again the home of Germany's parliament, the Bundestag. Foster's conception of the renovation as a 'dialogue between old and new', retaining old graffiti but adding modern touches like angled mirrors in the dome that reflect the workings of democracy below, is a delight, and in marked contrast to Berlin's other seat of democracy, the huge **Rotes Rathaus**. The 'red town hall' is literally that, its bright terracotta brickwork copied from the Marienkirche to create an elegant but imposing 19th-century edifice built in the style of the North Italian High Renaissance. Architect Hermann Friedrich Waesemann couldn't possibly have known how fitting the use of red bricks would be, giving the building an apt nickname for its role as East Berlin's town hall in communist times.

But if any one structure symbolised the city's – and country's – post-war partition of 1949, the **Brandenburg Gate** was surely it. As with so many of Berlin's structures, the gate, originally constructed as one of 18 city gates and as a triumphal arch for Prussia's capital city, has had a turbulent history since its 1791 construction, culminating perhaps with its being marooned in no man's land when the Berlin Wall was erected overnight in 1961. Since then it's been spruced up and makes a fittingly grand entrance to the Tiergarten park to its west and, to its east, the Unter den Linden, the boulevard lined with the lime trees it's named for. Today this area, Mitte, is greatly changed, but nearby are five cultural institutions that clearly descended from the age of enlightenment, beginning in the early 18th century with Frederick William, the Elector of Brandenburg, who made the city one of the most prominent, culturally vibrant and important cities in Europe.

The Altes, designed in the neoclassical Prussian tradition best exemplified by Karl-Friedrich Schinkel, along with the Pergamonmuseum, Alte Nationalgalerie, Neues Museum and Bode Museum, are all outstanding examples of 19th and early 20th-century architecture that house a world-class collection of works across the fine and applied arts, archaeology and architecture – unsurprisingly,

they were given UNESCO status in 1999. Equally arresting, though decidedly more challenging for traditionalists, is the **Kaiser Wilhelm Gedächtniskirche**, one of Berlin's best-known sights. The strangeness of the church's shape would be enough to make it remarkable, but taken together with the modern, mini-tower block belfry next door to it, it must surely qualify as one of Germany's strangest places of worship. Such a singular structure illustrates a willingness to embrace the new that can be seen through much of the city's 20th-century architecture, beginning with the 1933 **Olympiastadion**. Designed by brothers Walter and Werner March, it illustrates Hitler's understanding of the importance of propaganda more than any other building in Berlin. The head of state ordered its construction when the Nazis came to power in 1933, and in just two years the huge stadium with its iconic twin towers was ready for some of the city's most tumultuous scenes – including Jesse Owens' triumphant four gold medals in the Games. As an early form of brutalist architecture that was determinedly modern in both form and materials, the Olympiastadion shows the relationship between political power and modernism better than any other building in the city.

Post-war, and particularly post-reunification, Berlin has enjoyed an architectural renaissance of unparalleled vigour rooted in an early modernist ideal best exemplified in the elegant **Hansaviertel** complex of International Style buildings by Walter Gropius, Oscar Niemeyer, Alvar Aalto and Arne Jacobsen, constructed as part of the 1957 Interbau Exhibition for the 'city of tomorrow'. In the 21st century, the opaque glass box that is the Topographie des Terrors and Frank Gehry's DZ Bank are just two recent buildings that stand out of a fascinating crowd. But the last word in Berlin's skyline has to go to Daniel Libeskind's **Jüdisches Museum**. This troubling and disorientating building, in part based on an exploded Star of David, stands as a marker for so much that we associate with Berlin and Germany, but in its design and construction it looks forward as well as back, and as such acts as a beautifully fitting epitaph to the city, and Germany's, 20th-century history.

Olympiastadion

Hansaviertel

Reichstag

Berliner Fernsehturm

Marienkirche

L: Westend, Charlottenburg-Wilmersdorf
A: Walter and Werner March, 1933–6
FF: The capacity of the Olympiastadion was originally 110,000, now it's 74,000.

L: Between Großer Tiergarten park and the Spree
A: Various, incl. Walter Gropius, Alvar Aalto and Oscar Niemeyer, 1957–63
FF: The elevators servicing the nine-floor Walter Gropius apartment block stop only on the half-floors, so everyone has to take some stairs as well.

L: Platz der Republik 1
A: Paul Wallot, 1884–94
FF: The bronze letters of *Dem Deutschen Volke* (to the German People) were added in 1916 by Wilhelm II and cast from seized French cannons.

L: Panoramastraße 1a
A: Jörg Streitparth and Hermann Henselmann, 1969
FF: The tower is the tallest structure in Berlin and can be seen from almost anywhere in the city.

L: Karl-Liebknecht-Straße 8
A: Various, incl. Carl Gotthard Langhans, 1270, rebuilt 14th century, tower 1490
FF: The copper steeple replaced the wooden one in 1790 and was created by Carl Gotthard Langhans, best known for his design of the Brandenburg Gate.

Jüdisches Museum

Siegessäule Column

Brandenburg Gate

Rotes Rathaus

Kaiser Wilhelm Gedächtniskirche

L: Lindenstraße 9–4
A: Daniel Libeskind, 2001
FF: The first Jewish Museum was founded in 1933 but was closed by the Nazi regime.

L: Großer Stern
A: Johann Heinrich Stack, 1864–73
FF: The top of the Siegessäule has an observatory offering great views over Berlin.

L: Pariser Platz, at the end of Unter den Linden
A: Carl Gotthard Langhans, commissioned by Emperor Wilhelm II, 1778–91
FF: Napoleon removed the Quadriga statue on top of the gate and held it in Paris from 1806–14. On its return the whole statue was later turned around by the DDR so that its chariot faced west.

L: Rathausstraße
A: Hermann Friedrich Waesemann, 1861–7
FF: The building was modelled on the Old Town Hall of Toruń, now in Poland.

L: Breitscheidplatz
A: Franz Schwechten, 1891–5
FF: The church burned down after it was hit by an Allied bomb in 1943, leaving only the broken west tower.

Beijing

'The building is altogether so vast, so rich, and so beautiful, that no man on earth could design anything superior to it.'
Marco Polo's description of Kublai Khan's Summer Palace

The cityscape of Beijing is changing on an almost daily basis and, while some say that its architectural history is being demolished with it, this is nothing new. Kublai Khan, grandson of Mongol leader, Genghis, moved his court here in 1279 and, thanks to the myriad cultures and ethnic groups he ruled over, there was a great flowering of science and the creative arts, including architecture. His chief adviser, Liu Bingzhong, was responsible for the design and layout of the capital, and its palace – with 1,000 rooms, gold- and silver-covered walls and a dining hall that could accommodate 6,000 – was described by Marco Polo as 'the greatest palace that ever was'.

Most of Kublai's city was destroyed by the incoming Ming dynasty, though the rectangular shape, with a palace at the centre surrounded by temples and gardens, remains, along with the **White Dagoba Temple**, first built in 1096, and restored by Kublai's Nepalese architect in 1271.

The walled and moated **Forbidden City** is the largest palace complex in the world. It was the imperial palace from the Ming dynasty to the end of the Qing dynasty and Emperor Yongle commissioned young architect Kuai Xiang to create much of what can be seen today. Designed to emphasise his divine authority, buildings were orientated towards the south to 'channel the powers of the heavens' and symmetrical designs reflected balance, while the numbers of dragons, bridges, rooms (9,000 of a planned 9,999,

a particularly auspicious yang number), even roof ornaments, all had specific symbolism. Today, with the largest collection of preserved ancient wooden structures in the world, it's a UNESCO World Heritage Site.

Another of Yongle's great architectural feats is the Temple of Heaven, which, along with the Temples of the Sun, Moon and Earth, was a temple where sacrificial rites were performed at each winter solstice. The Temple of Heaven was built according to strict religious principles and the most impressive of its buildings is the **Hall of Prayer for Good Harvest**: three (another yang number) concentric circles of columns symbolise the four seasons, the 12 months and the 12 daily hours. In a remarkable feat of engineering, without the use of a single nail, they support three roof levels and a square brace representing the earth, a circular architrave symbolising heaven and a cupola decorated with dragons – Chinese symbols of good fortune.

There is no doubt that the egos behind the architecture have altered the physicality of the city. Take Mao Zedong's 'Ten Great Buildings' – built to celebrate ten years of the People's Republic. They were intended to represent modernism, communism and traditionalism. The National Museum and the Great Hall of the People were inspired by Soviet architecture, while those that recalled the pagoda style included Beijing railway station and the **Cultural Palace of Nationalities**. Ironically Mao saw no problem with tearing up the old city to make way for the new; Tiananmen Square, once a walkway from the Forbidden City to the Temple of Heaven, was expanded to become one of the largest squares in the world, flanked by the Great Hall of the People and the National Museum. The square takes its name from the highly ornate T'ai-ho Men, or Gate of Heavenly Peace, which was built during the Ming dynasty in 1420.

Deng Xiaoping's 'open-door' policies of the 1980s had mixed results (not least because of the Tiananmen Square protests) but by the 1990s a massive influx of foreign companies saw China gaining increased international interest. The 2008 Summer Olympic Games were an opportunity for China to show just how far the country had advanced, at least architecturally. Chinese artist Ai Weiwei, artistic consultant on the **National Stadium** and its bowl shape, was said to have been inspired by Chinese ceramics, while the structure of steel beams that hides the supports for a retractable roof, gave the stadium its 'bird's nest' appearance.

In spite of what sometimes appears to be wholesale destruction of the city's oldest buildings, some of the latest groundbreaking

constructions continue to nod to its rich cultural past, including the Olympic venues. While the National Stadium is in the shape of a circle, representing heaven, the cuboid shape of the **National Aquatics Centre** is said to represent the earth. The 'Water Cube' is also a technological wonder: with more than 100,000sq m (1.07 million sq ft) of ETFE foils – a lighter and more flexible alternative to glass – it's the largest, most complicated ETFE structure in the world. It's also sustainable: the cladding allows more light and heat to enter the building, resulting in a decrease in energy costs.

The latest swathe of buildings is continuing to push boundaries. Having pledged to 'kill the skyscraper', Rem Koolhaas's **CCTV Headquarters** recently won 'Best Tall Building Worldwide' from the Council on Tall Buildings and Urban Habitat, and Koolhaas himself considers the collaborative design, with Ole Scheeren, to be his best work. Some critics describe the breakaway anti-skyscraper structure – two connected and inverted 'L's – as 'the greatest work of architecture built in this century'.

Another modern low-rise wonder is Paul Andreu's **National Centre for Performing Arts**, a giant titanium egg set in the centre of an artificial lake next to Tiananmen Square. The ellipsoid shell is divided in two by a curved glass covering that allows light to flow through during the day and offers images of the interior at night.

One thing that all future new builds in Beijing should be concerned with is pollution. The problem isn't helped by the exponential rise in traffic and construction, but the recently opened **Parkview Green** looks like it might be part of a future solution. It's the first building to achieve platinum certification by the LEED (Leadership in Energy and Environmental Design) Green Building Rating System. The shopping centre comprises four separate buildings within a large pyramidal form of glass with ETFE pillows on a sloping roof. A buffer zone increases thermal insulation, so reducing energy consumption, with a shield limiting the need for air conditioning in summer and reducing heat loss in winter. Arup, the engineering firm behind the build, agrees: 'Its most significant long-term contribution is likely to be to the development of sustainable building design in one of the world's fastest-developing countries.'

Hall of Prayer for Good Harvest

National Stadium

White Dagoba Temple

Forbidden City

CCTV Headquarters

L: Yongdingmen Donji
A: Unknown, 1406–20, Ming dynasty
FF: Following a lightning strike in 1889 the original wooden building was burned down by fire. The current building was rebuilt several years later.

L: Olympic Green Chaoyang, Houhai
A: Herzog & de Meuron, 2008
FF: Now staging national and international sports events and concerts.

L: 171 Fuchengmennei Daiji
A: Araniko, 13th century
FF: Pollution has meant that the dagoba has had to be white washed, lest it become know as the Black Dagoba.

L: North of Tiananmen Square, Dongcheng
A: Kuai Xiang, 1407–20
FF: The famous Dragon Wall is a excellent example of pre-T'ang lead-glazed pottery.

L: N2 East 3rd Ring Road Middle, Chaoyang
A: Rem Koolhaas, Ole Scheeren, 2002
FF: Damaged by fire in 2009 shortly before completion, it took another three years for official construction to end.

L: 9 DongDaQiao Road,
Chaoyang District
A: Winston Shu, Principal of
Integrated Design Associates
(IDA), 2013
FF: Resident Hotel Eclat has the
largest collection of works by
Salvador Dali outside Europe.

L: 49 Fuxingmen Inner Street, Xicheng
A: Zhang Bo, 1959
FF: It contains a collection of cultural
relics of China's ethnic minorities
including arts and crafts, costumes
and musical instruments.

L: 42 West Chang'an Avenue, Xicheng
A: Paul Andreu, 2007
FF: The open space, water and trees,
were all designed to complement the
ancient buildings and the Great Hall of
the People nearby.

L: 11 Tianchen East Road, Chaoyang
A: PTW Architects, CSCEC, CCDI and Arup, 2008
FF: During the day the 'Water Cube' is a
translucent blue and at night LED lights make it
visually spectacular.

Delhi

'If there is a paradise on earth, it is this, it is this, it is this.'
Persian poet, Amir Khusrau's inscription on the wall of the Diwan-i-Khas in the Red Fort

A descendant of Genghis Khan, Babur, captured Delhi in 1526 and so began the Mughal Empire and a brilliant flourishing of Indo-Islamic art; though first off he reputedly built a pillar out of the heads of his decapitated enemies. More conventional architectural methods can be seen in the palace of the Mughal Emperors for 200 years, Shah Jahan's magnificent **Red Fort** complex, where the influence of Islam, India and Persia come together: the vaulted ceilings of the Chhatta Chowk (roofed arcade), with their geometric designs, are typical of Mughal architecture. The tracery work, such as the calligraphic inscriptions on the walls of the Diwan-i-Khas (Hall for Private Audiences), and the exquisite inlay work of coloured marbles known as *pietra dura*, are Persian features; projecting balconies (*chajjas*) and umbrella-shaped roof pavilions (*chhatris*) were adopted from Rajasthani architecture, and the curved roof is a Bengali style. Babur, who missed the gardens of Kabul, also introduced *charbagh* – four gardens intersected by gurgling water channels.

The fort also includes the superb Pearl Mosque commissioned by Shah Jahan's son, Aurangzeb. Constructed from white marble and surmounted with three domes that were once covered in gilded copper, the mosque has exterior walls that are symmetrical with the walls of the fort, while the inner walls were orientated to align with Mecca.

Delhi is not one city, but an amalgamation of many, each built in a different area and each with its own identity. The earliest was the city of Qila Rai Pithora established by the Mamluk sultans, the first Muslim dynasty. Their 12th-century Qutb complex, which includes India's earliest mosque, was built on the ruins of 27 temples and, though it's in ruins today, visitors can still admire the typically Islamic floral and geometric patterns, and corbelled (false) arches. The sandstone and marble **Qutb Minar** is considered to be one of the most perfect minarets ever built, and it's the tallest in India. It was built as a victory tower and signifies the start of Muslim rule in India.

Close to the Qutb Minar, and gateway to the Qutb complex, is the 14th-century **Alai Darwaza**, renowned for its ornamental facade and perfect proportions. 'Gateway' scarcely does it justice: the doorways, which are almost as high as the huge square building itself, were some of the first to utilise a 'true' arch, with a keystone (wedge-shaped block) and are beautifully embellished with geometric, floral and arabesque patterns, as well as a 'fringe' of lotus buds, typical of the Khilji period. Windows feature decorative *jaalis* (latticed screens) of carved stars and geometric shapes to diffuse harsh sunlight, as well as visually and audibly to connect two spaces while keeping them separate.

The architecture of the 15th-century Afghan Lodi dynasty, by comparison, has been described as 'prosaic' – instead of marble or sandstone, they used ordinary stone, but the use of coloured enamel tiles to decorate their **tombs** is distinctive, and domes, supported by either octagonal or sixteen-sided drums, are surrounded by *kangura* (crenellations), *guldastas* (spires) and *chajjas*.

Shah Jahan's last architectural wonder is the 17th-century **Jama Masjid**, India's largest mosque. It's situated on the top of a hill and so totally dominates the skyline. It was created by more than 5,000 workers, and is a vision of cusped arches, domes and richly carved *mihrabs* (Mecca-facing prayer niches), with precious stones originally used in much of the *pietra dura*. The two 40m (130ft) marble and sandstone minarets are five storeys high, each storey with its own balcony, and were once known as the 'shaking minarets' because of their movement; during the 1819 earthquake they lost half their height.

Architecture, mathematics and astronomy were all of great interest to the Maharaja Jai Singh of Jaipur, who oversaw the construction of the **Jantar Mantar** observatory in what is now New Delhi. The construction contained 13 architectural instruments including a 21m (70ft) high giant triangle that once acted as a sundial. Each of the instruments was used to predict the times and movements of the sun, moon and stars, but today are rendered inaccurate due to the large buildings that have grown up alongside them.

New Delhi was initially created to house the British governmental buildings and, in contrast to the narrow alleyways of the old city, it was developed with a European sensibility, with wide streets and open green spaces. Architects like Sir Edwin Landseer Lutyens and Sir Herbert Baker

tried to combine a Mughal past with colonial architecture. Typical is Lutyens's Viceroy's House (1912–31), neoclassical in design but paying homage to Mughal styling, with the addition of a dome and the use of red and yellow sandstone. Today it's known as the **Rashtrapati Bhavan** and is the official residence of the President of India.

Following independence there was a break with tradition. Some architects were influenced by the International Style and the likes of Walter Gropius. Habib Rahman was one such, renowned for creating buildings using reinforced concrete, with clean, simple lines, freestanding stairways and banks of horizontal windows and cantilevered porches. Others, like Ganesh Bhikaji Deolalikar, the first Indian to head up the Central Public Works Department, opted for an Indo-British style, imitating the lines of Lutyens and Baker, but adding the *chattris* and domes familiar in Mughal architecture. Raj Rewal, too, looks for a contemporary Indian identity while incorporating some traditional architectural forms. His **Parliament Library**, located next to Lutyens' Indian Parliament building, manages to harmonise with a colonial past while pointing to India's future. He used reinforced concrete as well as sandstone, created domes, but of glass, and utilised traditional techniques, such as handcrafted *jaalis*, to separate spaces.

A fusion of modern and traditional is certainly perfectly rendered in the **Bahá'í House of Worship**: made of concrete, the white marble-faced 'petals' make up a magnificent dome in the shape of a lotus blossom. Canadian architect Arthur Erickson described it as 'one of the most remarkable achievements of our time, proving that the drive and vision of spirit can achieve miracles'.

Jantar Mantar

Qutb Minar

Alai Darwaza

Bahá'í House of Worship

Rashtrapati Bhavan

L: Sansad Marg, Connaught
Place, New Delhi
A: Unknown, 1724
FF: There are Jantar Mantars
in several other locations,
including Jaipur and Varanasi.

L: Qila Rai
Pithora
A: Unknown,
12th century
FF: The Minar
is decorated
with intricate
carvings and
Koranic verses.

L: Qutb complex
A: Alauddin Khilji,
14th century
FF: The central arch, rising
to almost the height of the
building, is embellished
with geometric, arabesque
and floral patterns.

L: New Delhi
A: Fariborz Sahba, 1986
FF: All Bahá'í Houses of Worship
share certain architectural elements,
including its nine-sided circular shape.

L: New Delhi
A: Edwin Landseer Lutyens, 1929–31
FF: It's the third largest residence (for a head of
state) in the world after Rome's Quirinal Palace
and London's Buckingham Palace.

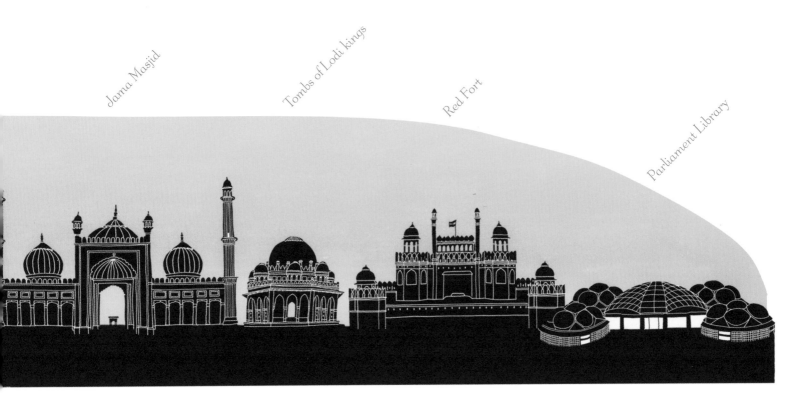

Jama Masjid

Tombs of Lodi kings

Red Fort

Parliament Library

L: Chandni Chowk, New Delhi
A: Unknown, 1656
FF: The mosque's courtyard can hold 25,000 devotees.

L: Lodi Gardens
A: Various, 15th–16th centuries
FF: The gardens surrounding some of the tombs were originally known as 'Lady Willingdon Park', having been landscaped by Lady Willingdon, wife of the Governor-General of India, Marquess of Willingdon in 1936. After independence, the park's name was changed to Lodi Gardens.

L: Netaji Subhash Marg, Chandni Chowk, Old Delhi
A: Unknown, 17th century
FF: The name comes from the red sandstone used as facing on the brick-built walls, but according to the Archaeological Survey of India, the Mughal lime plaster was originally white and possibly painted over by the British.

L: Gokul Nagar, Central Secretariat, New Delhi
A: Raj Rewal, 2002
FF: The building is much bigger than it appears as two of the four floors are underground.

Istanbul

'On cold winter mornings, when the sun suddenly falls on the Bosphorus and that faint vapour begins to rise from the surface, the hüzün is so dense that you can almost touch it, almost see it spread like a film over its people and its landscapes.'
Orhan Pamuk

In *Istanbul: Memories and the City*, the Nobel Prize-winning author and Istanbul resident Orhan Pamuk attempts to convey the *hüzün* that he feels imbues his home city. This state is best summed up as a willingness to embrace failure, indecision, defeat and introspection philosophically, with pride and even honour. A visitor to 21st-century Istanbul might have difficulty finding the *hüzün* that Pamuk describes, or simply decide that modern Turkey has finally shaken off the perceived sense of failure. Indeed, in the 21st century, the most prominent buildings on the city's skyline are as arrogantly brash as they come; when the Skyland towers are completed in 2016 they will soar to 284m (932ft) to become Turkey's tallest buildings, while RMJM architects's **Metropol Istanbul** is comprised of two towers around a central 250m (820ft) skyscraper that already dominate the skyline. J-Lo bagged an apartment here back in 2012, and doubtless others of the city's 17 million residents will rush to follow suit.

What they'll see, among the 21st-century megalopolis and the opulence of the Ottomans, is a broad array of buildings that stretch back 1,500 years, to Istanbul's most famous building, the **Hagia Sophia**. To enter it now, and gaze up at what was the largest dome in the world until the building of the Vatican a thousand years later, is to experience the interior space largely as it was in AD 537, when Emperor Justinian conceived it as a physical impression of the kingdom of God. Its spiritual ambitions clearly worked on one man, Mimar Sinan, who, a thousand years later would become regarded by many as the greatest Ottoman architect ever, and certainly one of the most prolific. Sinan was responsible for designing or overseeing the construction of 470 buildings in Istanbul.

The dimensions and refined classicism of the Hagia Sophia strongly influenced Mimar Sinan's mosque design. His **Süleymaniye Mosque**, the largest in the city and visible for miles around, sports the same large domed buildings supported by half-domes and a central soaring prayer room lit by 200 windows. And the Şehzade Mosque, built ten years earlier, uses the same square plan, central dome and colonnaded galleries to hide the supporting buttresses. But to say that Sinan was a copyist would be unfair; as chief royal architect to three sultans over 50 years, his mosques, palaces, colleges, bathhouses, bridges, schools, mausoleums and perhaps most of all, Selimiye Mosque in Edirne, all mark him out as a truly innovative and original architect, one who received the highest honour by being copied profusely; far afield, the Taj Mahal bears architectural concepts drawn from Sinan, and closer to home, Istanbul's second-best-known mosque, the **Sultan Ahmed (Blue) Mosque**, is as grand as they come, but is still little more than a copy of the Süleymaniye mosque.

While the huge dome and six minarets of the Blue Mosque are undoubtedly a glorious sight on Istanbul's skyline – no mean feat when religious buildings like the Beyazit Mosque and the 11th-century **St Saviour in Chora**, considered to be one of the most beautiful surviving examples of a Byzantine church, are also part of the skyline – there's a secular building that is even more impressive; the **Topkapi Palace**, whose diminutive height belies its vast scale. Yes, the Palace's Tower of Justice, while visible from the Bosphorus, is less prominent than others in the city, such as the 14th-century nine-storey Galata Tower, built by the Genoese as part of the defence wall surrounding their district of Galata, directly opposite. But the Topkapi Palace, the seat of the Ottoman Empire for more than three centuries, is massive, with four huge courtyards surrounded by numerous halls, extensive harem quarters and kitchens that could serve more than 6,000 meals a day.

The Topkapi marks the apotheosis of Ottoman extravagance, but also the decline that shaped the *hüzün* that Pamuk talks of. Reflecting the more confused but arguably more interesting social and political shifts in the city as the Ottomans' power waned, buildings that came after the Byzantine and Ottoman churches, mosques and palaces lacked the vision and grandeur of their predecessors, but made up for it with a wealth of fascinating styles and architectural flourishes, including the Turkish baroque style seen in the 18th-century Nuruosmaniye Mosque. Squat yet elegant and restrained, its Ottoman heritage is clearly visible among its more ostentatious interior decoration.

The later **Dolmabahçe Palace** however, bears little relationship to its forebear, the Topkapi. This new, modern residence of the Sultan clearly drew its influences of neoclassical, Baroque and rococo styles from the salons and palaces of new Europe rather than the medieval Ottoman palace it was built to replace. It featured many mod cons unseen outside Europe, including gas lighting and toilets imported from Britain, and later, electricity, a central heating system and even an elevator. The 20th century had arrived, and brought with it rail links to Europe via the Orient Express, which needed an appropriately stylish terminus. It got it in the **Sirkeci Station**, an elegant, stately yet accessible building that marries European and Oriental styles to offer a fascinating example of European Orientalism. In the years that followed, even Art Nouveau would take its place in the city; the Şeyh Zafir, a complex of library, tomb and fountain, is a small but striking monument designed in Art Nouveau style by Italian Raimondo D'Aronco, who designed a number of beautiful Art Nouveau buildings in the city's suburbs.

Istanbul's architects have always been at the forefront of design, and show no signs of slowing down. The construction of innovative mosques continues apace with the likes of the beautiful, modernist-influenced Sancaklar Mosque, a tower in the suburban neighbourhood of Büyükçekmece, and **Şakirin Mosque**, built by Hüsrev Tayla with interior design by Zeynep Fadillioglu, making it, it's believed, the first mosque to be designed by a woman. Fadillioglu is now on her third mosque, but in this one, in her home town, she has said she 'purposely placed the women's section in one of the most beautiful parts of the light-flooded dome'. Such an approach, while innovative, sees Fadillioglu eliptically referencing Istanbul's past; scholars like Pamuk will know well the female influence that has woven through the city's history; after all, how many cities can lay claim to an 80-year 'rule of women' – led by a Sultan's wife?

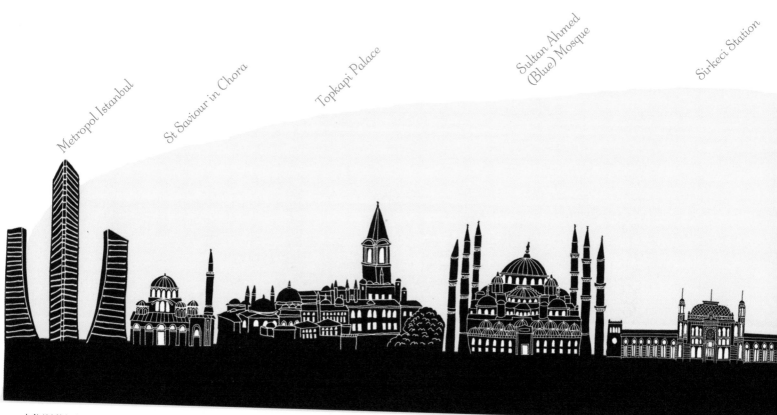

Metropol Istanbul

St Saviour in Chora

Topkapı Palace

Sultan Ahmed (Blue) Mosque

Sirkeci Station

L: Atatürk Mah., Atasehir Boulevard
A: RMJM Architects, 2016
FF: It's predicted the main tower will have 23 million visitors a year.

L: Kariye Camii Sokak, Edirnekapi
A: Various architects, 1077–1328
FF: Allow lots of time if you visit as the near-intact internal 14th century mosaics and frescoes are stunning.

L: Entrances off Soğukçesme Sokaği or through Gülhane Park
A: Mehmed the Conqueror, Mimar Sinan, Acem Ali, Davud Aga, Sarkis Balyan, 1459–1560s
FF: The distinctive conical roof replaces the 1846 original, and was built between 1965–7.

L: Sultanahmet Cami, 34122 Sultanahmet, Fatih
A: Sedefkar Mehmed Agha, 1616
FF: The tomb of Sultan Ahmed I is sited in the garden. He abandoned the practice of strangling undesirable heirs in favour of preferred sons.

L: Sirkeci Istasyonu Cad., Eminönü
A: August Jachmund, 1890
FF: The original Orient Express restaurant is located next to platform 1.

Şakirin Mosque

Hagia Sophia

Dolmabahçe
Palace

Süleymaniye
Mosque

L: Barbaros Mah., 34662
Üsküdar
A: Hüsrev Tayla and
Zeynep Fadillioglu, 2009
FF: The spectacular
chandelier's light bulbs
in the shape of raindrops
represent a prayer that
says Allah's light should
fall like rain.

L: Ayasofya Meydanı, Sultanahmet Fatih
A: Isidore of Miletus, Anthemius of Tralles,
AD 537
FF: Justinian is said to have used
mathematicians to help him with the
huge scale of Hagia Sophia. Until 1520 it
was the biggest cathedral in the world.

L: Dolmabahçe Caddesi Beşiktaş
A: Balyan family, Evanis Kalfa, 1856
FF: Beloved Turkish leader Atatürk died
here on 10 November 1938. A clock in the
room he died in permanently marks the
time of his death: 9.05am.

L: Süleymaniye Mah., 34116 Fatih
A: Isidore of Miletus, Anthemius of Tralles, AD 537
FF: Recent cleaning has shown that Sinan
experimented first with blue, before turning the
dominant colour of the dome red.

Washington DC

'Power tends to corrupt, and absolute power corrupts absolutely.'
John Dalberg-Acton, 1st Baron Acton, in a letter to Bishop Mandell Creighton,
from *Historical Essays and Studies*

British parliamentarian John Dalberg-Acton wrote his famous line about power 22 years after the end of the American Civil War. During that war, he'd been vociferous in his support of the Confederacy and its defence of states' rights and powers, certain that a victory for the north would result in a centralised government that would by its nature be tyrannical.

Power of course does often corrupt, but it also frequently has a fascinating and hugely productive relationship with culture, and nowhere in the modern world is this more true than in Washington DC. The National Mall alone has 14 galleries and museums on it, and in 1962 President John F. Kennedy's administration even set out Guiding Principles for Federal Architecture to encourage modern design that would 'reflect the dignity, enterprise, vigour and stability of the American national government' and 'embody the finest contemporary American architectural thought'.

For most international visitors, the first such encounter begins 26 miles outside the capital. Flying over the suburbs of Chantilly, Virginia into **Dulles International Airport**, the sight of Eero Saarinen's main terminal building, with its elliptical swooping roof, graceful structure and monumental colonnades, calls to mind nothing less than a bird's wing rendered in vast glass, steel and concrete – a deliberate reference to flight. It acts as a delightful introduction to the capital, and is a fine example of modernism in the city.

But two equals sit on the aforementioned National Mall, both of them bound up with Washington's position as the western world's most powerful city. The brutalist concrete cylinder that is the **Hirshhorn Museum** would be a standout building anywhere, but here on the Mall, among its neoclassical neighbours, it's eye-popping in its resolute modernity. Established in 1966 by an Act of Congress and housing the art collection of self-made Wall Street millionaire Joseph Hirshhorn in the 1970s, it is the acme of the American dream made real – especially as Hirshhorn was a child immigrant from Latvia.

Next door to the Hirshhorn, appropriately enough, lies a cathedral to another favourite American theme: the conquest of space. The **National Air and Space Museum** bears an exterior as blank as that of the Hirshhorn, made up of pink Tennessee marble cubes linked by glass, with artist Richard Lippold's thrusting sculpture outside it the only suggestion of what might lie inside.

Like the Hirshhorn, the museum is part of the Smithsonian Institution, many of whose 19 cultural institutions exist because they were endowed by politicians and businessmen possibly craving a degree of immortality, but also keen to give something back to their nation. The National Gallery of Art's West Building was a gift from Pittsburgh industrialist Andrew Mellon, his Irish father's immigrant status proving no barrier to the acquisition of wealth or power. Mellon went on to become the US Secretary of the Treasury from 1921 to 1932, and his son to create I. M. Pei's East Building in 1978 and endow the gallery with a staggering collection of art on his death in 1999.

The tradition of such philanthropic acts allied with Federal largesse continues to this day: in 2013, Oprah Winfrey donated $12 million to the **National Museum of African American History and Culture** (NMAAHC), which is due to open in 2016. Assuming approval without too much dilution by the various government agencies involved, including the National Capital Planning Commission, the building's glistening horizontal tiers, intended to act as a 'celebration crown' atop an elevated 'mound', according to lead designer David Adjaye, will make a stunning addition to the Mall. It has stiff competition – not least from the other modern buildings around it, including the hugely popular seven-storey **Newseum**. Designed in 2008 by James Polshek, the glass cube aims to physically represent the openness and transparency promoted by the Freedom Forum, the non-partisan foundation funding much of the museum.

Set against these newcomers are much-loved elder statesmen such as the **Smithsonian Castle**, the National Mall's oldest structure and a fetching red-brick building mixing late Romanesque with Gothic Revival. Its distinctive turrets and tower stand up surprisingly well to the competition around it, though is definitely overshadowed by the daddy of Washington's obelisks, the **Washington Monument**, just over 600m to its west and actually the the tallest obelisk in the world at a touch above 169m (555ft).

North of the Monument, the **White House**'s 132 rooms constitute what must surely be one of the world's most recognisable buildings – despite the neoclassical structure having little architectural merit, possibly because of its immediate expansion by Thomas Jefferson the year after its completion; near demolition by the British in 1814; and, over the decades, a hotch-potch addition of various porticoes, wings, offices and galleries, including the Oval Office, created by President William Howard Taft. Still, it's an appropriately Palladian edifice, and matched nicely to the west by the **US Capitol**, constructed in the same year as the White House and in the same

neoclassical style by, among others, the same architect, James Hoban. If both leave something to be desired in terms of architectural interest, there's plenty further afield in the city to engage and enthrall.

Philip Johnson's Kreeger Museum, designed in 1963 with Richard Foster, and Ludwig Mies van der Rohe's Martin Luther King Jr Memorial Library, opened in 1972, offer strong interpretations of the International Style, while Marcel Breuer's expressionist **Robert C. Weaver Federal Building** is, along with his Hubert H. Humphrey Building, one of the most significant modernist landmarks in the city. Combined, these two buildings, respectively housing the headquarters of the US Department of Housing and Urban Development and the US Department of Health and Human Services, physically embody the might of federal government, and offer an arresting flipside to the classical Romanesque architecture for a classical Roman Empire-based ideology of central government.

Just as interesting as these examples of 20th-century architecture is the work of German-born Adolf Cluss, who would go on to become one of Washington's most important architects – despite friendships with Karl Marx and Friedrich Engels and an early belief in the tenets of communism. After emigration in 1848 to the US, Cluss created most of the city's schools, including the **Charles Sumner School**, one of the first schools for black children in Washington DC, and the first teachers' college for black citizens in the city. With its stocky footprint dominated by an elegant front tower, the block is a fine example of late 19th-century Arts and Crafts styling, and deservedly won Cluss a design award at the 1873 Vienna Exposition. If any one building speaks of the more human side of Washington DC, it is possibly this one, miles away from the grandeur and might of central government, and still quietly going about its business as an educational archive for the District of Columbia Public Schools, a centre for community events and yes, this being Washington DC, a museum.

L: 1400 Constitution Avenue, NW
A: Freelon Adjaye Bond/ Smith Group, 2016
FF: The bronze and glass-panel facade, called the Corona, is a representation of traditional African architecture using modern materials.

L: 600 Independence Avenue SW
A: Gyo Obata, 1976
FF: The sculpture on the Jefferson Drive entrance of the museum is called Ad Astra, which means 'To the Stars' in Latin. It pierces three stars at its summit, and is by American artist Richard Lippold.

L: 1000 Jefferson Drive SW
A: James Renwick Jnr, 1855
FF: The Smithsonian's benefactor James Smithson, who bequeathed his fortune to the US government despite never having set foot in the US, is buried in the Castle.

L: 1 Saarinen Circle, Dulles, VA 20166
A: Eero Saarinen, 1958–62
FF: Saarinen's original departure gates consisted of luxury mobile lounges transporting passengers from the terminal to their plane.

L: East Capitol Street NE & First St SE
A: Benjamin Henry Latrobe, William Thornton, plus others, 1793–1800
FF: The Capitol's iron dome is painted each year with 600 gallons of paint to make it look like marble.

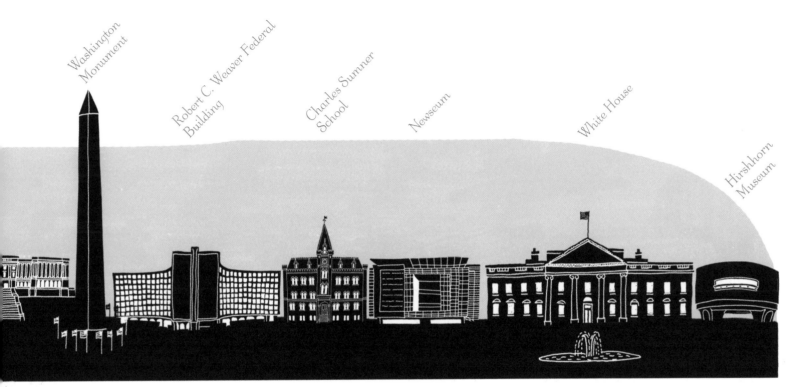

Washington Monument

Robert C. Weaver Federal Building

Charles Sumner School

Newseum

White House

Hirshhorn Museum

L: 2 15th Street NW
A: Robert Mills, 1848–84
FF: At 169m (555ft), the monument is popularly cited as the tallest free-standing masonry structure in the world – despite actually being the second tallest, after the chimney stack of the Anaconda Copper Mine near Butte, Montana.

L: 451 7th Street SW
A: Marcel Breuer & Herbert Beckhard, 1965–8
FF: In 1999, the HUD building was officially named to honour Dr Robert C. Weaver for his service as the first African American cabinet member.

L: 1201 17th Street NW
A: Adolf Cluss, 1872
FF: Cluss is represented on the National Mall by his Arts and Industries Building.

L: 555 Pennsylvania Avenue NW
A: James C. Duff, 1997
FF: The marble stone outside the museum is inscribed with the 45 words of the First Amendment.

L: 1600 Pennsylvania Avenue NW
A: James Hoban, 1792–1800
FF: Various presidents over the years have added the West Wing, the Oval Office, a zoo, a pool, a horseshoe-throwing lane and a jogging track.

L: 700 Independence Avenue SW
A: Gordon Bunshaft, 1969
FF: Founder Joseph Hirshhorn bought his first works of art aged 18: two etchings by German artist Albrecht Dürer for $150.

Budapest

Black Widow: *'It's like Budapest all over again.'*
Hawkeye: *'You and I remember Budapest very differently.'*
The Avengers (2012)

Two years after the Russians moved in to Budapest, they erected a **Freedom Statue** on Gellért Hill 'To the memory of the liberating Soviet heroes [erected by] the grateful Hungarian people [in] 1945'. Following their final departure in 1991, Budapest was keen to rid itself of any reminders of the occupation; location names, such as Lenin Boulevard and Marx Square, were changed, and the idealised statues of socialist workers, Lenin and Stalin, were consigned to an outdoor museum on the edge of the city known as **Memento Park**. Only the Freedom Statue remains, with a slightly altered inscription: 'To the memory of all those who sacrificed their lives for the independence, freedom, and prosperity of Hungary'.

Since that time, Budapest has been reclaiming its glorious fin-de-siècle past. The 'Paris of the East' boasts plenty of Hungarian Secession architecture – a mash-up of Art Nouveau and Transylvanian folk art – with architect Ödön Lechner as its best-known proponent. The first Secession work by Budapest's answer to Barcelona's Antoni Gaudí was the **Museum of Applied Arts**. Opened in 1896 for the Millennial Exhibition, it's the third oldest applied arts museum in the world, and the first in Europe to be constructed on a steel frame. Heavily influenced by the folk art of the Magyars, who came from the East, Lechner's work also features Hindu and Islamic designs, with pointed arches, and roof spires that resemble those on Indian temples. But perhaps the best example of Lechner's

work is the Former Royal Post Office Savings Bank – the roof is a fairy-tale riot of colourful Zsolnay tiles sourced from a factory in Pécs, where innovative firing techniques earned Vilmos Zsolnay the French Legion of Honour. Ceramic bees, ancient symbols of thrift, decorate exterior pillars and appear to be making their way towards the beehives at the corners of the building.

Another Art Deco landmark is the **Four Seasons Gresham Palace**, originally built as an office for the London-based Gresham Life Assurance Company. Architect Zsigmond Quittner employed skilled artisans to decorate the interior, among them Miksa Róth, who created the exquisite stained glass windows, while the exterior features fine ironwork, including peacock gates. During the Second World War the building fell into decline as it was used as a barracks by the Red Army. The following four decades of communist rule led to even further neglect. But, with the help of workers from the Zsolnay tile factory, who provided production details for the beautiful glazed tiles, the building was painstakingly restored and is now the luxurious five-star Four Seasons.

Róth's exquisite glass mosaics and windows are also found in the Gothic Revival **Parliament** where he uses the grotesque style that originated in the Renaissance period. The building is the seat of the National Assembly of Hungary and one of Europe's oldest legislative buildings. It was reputedly built over several years using 40 million bricks, half a million precious stones and 40 kg of gold, and also features a hexadecagonal (sixteen-sided) central hall and a Renaissance Revival dome.

The Four Seasons hotel overlooks the city's **Chain Bridge**, the brainchild of Count István Széchenyi, which was inaugurated in 1849. The story goes that, unable to cross the frozen Danube to attend his father's funeral, Anglophile Széchenyi had raised the funds to hire William Tierney Clark, designer of London's Hammersmith Bridge, to create a wrought iron and stone bridge to link residential Buda to industrial Pest. He was a visionary: the two towns have only been officially united, along with historic Óbuda, since 1873. Tierney's design, a larger version of his earlier Marlow Bridge that crosses the River Thames, was built in sections and shipped to Hungary for construction by Scottish engineer, Adam Clark.

Buda has been populated as far back as Neolithic times, probably thanks to the extant hot springs that the Romans were certainly grateful for, but it was the Ottoman Turks who turned bathing into an art form. The architecture of the **Király Baths**, dating back to the 16th century, is typical, with a low dome and octagonal pool that reveals an Iranian influence. The Turks had arrived in 1541 and made Buda their capital, converting the neo-Gothic **Matthias Church**, which dated back to the 13th century, into the Great Mosque. It was reconstructed in the 19th century by Frigyes Schulek, who returned the building to its original plan, adding diamond-patterned Zsolnay tiles and a gargoyled spire.

Schulek was also responsible for the castle-like **Fisherman's Bastion** – a viewing terrace overlooking the Danube that takes its name from the guild of fishermen that defended the city walls in the Middle Ages. The seven white stone towers, representing the seven Magyar tribes that settled the area in 896, are a flurry of neo-Gothic turrets, stairways and parapets.

In the mid-19th century Europe became fascinated with all things oriental, leading to what became known as the Moorish Revival – Islamic arches, minarets and pointed domes – that, surprisingly, became the preferred style for synagogues. The **Dohány Street Synagogue**, the largest synagogue in Europe, was designed by Ludwig Förster, who believed that, since there was no identifiable Jewish architecture, per se, it was appropriate to use 'architectural forms that have been used by oriental ethnic groups that are related to the Israelite people, and in particular the Arabs'. The onion domes are complemented by decorative brickwork that uses the city's heraldic colours of red, yellow and blue.

Today's architecture is even more eclectic, with one of the city's most popular contemporary buildings being the headquarters of **ING Bank**. The facade is made up of three sections of dazzling glass that appear to be held together with haphazardly tied stainless steel 'string'. Continuing a theme of 'wrapping', the HQ of Autoklub is another statement building; shaped like the letter 'A', the architects designed 'a ribbon that wraps around the office spaces on seven floors'.

If it goes ahead, Sou Fujimoto's House of Hungarian Music is likely to be a talking point for many a year. His proposition is a mushroom-shaped canopy over a glass-walled building that will have light wells running down through several floors. It will be located at the site of the old Hungexpo, along with the Hungarian Museum of Photography (FotoMuzeum Budapest) and Hungarian Museum of Architecture. Once again, it seems, Hungary is keener to look to its future than its past.

Király Baths

ING Bank HQ

Freedom Statue

Museum of Applied Arts

Dohány Street Synagogue

Four Seasons Gresham Palace

Fisherman's Bastion

L: Fő utca 84
A: Unknown, commissioned by Arszlan Pasha, 1565, finished by Sokoli Mustafa Pasha
FF: The entrance is decorated by three Turkish-style reliefs.

L: Dózsa György út 84/B H
A: Erick Van Egeraat, 2004
FF: The design was a contemporary solution that aimed to fit between the modernist building on one side and 19th-century villas on the other.

L: Gellért Hill
A: Zsigmond Kisfaludi Stróbl, 1947
FF: Two small statues at the base were relocated to Memento Park.

L: Üllői út 33–37
A: Ödön Lechner, 1896
FF: As well as a museum, it was built to house a library and school.

L: Dohány utca 2
A: Ludwig Förster, 1859
FF: The leaves of a weeping willow memorial feature the names of concentration camp victims.

L: Roosevelt tér 5–6
A: Zsigmond Quittner and József Vágó, 1907
FF: Before the Second World War it also functioned as a residence for visiting royalty, including the Romanov, Habsburg and Windsor families.

L: Castle Hill
A: Frigyes Schulek, 1902
FF: The bastion offers panoramic views of the Danube, Margaret Island, Pest and the Gellért Hill.

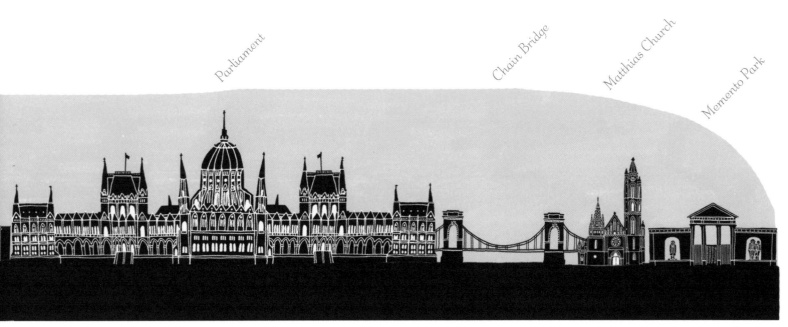

Chain Bridge

Matthias Church

Memento Park

L: Kossuth Lajos tér 1–3
A: Imre Steindl, 1904
FF: It is currently the largest building in Hungary and the highest building in Budapest.

L: Széchenyi Square to Clark Ádám Square
A: William Tierney Clark & Adam Clark, 1849
FF: Széchenyi, who commissioned the bridge, lost his mind and ended his life in an asylum. He never got to cross his own bridge.

L: Szentháromság tér 2
A: Frigyes Schulek, 1896
FF: During the summer the church hosts evening classical concerts.

L: Balatoni út–Szabadkai utca sarok
A: Ákos Eleöd, 1993
FF: The Barracks Theatre holds an exhibition about popular uprisings around Europe, along with recordings of communist leaders around the world.

Rome

'I found Rome built of bricks; I leave her clothed in marble.'
Augustus, founder of the Roman Empire

Is there another city in the world that reveals so much of its 2,800-year history through its buildings and monuments as Rome? In 700 BC, in a cave on the Palatine Hill, twins Romulus and Remus were suckled by a she-wolf and, following the death of Remus, Romulus gave his name to the city he went on to create here. So goes the myth at least, but there is evidence of occupation as far back as 800 BC, and in 2007 a cave was discovered that was believed to be the Lupercal (from *lupa*, Latin for she-wolf) and the site of the Lupercalia – an annual fertility festival in which young men, half-naked save for a goatskin, were known to thrash young virgins in the hope that this would improve fertility, reduce sterility and ease the pangs of childbirth.

From 500 BC, the Palatine was also the place where wealthy Romans built the extravagant villas that gave rise to the English word 'palace'. Romans adopted some of the techniques of the Etruscans and Greeks before them, but by the 1st century BC, they were using an early form of concrete known as *opus caementicium*. From the Palatine Hill, residents would have had a great view of the Forum below and, in spite of the constant raiding by those looking for building materials, plenty of the structures survive or have been restored, including the remains of the Greek-style **Temple of Vesta**, where Vestal Virgins tended the fire to ensure fertility.

The Appian Way, begun by Appius Claudius Caecus in 312 BC, stretched from the Forum to the port at Brindisi – over 500 miles. It's imprinted on most minds as the road along which 6,000 slaves involved in the Spartacus slave rebellion were crucified, but it is also lined with the tombs of Rome's ancient patrician families. Among the most impressive – an enormous rotunda with a castle behind – is the **Mausoleo di Cecilia Metella**, wife of Marcus Licinius Crassus, son of the more famous Marcus Crassus, political and financial patron of Julius Caesar.

In AD 64 Nero was rumoured to have played the lyre from the Palatine Hill while he watched Rome burn. This was never proven, but it is thought he blamed the Christians for the blaze and so began their first persecution, including their sacrifice in Vespasian's **Colosseum**. Ancient Rome's great amphitheatre was constructed using the Greek system of architectural order, with Doric columns to support the building, more elegant Ionic in the middle and topped by decorative Corinthian columns. During its 100-day inauguration in AD 75, 9,000 wild animals were slaughtered here, along with slaves, prisoners of war and Christian martyrs.

The **Pantheon**, dedicated to 'all the Gods' was commissioned by Marcus Agrippa in 27 BC and rebuilt by the Emperor Hadrian around

AD 126. Considered to be the best preserved of all Rome's temples, it's also an exceptional feat of engineering – the diameter of the dome is exactly equal to the height of the entire building and could accommodate a perfect sphere. This was made possible by covering a light interior of pumice and volcanic tufa with a thin layer of concrete. Archaeoastronomers believe that the Pantheon was designed so that the portico would flood with light at the equinox.

In the 3rd century Emperor Aurelian commissioned the building of a defensive wall around the city, and the largest, most important and best-preserved entrance is the **Porta San Sebastiano**. It has two arches surmounted by bow windows between two semi-cylindrical towers and today it houses the Museo delle Mura, detailing Roman construction methods, but during the Second World War it was the home of the Fascist Party secretary Ettore Muti.

In AD 313 Constantine declared an Edict of Toleration, and the following year ordered the building of **St Peter's Basilica**, a five-aisled classical basilica, on the site where Peter the apostle was believed to have been crucified 250 years earlier. It stood here until the 16th century, when Julius II commissioned its restoration by Donato Bramante, who opted for a Greek-cross plan, basing his dome on that of the Pantheon. After his death, Michelangelo took command and began, with Giacomo della Porta finishing, the spectacular dome – the largest ever created – that today still dominates the skyline. Much of the masonry for its construction was purloined from the Colosseum, and Gian Lorenzo Bernini's extraordinary Baroque canopy above the high altar was cast from bronze stolen from the Pantheon. The church was further altered with the creation of Bernini's colonnade that encloses the square.

Like the Roman emperors before him, fascist dictator Benito Mussolini had ambitious plans for Rome. Marcello Piacentini was commissioned to create a brand new district that would include numerous architectural exhibition spaces to rival Imperial and Papal Rome. The Esposizione Universale Roma (EUR) was never fully realised, but the extant **Palazzo della Civiltà del Lavoro** is a fine example of the *razionalismo* vision – fiercely modern but classically inspired, it is known as the square Colosseum.

Also credited with bringing the past and the future together was Pier Luigi Nervi. Known as the 'God of Concrete', Nervi drew upon the geometry-based domes of ancient Rome and used reinforced concrete to create the wonderfully modernist **Palazzetto dello Sport**. Designed by architect Annibale Vitellozzi, the elegant venue was built for Italy's 1960 summer Olympics and had a reinforced ribbed concrete shell braced by concrete flying buttresses. Made from 1,620 prefabricated concrete pieces, it was put together in just 40 days.

Striking out with seemingly little reference to the past, Zaha Hadid won the Stirling Prize for her **MAXXI** contemporary art museum – a building that has been described as being made 'entirely of swooshes'. And, while Massimiliano Fuksas's 'Cloud' project – a new conference centre in EUR – is currently on hold, Rem Koolhaas has grand plans for the ex-Mercati Generali. Koolhaas, who once described the Pantheon as 'the most beautiful building in the world', believes that architecture was at its best in antiquity. His plan for this enormous commercial site is likely to fuse the traditional fabric of the original building with a variety of contemporary, designed fabrics, bringing it bang up to date.

Temple of Vesta

MAXXI

Pantheon

Porta San Sebastiano

L: Via dei Fori Imperiali
A: Unknown, 7th century BC
FF: The building was completely demolished in 1549 and the section standing today was reconstructed in the 1930s.

L: Via Guido Reni 4a
A: Zaha Hadid, 2009
FF: The outdoor courtyard is used to display large-scale works of art.

L: Piazza della Rotonda
A: Apollodorus of Damascus, AD 126
FF: The Pantheon holds the tombs of the artist Raphael and several Italian kings.

L: Museo delle Mura, Via di Porta San Sebastiano
A: Unknown, AD 275
FF: On the right jamb of the gate there is a carved figure of the Archangel Michael killing a drake, with an inscription written in medieval Latin.

St Peter's Basilica

Palazzo della Civiltà del Lavoro

Colosseum

Mausoleo di Cecilia Metella

Palazzetto dello Sport

L: Vatican City
A: Donato Bramante, Antonio da Sangallo the Younger, Michelangelo, Jacopo Barozzi da Vignola, Giacomo della Porta, Carlo Maderno, Gian Lorenzo Bernini, 1506–1626
FF: St Peter is believed to be buried in the Necropolis, which lies under the Vatican grottoes.

L: Quadrato della Concordia
A: Giovanni Guerrini, Ernesto Bruno Lapadula and Mario Romano, 1943
FF: From 2015, luxury fashion label Fendi will house its headquarters here.

L: Piazza del Colosseo
A: Vespasian, AD 70
FF: When it was built the Colosseum was clad in marble with 160 larger-than-life statues in many colours standing within the arches on the upper floors.

L: Via Appia Antica 125–127
A: Unknown, 1st century BC
FF: The particular bull heads and garlands on the upper section of the rotunda have dated the creation of the monument.

L: Piazza Apollodoro, 10
A: Annibale Vitellozzi, Pier Luigi Nervi, 1957
FF: Today the arena now hosts volleyball matches.

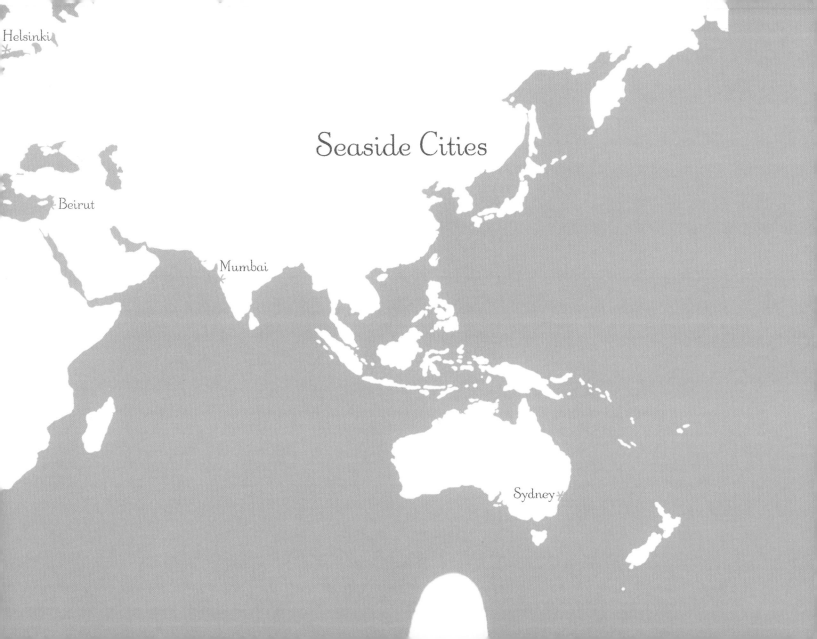

Seaside Cities

Helsinki

Beirut

Mumbai

Sydney

Cape Town

'During the many years of incarceration on Robben Island, we often looked across Table Bay at the magnificent silhouette of Table Mountain. To us on Robben Island, Table Mountain was a beacon of hope. It represented the mainland to which we knew we would one day return.'

Nelson Mandela, 1998

It's one of the most vibrant and cosmopolitan cities in the world, but the most dramatic feature of Cape Town's skyline is not man-made. The entirely natural, flat-topped **Table Mountain**, which rises regally to a lofty 1,086m (3,563ft) above the sea is possibly 600 million years old, six times older than the Himalayas, the oldest rock in the world and one of the seven natural wonders of the world. It's a stunning backdrop to a waterfront city that has been attracting visitors, friendly and otherwise, for over 350 years, and telling a story of an empire through the architecture of its colonisers.

At the southernmost tip of Africa, lying between two oceans and with 150km (93 miles) of pristine sandy beaches, Cape Town is simply spectacular. Portuguese seafarer Bartolomeu Dias described it as the 'Cape of Good Hope' in 1488, and 100 years later Sir Francis Drake called it 'the most stately thing and the fairest cape we saw in the whole circumference of the earth'. But it was its physical situation, rather than its beauty, that first attracted settlers. The Dutch East India Company set up a trading post in 1652 and the town began to take physical shape. Though much of the distinctive Dutch colonial architecture was destroyed by developers during the 1960s, bustling Long Street, which seems to stretch from the sea to the base of the mountain, is a mix of Victorian and Cape Dutch, with its wrought iron balconies and ornate gabled roofs. Nearby, the 17th-century **Castle of Good Hope** – the oldest building in South Africa, built to protect the interests of the Dutch East India Company – is an excellent example of a star-shaped fort and now houses a military museum.

The Dutch colonialists quickly began a vigorous campaign to enslave the indigenous population, as well as using slaves brought in from other parts of Africa and Asia. A '**Slave Lodge**' was built in 1679 where thousands of slaves were held during its time. It also gained a reputation as the Cape's biggest brothel, before becoming the Supreme Court. Today it's a museum. Some of the slaves' descendants created their own architectural style, which can best be found in the Bo-Kaap area; steep and narrow streets full of brightly painted houses featuring a mix of Cape Georgian and Cape Dutch styles and, reflecting the predominant religion of the area, interspersed with many beautiful mosques, including the **Auwal Mosque**, thought to have been in use since 1798.

But it was the discovery of diamonds in 1867 that brought some of the greatest changes to the Cape's skyline. By the 1870s the country was producing 95 per cent of the world's diamonds, securing the fortune and career of English-born Cecil John Rhodes. The successful mining magnate went on to become Prime Minister of the Cape, but Rhodes was a controversial figure who constructed the very first segregation law that led to the creation of the apartheid system. He is commemorated by the huge hillside **Rhodes Memorial** that overlooks the city, including the imposing Victorian bronze sculpture 'Physical Energy', with Doric columns and eight lions modelled on those surrounding Nelson's Column in London, was designed to impress. Following his death, much of the land he owned was returned to the nation, including Kirstenbosch, one of the most impressive botanical gardens in the world.

During the 'Scramble for Africa', Rhodes and his fellow British imperialists had been keen to promote their own architectural style. Lord Charles Somerset, Cape Governor, made his mark by restyling the 17th-century Governor's Building, the **Tuynhuys**, with a more fashionable Regency look. It was on the steps of the Tuynhuys that F. W. de Klerk announced that South Africa had finally 'closed the book on apartheid'.

The shameful era of apartheid is best encapsulated by Robben Island, where Nelson Mandela, leader of the African National Congress, spent 18 of his 27 years of imprisonment. The island's prison, in use since the 17th century, was variously a hospital for the insane, lepers and other socially unacceptable groups, and a military base. Today the entire island is a UNESCO World Heritage Site, and its

turreted **Anglican Church**, built by prisoners in 1841, is an early example of Cape Gothic style. Robben Island and Table Mountain are the only two World Heritage Sites that are visible from each other.

Mandela's election as President of South Africa ushered in a period of reconciliation, regeneration and renewal. No longer a pariah, the country hosted the 2010 FIFA World Cup and its new **Cape Town Stadium** was built to encapsulate the optimism of the country.

When Mandela was finally released, he made his speech from the balcony of the neoclassical **City Hall**. Built in 1905, it was designed in Renaissance style and features a 61m (200ft) tower with 39 bells, and now it houses the Cape Town Municipal Library.

Today the V&A Waterfront, between Robben Island and Table Mountain, is the city's most popular symbol of success: the reclaimed harbour area is home to hundreds of restaurants, shops and entertainment complexes, with a backdrop of sea and mountain views. As Capetonians move further away from their troubled past, and relax at spots like this and Camps Bay – the beautiful beachfront below the Twelve Apostles mountain range – it's perhaps fitting that the ambitious project to convert the Waterfront's now-derelict grain silos into a contemporary art museum will be completed this year by Thomas Heatherwick, one of the world's most visionary designers.

Anglican Church

Auwal Mosque

Rhodes Memorial

Castle of Good Hope

Table Mountain

L: Robben Island
A: Unknown, 1841
FF: The church is now a multi-denominational place of worship for the island's residents.

L: Dorp Street
A: Unknown, 1798
FF: The first mosque in South Africa was built on land belonging to the ex-slave, Coridon van Ceylon. The original building collapsed in the 1930s and only two of its walls remain.

L: Rhodes Memorial Street
A: Sir Francis Macey and Sir Herbert Baker, 1912
FF: The 49 steps up to the monument represent each year of Rhodes' life. There is a tea room behind the memorial.

L: Buitenkant Street
A: Louis Michel Thibault, 1666–79 (rebuilt in its current form between 1786 and 1790)
FF: Today the castle is a military museum.

L: Cape Point
A: N/A
FF: The mountain has an unusually rich biodiversity, including the Cape fynbos (shrubland). Take the cable car to the top for the best views in Africa.

L: St Johns Street
A: Unknown, 1674, Josephus Jones, 1790 (redesigned in 1824 and 1967)
FF: The nearby parliament buildings offer guided tours as well as tickets to sit in the public gallery during assemblies.

L: Wale Street
A: Unknown, 1679
FF: The upper galleries are open to the public, exhibiting ceramics, silverware and Egyptology collections, but no history of South Africa's slave trade.

L: City Street
A: Henry Austin Reid and Frederick George Green, 1905
FF: Messrs Norman and Beard of London and Norwich built the organ to the specifications of Sir George Martin, organist of London's St Paul's Cathedral. The honey-coloured oolitic limestone was imported from Bath in England.

L: Fritz Sonnenberg Road
A: GMP Architects, Louis Karol Architects, Point Architects, 2009
FF: The construction costs were £415 million and the stadium capacity is 55,000. It is surrounded by a 60-hectare urban park.

Rio de Janeiro

'Her name is Rio and she dances on the sand, just like that river twisting through a dusty land.'
Duran Duran, *Rio*

Football, favelas, Carnival, Christianity, shanty towns and soap opera: those endless beaches stretching out under a glittering sky and the gaze of **Christ the Redeemer**. Rio is a city of contrasts – hardly surprising, considering it's had more drama than any *telenovela*; from conquistadores and colonialism, through slavery, gold rushes and republicanism, to dictatorship, boom and busts, drugs and endemic violence. Yet the *Carioca* know how to party; even the drug gangs or *traficantes* have been known to cordon off streets, turning the favela into an enormous open-air nightclub with loudspeakers belting out *baile funk proibido*, drugs being sold on every corner and dancing until dawn. And that location really helps...

Overlooking the good, the bad and the ugly is Rio's iconic statue of Christ the Redeemer. Built on a 710m (2,329ft) peak known as Corcovado ('hunchback') in the forested hills behind the city, the Art Deco mosaicked Christ appears to open his arms to enfold everything below: from luxury high-rises to sprawling favelas, and golden beaches stretching along the endless Atlantic Ocean. The idea for a city statue was first mooted in the mid-1850s but it wasn't until the 1920s when the Catholic Church, keen to encourage the city's population back to God, raised donations in support of it. Its statistics are impressive; it needed to be huge so that it could be seen from the city centre 4km (2.4 miles) away, and strong enough to support a head weighing 30 tons and hands weighing 8 tons each. Heitor Da Silva Costa's original design showed Christ holding a large cross and a celestial globe, but

it was thought to look like 'Christ with a ball' and the idea was thrown out. Oh the irony, for a city with another religion… football.

Surrounded by mountains and tropical forests with beaches – 90km of them – Rio is naturally one of the world's most beautiful cities and in 2012 UNESCO awarded it World Heritage status for its iconic landscape and setting. When the Portuguese first arrived at Guanabara Bay in January 1565, believing the bay to be an estuary, they named it 'January River' and in 1763, following the discovery of gold and diamonds, the colonial administration moved their capital to Rio, where it remained until 1960. The governors resided in the Baroque **Paço Imperial** (Imperial Palace), designed in typical Portuguese style, until 1808 when, following Napoleon's invasion of Portugal, it became the royal residence of King John VI. The palace remained one of the main political centres of Brazil for nearly 150 years until 1889, when it became the central Mail Office. Today it's a cultural centre.

The city was surrounded by swamps where the water quality was poor, so fresh water was transported from the Carioca River via an impressive example of colonial architecture and engineering. The **Arcos da Lapa** was built in the middle of the 18th century and, between the hills of Santa Teresa and Santo Antônio, it stretches 270m (886ft) with two storeys of 42 enormous arches rising to a height of 17.6m (58ft). Since it was decommissioned at the end of the 19th century, it has served as a bridge for a popular tram that connects the city centre with the Santa Teresa neighbourhood.

Another piece of engineering to radically change the future of the city was the opening of the Túnel Velho in 1892, connecting the tiny fishing village of Copacabana with the rest of the city. The 4km beach area soon became a playground for the rich and famous, and the **Copacabana Palace Hotel**, facing the sea, hosted the likes of Marilyn Monroe, Brigitte Bardot, Gina Lollobrigida and Frank Sinatra. The neoclassical hotel, designed by French architect Joseph Gire, was inspired by hotels on the French Riviera and featured in the 1933 film *Flying Down to Rio*, which did nothing to dint its popularity. But it was Antônio Carlos Jobim's bossa nova hit *The Girl from Ipanema*, about a tall, tanned, young and lovely local girl walking along the beach down to the sea – the second most recorded song of all time – that really alerted the world to the fact that Rio's beaches were the place to see and be seen.

In the early 20th century, there was a push to move from the 'old' conservative post-colonial architecture to a new modernist style. One of the leaders of the left-leaning Brazilian modernists, Lúcio Costa, along with Oscar Niemeyer, called on Le Corbusier to consult upon the **Gustavo Capanema Palace**, considered by some to be one of the most influential buildings of the 20th century, and certainly one of the finest examples of Brazilian 1930s modernist architecture. It stands on 12m (39ft) pilings and has an internal concrete frame that supports two sides made entirely of glass. The blue and white *azulejo* tiled murals reference Portuguese colonial tradition, while the Le Corbusier-designed adjustable shades on the windows, to combat the effects of the sun, were a world first.

Affonso Eduardo Reidy was part of the architectural team that worked on the Gustavo Capanema Palace, and his own **Museum of Modern Art** is another modernist landmark, with dramatic slanted concrete pillars and aluminium shutters to maximise light entering the building during the winter. It is situated in Flamengo Park, created under the direction of modernist landscape designer and artist Roberto Burle Marx.

Across Guanabara Bay lies Niterói, blessed with its own spectacular, but quieter beaches, and the extraordinary visual landmark of the **Niterói Contemporary Art Museum**. The futuristic cultural centre rises up from a reflecting pool 'like a flower', in the words of its architect, Oscar Niemeyer. Its narrow cylindrical base, a mere 9m (29ft) wide, gives the impression that the museum is hovering, like a UFO, over the bay.

The Porto Maravilha dock area of Rio is being revitalised with projects like the **Museu de Arte do Rio** (MAR), an impressive structure that combines old and new architecture with a wave-like roof, reminiscent of the sea, joining the old colonial building with the new galleries. It sits close to the Cais do Valongo (Valongo Quays), an African heritage site, where roughly one million slaves are thought to have arrived in Brazil.

The 20th World Cup was held here in 2014 and seven new venues were built. The **Maracanã Stadium**, built for the 1950 World Cup, was updated and is the largest in the world. It also holds the record for the largest attendance – almost 200,000 saw Uruguay beat Brazil in 1950 – and it's where Pelé scored his 1,000th goal.

Rio's redevelopment of the port area continues with Spanish architect Santiago Calatrava's forward-thinking **Museum of Tomorrow**. The focus will be on science and sustainability, exploring how to live in harmony with the environment. Calatrava is inspired by the natural landscape and the two-storey eco-friendly museum, with photovoltaic panels protruding, like fins or sails, from a steel roof, will appear to float out into the bay – site of the sailing events of the 2016 summer Olympics.

Niterói Contemporary Art Museum

Paço Imperial

Museu de Arte do Rio

Museum of Tomorrow

Christ the Redeemer

L: Mirante da Boa Viagem, Niterói
A: Oscar Niemeyer, 1996
FF: In the documentary *Oscar Niemeyer, an Architect Committed to his Century*, Niemeyer is seen flying over Rio in a UFO which then lands on the site.

L: Praça XV
A: José Fernandes Pinto Alpoim, 1738
FF: The Baroque portal is made from Portuguese marble.

L: Praça Mauá, 5, Centro
A: Bernardes & Jacobsen, 2013
FF: On the nearby Valongo Quays, around one million slaves are thought to have arrived in Brazil.

L: Pier Mauá
A: Santiago Calatrava, 2015/6
FF: The water of the Guanabara Bay will be used in a heat exchange to cool the building.

L: Corcovado
A: Heitor da Silva Costa, Paul Landowski, Gheorghe Leonida, 1931
FF: There are lightning rods located in the statue's head and arms as tropical storms have resulted in the statue being hit several times over the years.

Arcos da Lapa

Gustavo Capanema Palace

Museum of Modern Art

Copacabana Palace Hotel

Maracanã Stadium

L: Santa Teresa–Rio
A: José Fernandes Pinto Alpoim, 1750
FF: At the time of writing the tramway had been suspended owing to an accident in 2011 that killed 11 people.

L: Rua da Imprensa, 16
A: Lucio Costa, Le Corbusier, 1943
FF: The modernist tropical gardens were laid out by the landscape architect Roberto Burle Marx.

L: Avenida Infante Dom Henrique, 85, Parque do Flamengo
A: Affonso Eduardo Reidy, 1955
FF: The on-site restaurant, Laguiole, serves a dessert that replicates the museum's architecture.

L: Avenida Atlântica 1702, Copacabana
A: Joseph Gire, 1923
FF: Roberto Burle Marx's stunning black-and-white mosaic promenade stretches the entire length of the beach.

L: Avenida Presidente Castelo Branco
A: Oscar Valdetaro, Pedro Paulo B. Bastos, Orlando Azevedo, Antônio Dias Carneiro, 1950
FF: By Gate 18 the Museu do Futebol has plenty of footballing highlights.

Vancouver

'If Paris is a city of monuments, and if Tokyo is a city of small beautiful moments, Vancouver is a city of scenery.'
Douglas Coupland, *City of Glass*

By the beginning of the 1990s, Vancouver's steel-and-glass aesthetic led Douglas Coupland to describe his hometown as a 'City of Glass' – a skyline of 'see-throughs', a 'voyeur's paradise', 'large glass totems that say "F-you"' to the city's inhabitants. Occasionally this has caused tension between architects and city planners, as happened with **One Wall Centre**, winner of the Emporis 'Best Skyscraper of the Year' award in 2001. For seven years the narrow, elliptical building was the tallest skyscraper in Vancouver and renowned for its two-toned glass exterior: dark reflective glass on the lower levels and lighter on the upper floors, appearing to blend with the sky. Controversially, that was not the architects' original intent but at the insistence of the city planners, who thought that dark glass all the way up would dominate the skyline. More than a decade later it looks as though the architects will get the glass they originally wanted, and the occupants will be happy as the darker glass will probably result in a 40 per cent drop in energy costs.

Still in Downtown, the impressive **Jameson House** – a high-spec residential tower – was Foster + Partners' first North American project: distinctive curved glass towers rise above two preserved Art Deco buildings and its floor-to-ceiling glass windows offer spectacular views over the city. Controversially, they might also have overlooked the new Swiss Real office building that had been given the go-ahead, highlighting the downside of allowing residential properties into the commercial district.

Surrounded by sea and bordered by a wilderness of woods and mountains, Vancouver is regularly voted 'World's best city', but back in the 19th century it was the ready supply of wood, and water with which to process and move it, that attracted settlers. 'Gastown' grew up around a sawmill in 1867 and, when the mill was slated for demolition, the **Old Hastings Mill Store** – the only survivor of the 19th-century Great Fire of Vancouver – was taken down and moved, by barge, to Point Grey.

In the 1940s the influence of European modernism and an admiration for Japanese open-plan design came together in what became known as the West Coast Style. In the 1949 'Design for Living' exhibition, one of its pioneers, Ned Pratt, cited five principles of the style they espoused, which included the extensive use of natural materials, especially wood, and glass to allow the visual integration of the house into its surrounding landscape – in other words, 'don't fight nature, use it to your advantage'. Their buildings were modest in size as well as budget and, after the Second World War, such sentiments chimed well with the need for austerity, and a desire for pared-back architecture. Fellow modernist Arthur Erickson advanced the West Coast Style with his monolithic **MacMillan Bloedel Building**. Believing concrete to be the new marble, he used poured-in-place load-bearing concrete instead of the usual curtain-wall construction, giving rise to the building being nicknamed the 'concrete waffle'.

By the 1970s the age of the skyscraper was in full swing. The boxy

Harbour Centre with its distinctive flying saucer top can be seen from pretty much everywhere in Vancouver and, thanks to a 30m (100ft) pylon, it's one of the tallest buildings in Vancouver. The city had been on the verge of building a contender for the 'tallest skyscraper' record, but the plan was scrapped and Erickson was brought in to create a radical new development. Instead of building up, Erickson proposed to put the skyscraper on its side so that people could walk over it. The Robson Square project, which covers three blocks, included the remodelling of the city's neoclassical courthouse by overlaying it with an entirely modernist glass and steel structure. The complex includes Law Courts, the **Vancouver Art Gallery** and a central section for government buildings where three waterfalls cascade through the complex providing natural air-conditioning. Erikson's **Museum of Anthropology** too, is a triumph: inspired by aboriginal dwellings, the building references traditional wooden post-and-beam structures; soaring glass windows look out on to two reconstructed Haida houses.

The 1986 World Exposition saw a veritable explosion of building projects, focusing especially on the redevelopment of former industrial sites. **Canada Place**, built on the site of an old cargo pier, was created as a way of focusing visitors on the beauty of the harbour and it bears comparison with the Sydney Opera House, not least because of its five enormous white Teflon sails.

The building frenzy was complemented by the first lines of the rapid transit **SkyTrain** which runs on elevated tracks, giving passengers unparalleled views across the city. The stations, renowned for their innovation, are often designed by prominent architects and structural engineers. The transit also uses the SkyBridge – the world's longest cable-supported transit-only bridge – to cross the Fraser River.

The city's most famous bridge, connecting Downtown Vancouver to the North Shore, is the delicate **Lions Gate Bridge**. The three-lane suspension bridge takes its name from a pair of mountain peaks north of Vancouver and, to labour the point, a pair of cast concrete (budget restrictions wouldn't allow for bronze) lions, designed by sculptor Charles Marega in 1939, can be found on either side of the south approach to the bridge. In the same year the third incarnation of the **Hotel Vancouver** was built by the Canadian National Railway. The grand railway hotel had a uniquely Canadian architectural style: historian Harold Kalman wrote: 'Inspired by the picturesque castles of France and Scotland... Vancouver's version, resplendent in its gargoyles, Renaissance detail, and fine relief sculpture, was built by the CNR.'

Another important character in Vancouver's architectural history is the Toronto entrepreneur, Lt Commander J. W. Hobbs. Following the opening of the Panama Canal in 1914, Hobbs saw that, in order to boost Vancouver's position on the international shipping map, it needed an impressive skyscraper along the lines of New York's recently built Chrysler Building. And that's exactly what it got with the **Marine Building**: the sea-green edifice facing the harbour is decorated with flashes of gold and beautiful nautical motifs that symbolise the city's maritime history. English poet and architectural critic, Sir John Betjeman, declared it to be the 'best Art Deco office building in the world'.

While the passion for glass continues, the city's love of simple West Coast design is also still evident: a recent architectural hit is the **UBC Pharmaceutical Sciences Building** that seems to combine both. The design was based on the concept of a tree, and the blocky, staggered facade of dark glass cubes forms a sort of floating 'canopy', while the natural wood-clad lobby provides an open and flexible exhibition space.

Old Hastings
Mill Store Museum

UBC Pharmaceutical
Sciences Building

Vancouver
Art Gallery

Museum of
Anthropology

Hotel Vancouver

MacMillan
Bloedel
Building

L: 1575 Alma Street
A: Unknown, 1865
FF: It was the city's first post office, library and community centre.

L: 2405 Wesbrook Mall
A: Saucier + Perrotte Architectes and Hughes Condon Marler Architects, 2012
FF: Materials with a high level of recycled content were prioritised in the procuring and specifying process.

L: 750 Hornby Street, at Robson Street
A: Sir Francis Mawson Rattenbury 1907–11, Arthur Erickson, 1983
FF: There's an excellent collection of artworks by the 1920s modernist Emily Carr.

L: 6393 NW Marine Drive, at West Mall
A: Arthur Erickson, 1976
FF: The enormous doors were created by four Gitxsan woodworkers.

L: 900 West Georgia Street
A: John S. Archibald and John Schofield, 1928–39
FF: The hotel was used as the Heathman Hotel in the film *Fifty Shades of Grey* (2014).

L: 1075 West Georgia Street
A: Arthur Erickson, 1968
FF: The building is composed of two towers around a central core in order to allow for more offices with outside windows.

One Wall Centre

Harbour Centre

Jameson House

Marine Building

SkyTrain

Lions Gate Bridge

Canada Place

L: 1088 Burrard Street
A: Perkins + Will, 2001
FF: Due to the high air conditioning costs owing to the light-coloured glass, the windows are gradually being replaced with dark glass that will match the rest of the building.

L: 555 West Hastings Street
A: WZMH Architects, 1977
FF: When the observation deck was officially opened in 1977, Apollo 11 astronaut Neil Armstrong was guest of honour and there is a cement mould of his footprint.

L: 838 West Hastings Street
A: Foster + Partners, 2011
FF: Lord Foster said of Jameson House, 'The design makes the most of the city's fantastic natural setting, with balconies and deep bay windows looking out towards the landscape'.

L: 355 Burrard Street
A: McCarter Nairne, 1930
FF: The building doubled as the *Daily Planet* headquarters in the TV show *Smallville*.

L: 4720 Kingsway
A: Various, 1985
FF: The Evergreen line is due to open in 2016.

L: Across Burrard Inlet
A: Charles Nicholas Monsarrat, Philip Louis Pratley, 1938
FF: In 1986, the Guinness family, as an Expo gift, added lights to the bridge to make it a distinctive nighttime landmark.

L: Howe Street
A: Eberhard Zeidler and Barry Downs, 1986
FF: The 'Promenade into History' is a walkway providing a self-guided exploration of Vancouver's past.

Miami

'If you create a stage and it is grand, everyone who enters will play their part.'
Morris Lapidus

When old-school architecture fans come to Miami, they head for one area: South Beach. Filled with some 800 fine examples of rounded white concrete and pastel blocks featuring eyebrows over porthole windows, the winterbird destination of choice for many North Americans is famous for its Art Deco legacy. But increasingly, architecture fans are also coming to explore a very different skyline, one filled with surreal, innovative new structures by modern 'starchitects' who, rather than reject the past, are wisely drawing on it to sell the idea of a fantasy island to affluent sunseekers looking for a beach retreat with real flair – just as their 19th-century counterparts did.

Since its conception, Miami has always had a fresh and lively take on architecture, happily plundering European and South American styles to create buildings you wouldn't see anywhere else in the US. Take 1920s Mediterranean revivalism, a winning pastiche that deftly blended the shady balconies, loggias, colonnades, barrel tile roofs, grand stairways and cool courtyards of Spanish, Moorish and Venetian villas to create buildings perfectly suited to the hot and humid Florida climate. Largely the work of two men, August Geiger and Addison Mizner, these stately but fun homes set the standard for a style of building that is visibly echoed in today's buildings.

At the turn of the century, it was Geiger who set about creating the dream palaces desired by the property developers, well-to-do locals and growing numbers of winterbirds arriving in the fledgling city. But Geiger was capable of understated grandeur, too; his **Miami-Dade County Courthouse** offers a view of the style that is stately rather than fanciful; suggesting that while the tourists and settlers saw Miami as a playground, its elder statesmen were aiming for something a little more imposing. What they made of Mizner's work is anyone's guess; this high-society architect, bringing influences from a childhood spent travelling the world, was responsible for a number of imaginative houses and hotels, including the Boca Raton Resort & Club and the **Everglades Club**. Mizner's money enabled him to create a work that didn't just pastiche his influences; he built a factory in which he could create the clay roof tiles, cast stone, forged iron, pottery, stained glass and floor tiles that decorated this and his other buildings.

Ostentation was the order of the day, with areas like Coral Gables, a 10,000-acre development featuring gondolas on waterways and imported foxes (for hunting), sending critics into paroxysms of delight, and occasionally disdain. The district was epitomised by the **Biltmore Hotel**, whose lavish touches – from hand-painted frescoes on barrel-vaulted ceilings indoors to polo fields and a 68m (207ft)-long pool out – attracted a celebrity clientele that included English royalty, Hollywood A-listers and global leaders. It was all going so well – until the Depression.

But this being Miami, even the Depression was to create an unexpected fillip for the sunny – and sunnily minded – city, with a move towards austerity ushering in the outwardly understated Art Deco style that Miami Beach is now so famous for. Architects like L. Murray Dixon and Henry Hohauser filled creations like the former's **Ritz Plaza Hotel** and the latter's Essex House Hotel and Park Central Hotel with motifs of local flora, fauna and animal life in frescoes, friezes, marquetry and frosted glass panels, to create interiors that were often as dazzling as their exteriors were plain; even Howard Lovewell Cheney's utilitarian **Miami Beach Post Office** features an interior studded with elegant brass details and a frescoed sunburst-and-stars motif.

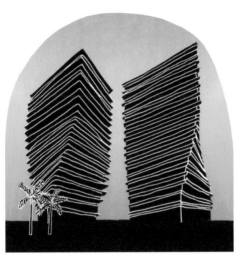

Even the prospect of a Cold War married with the more austere International Style did little to dampen the exuberance of Miami's built environment. Instead of straight lines, utilitarian construction materials and functionalist blocks, Miami's modernism featured colour, curves and kitsch – so much so that even religious buildings like **Temple Menorah**, with its mustard and cream paintwork and cheesegrater shape, looked, well, fun – though in this case, that's hardly surprising, given that it was designed by Morris Lapidus. This MiMo giant is without doubt one of Miami's most famous sons, and, with the design of **Fontainebleau**, the creator of one of its most famous historic buildings. The star of numerous films, including *Scarface*, *Goldfinger* and *The Bodyguard*, the white tower block played host to Frank Sinatra regularly and was the site of Elvis Presley's first post-army performance, but the real star of the show has always been the building itself. Despite critical rejection by American architecture at the time, Lapidus single-handedly shaped MiMo, aided by protégés like Melvin Grossman, whose Deauville Beach resort is another fine example of the style, and Enrique Gutierrez, whose boisterous **Bacardi Building** was only strengthened by the arrival, ten years after it was built, of a high-rise older brother.

By the time Gutierrez came to work on One Biscayne Tower, the hallmark fins and pizazz of the MiMo style were giving way to a slightly more grown-up form of architecture, the sense of playfulness finally tempered by the more sober aspects of the International Style it had subverted. And the trend has continued to this day; for each identikit skyscraper mushrooming on Biscayne Bay a more interesting counterpart exists or is in development: the **Adrienne Arsht Center for the Performing Arts** blends what was left of a 1929 Art Deco tower into a dramatic building that looks like an origami abstract writ large on the landscape; Herzog & de Meuron's **1111 Lincoln Road** subverts that most ubiquitous of Miami spaces – the parking garage – with irregularly spaced slabs and columns to create a mixed-use space which Jacques Herzog says reinterprets the essence of tropical modernism.

If he's looking back with a wry smile, a clutch of other starchitects on his heels are doing so with perhaps more restraint but equal amounts of touching homage; Zaha Hadid's **1000 Museum**, a residential tower complete with helipad, calls to mind the Bacardi Building with its horizontal base and vertical fins given a 21st-century twist. And **Grove at Grand Bay** literally twists elements of both the Miami parking garage and tropical modernism with its two arresting tower blocks. These, along with new starchitect structures like Frank Gehry's New World Center and Grimshaw's Miami Science Museum, pay homage to the idea of Miami's fantastic futuristic as imaginatively as you'd expect. Flights of fancy, certainly, but joyful ones that are revitalising downtown in ways that could only have been imagined back in the 1950s… and probably were.

Everglades Club

Temple Menorah

Miami Beach Post Office

1111 Lincoln Road

Biltmore Hotel

Miami-Dade County Courthouse

L: 356 Worth Avenue, Palm Beach
A: Addison Mizner, 1919
FF: Sewing machine heir Paris Singer conceived the club as a convalescent hospital for military officers injured in the First World War, but by the time it was finished it was obsolete, and so became a private club with a private suite for Singer.

L: 620 75th Street, Miami Beach
A: Morris Lapidus, 1962
FF: In the early 1960s, the temple was among only a handful of synagogues in South Florida to open its doors to the Jewish exiles from Cuba.

L: 1300 Washington Avenue, Miami Beach
A: Howard Lovewell Cheney, 1937
FF: Surrounding the fountain in the drum-shaped rotunda, the post office contains murals by Charles Hardman depicting Ponce de Leon's invasion of Florida, an attack on Hernando de Soto and a clash between Seminoles and the US Army.

L: 1111 Lincoln Road, Miami Beach
A: Herzog & de Meuron, 2008–10
FF: Interior courtyards by landscape architect Raymond Jungles punctuate a mix of shops and luxury residences, with the building topped and tailed by two restaurants at ground level and on the roof.

L: 1200 Anastasia Avenue, Coral Gables
A: Leonard Schultze, 1924–6
FF: Aquatic shows in the 45x68m (150x225ft) pool attracted up to 3,000 spectators to watch synchronised swimming, alligator wrestlers and record-breaking swims by Johnny Weissmuller, who was a Biltmore swimming instructor before he became famous as Tarzan.

L: 73 West Flagler Street
A: August Geiger and A. Ten Eyck Brown, 1925–8
FF: On its completion, the 110m (360ft)-high courthouse was the tallest building in Florida.

1000 Museum

Grove at Grand Bay

Bacardi Building

Ritz Plaza Hotel

Adrienne Arsht Center for the Performing Arts

Fontainebleau

L: 1000 Biscayne Boulevard
A: Zaha Hadid, 2014–16
FF: The 215m (706ft) residential tower will be topped by a helipad, and feature both sunrise and sunset pools.

L: 2675 South Bayshore Drive, Coconut Grove
A: Bjarke Ingels and BIG, 2015
FF: Residents have access to a polyglot butler, an on-site chef, a pet spa, a gym and five pools, including one rooftop pool on each tower, both of which are twisted 38 degrees.

L: 2100 Biscayne Boulevard
A: Enrique Gutierrez, 1963 (tower), Ignacio Carrera-Justiz, 1973 (square block)
FF: The two huge *azulejos* murals by Brazilian artist Francisco Brennand are comprised of 28,000 hand-painted, glazed, baked, 6x6in tiles surrounded by a marble border. The square building added in 1973 features four massive glass mural tapestries made of 1in-thick hammered glass designed to withstand hurricane-force winds.

L: 1701 Collins Avenue
A: L. Murray Dixon, 1940
FF: When the Ritz Plaza opened as the Grossinger Beach Hotel, it was the first air-conditioned hotel on Miami Beach. It became the Ritz Plaza in 1946, after being used during the Second World War to house high-ranking officers, and its current name is the SLS Hotel South Beach.

L: 1300 Biscayne Boulevard
A: Cesar Pelli, 2006
FF: The seven-storey Art Deco Sears tower from 1929 is dwarfed by the center's two main concert halls, the Sanford and Dolores Ziff Ballet Opera House, and John S. and James L. Knight Concert Hall.

L: 4441 Collins Avenue
A: Morris Lapidus, 1954
FF: The curved shape of the building carried ocean breezes along its length before air conditioning became ubiquitous, and cut short the sense of interminable hotel corridors hated by most hotel guests.

Mumbai

'Bombay was central, had been so from the moment of its creation:
the bastard child of a Portuguese-English wedding, and yet the most Indian of Indian cities.'
Salman Rushdie's Moraes Zogoiby narrator in *The Moor's Last Sigh*

Mumbai – previously called Bombay – is an inherently colonial city. The land that was originally composed of an archipelago of seven islands first started to morph into one distinct form in the 18th century, through the endeavours of the East India Company, the powerful trading force of the British Empire. Now one of the world's largest urban centres, Mumbai's skyline represents its colonial roots, its formative industries and its post-colonial ambitions. From the imposing Gothic public architecture of The Raj, to the Art Deco cinemas of the 1930s, to the gleaming residential skyscrapers of recent times – all seek to assert the city's multifaceted story against a backdrop of slums and urban decay.

As Bombay-born Salman Rushdie alludes to in the above quote, the British weren't, however, the first Europeans to set their covetous sights on the region; that particular exploit lay with the Portuguese explorers who wrestled the land from the reigning indigenous rulers in the 1500s, calling it 'Bom Baim'. It was the Portuguese who started to alter the area's visual appearance, through the construction of forts and churches and by influencing the vernacular architecture of the local Koli fishermen. But it wasn't until the British bought the islands from the Portuguese in the 1660s – after the East India Company had identified the natural harbour's trading potential – that a successful mercantile hub started to emerge. This in turn made the area a beacon for surrounding communities, and by the 1800s, a single landmass had been created by means of causeways and reclamation from the sea, and Mumbai's monumental architecture began to emerge.

The first British colonial architecture was neoclassical in form, with the Asiatic Society Building, in the Horniman Circle area – then the heart of the city's important cotton-trading district – a remnant of this era. But the stone-breaking really got underway when the British crown took over governance from the East India Company in 1857 – an event that would have a marked impression on the emerging city's skyline. Seeking to undermine local uprisings, British rulers under the Raj began an ambitious construction drive, erecting dozens of monuments to British power over the following three decades – kicking off with the **Flora Fountain**, a central monument that combined neoclassical form with the decorative Gothic Revival style popular in England at the time.

Through its incorporation of Eastern materials and motifs, Gothic Revival architecture in Bombay then began to take on a distinct local flavour, morphing into a style known as 'Bombay Gothic' – a style that still defines South Mumbai (the city's nucleus) today. Imposing public buildings exhibiting this style include the Maharashtra Police Headquarters and the University of Mumbai, with the latter also home to the landmark **Rajabai Clock Tower**; modelled on Big Ben, built from local kurla stone and incorporating Venetian flourishes, the clock tower was India's tallest building in the late 1870s. Mumbai's most-celebrated Bombay Gothic building, however, is also its most important for the city's functioning: **Chhatrapati Shivaji Terminus** (formerly Victoria Terminus), completed in 1887, is a perfect example of this East-meets-West style, and representative of the mass migration that has occurred here over the past century.

The Eastern elements of Bombay Gothic became more pronounced in the city as time went on, and by the turn of the 19th century a new style known as 'Indo-Saracenic' was emerging. A melding of Victorian, Hindu and Islamic styles, Indo-Saracenic reflects the tolerance (albeit an uneasy one) exhibited between the city's different communities at this time. **The Taj Mahal Palace Hotel** and the **Gateway of India** – two landmark buildings that sit metres from each other near the Colaba waterfront – are pre-eminent examples of Indo-Saracenic. The first, an amalgamation of Moorish and Renaissance styles, with a modern **tower** added in 1973, is a key symbol of the city – one reason why it was a target during the Mumbai terrorist attacks of 2008. The latter, a grandiose basalt arch built by the British to commemorate the 1911 visit of King George V, combines Classical Roman and Gujarati architectural forms, and remains the city's best-known visitor attraction.

This blending of styles continued in the city in alternative forms over the next few decades – most notably in the 1930s and 1940s, when Art Deco exploded here. This was also the era when the Indian film industry, which has always been based in Mumbai, was really finding its legs, and the two elements came together beautifully in the city's cinemas. Combining classic Art Deco industrial forms with fanciful Hindu and Islamic aesthetics (such as domes and minarets), Art Deco – like Gothic architecture before it – became a localised style here, evolving into what is referred to as Deco-Saracenic. The style was most visual in the city's many cinema buildings that were sprouting across the skyline at this time, such as the cream and maroon **Eros Cinema**, built in 1938 in the newly reclaimed Back Bay area.

Further land reclamations after Independence, in 1947, allowed for a new construction boom in the 1970s – one exhibiting a different symbolism to the preceding colonial-influenced styles: one of self-reliance and new wealth. The flourishing of the skyscraper, in particular, reinforced Bombay's status as the nation's economic powerhouse – especially in the case of the modernist **Phiroze Jeejeebhoy Towers**, built to house the Bombay Stock Exchange. At 118m (387ft), the building was India's tallest when completed in 1980, though it has since been surpassed by hundreds of newer towers. Most skyscrapers were, however, residential, with the most notable being Charles Correa's concrete **Kanchanjunga Apartments** – a totem for Mumbai's newly emerging middle classes.

The skyscraper trend took off again with gusto in the mid-1990s, since when the newly named Mumbai's geographic limitations have seen hundreds of new office and residential buildings being built upwards; Mumbai now has the 12th-highest number of skyscrapers in the world. However, the megacity's flashy new skyline is seen by many as a symbol of its unplanned growth and of the increasing gap between rich and poor, in a place that now contains Asia's worst slums. This is most extreme in Mumbai's most controversial skyscraper, **Antilia**, a 27-storey private home built in 2010 that is one of the world's most expensive residences. Residents in the nearby twinned **Imperial Towers**, at the time of writing India's tallest buildings at 400m (1,312ft), look down upon Antilia and beyond to the waterways that initially fuelled the city's economic growth as a global trading hub.

Flora Fountain

Eros Cinema

Taj Mahal Palace Hotel

Taj Mahal Palace Hotel Tower

Kanchanjunga Apartments

Imperial Towers

L: Hutatma Chowk (Martyrs' Square), South Mumbai
A: Richard Norman Shaw, 1864
FF: The fountain – named after the Flora goddess statue that graces its top – was originally to be named after the Governor of Bombay of the time, who was responsible for the drive to construct many new public buildings.

L: Maharshi Karva Road, Churchgate
A: Shorabji Bhedwar, 1938
FF: The cinema's circular foyer is finished in black and white marble, and includes a domed ceiling, Art Deco reliefs and two grand staircases.

L: Apollo Bunder, Colaba, South Mumbai
A: Sitaram Khanderao Vaidya (for Jamsetji Tata), 1903 (Taj Mahal Tower added 1973)
FF: Many famous guests have stayed at 'The Taj', including Queen Elizabeth II, John Lennon and Barack Obama; the latter was the first foreign head of state to stay here after the 2008 terrorist attacks, when 31 people were killed in the hotel.

L: 72 Peddar Road, South Mumbai
A: Charles Correa, 1970–83
FF: These sky-high apartments run from one side of the building to the other; with their veranda-inspired courtyards, this creates through-drafts that are much desired in Mumbai's heat.

L: M. P. Mills Compound, Tardeo
A: Hafeez Contractor, 2010
FF: The towers were built on a former slum in accordance with a modern developmental policy, where developers rehouse slum dwellers in exchange for rights to use the land.

Antilia

Phiroze Jeejeebhoy Towers

Chhatrapati Shivaji Terminus

Rajabai Clock Tower

Gateway of India

L: Altamount Road, off Pedder Road, South Mumbai
A: Perkins + Will, 2010
FF: This private residence was built for Mukesh Ambani, chairman of Reliance Industries Ltd, and includes three helipads and a staff of 600.

L: Dalal Street, Fort area
A: Larsen & Toubro Ltd (contractor; architect unknown)
FF: The Bombay Stock Exchange was established in 1875. Its new home was originally called BSE Towers, but the name was changed in the 1980s, when it was named after the late, long-serving chairman of the BSE.

L: Nagar Chowk, South Mumbai
A: Frederick William Stevens, 1888
FF: Around three million people pass through this terminus every day, making it Asia's busiest railway station.

L: University of Mumbai Fort Campus, South Mumbai
A: Sir George Gilbert Scott, 1878
FF: During the era of the Raj, the clock tower played the tunes of 'God Save the King' and 'Rule Britannia', among other imperial numbers, four times a day. It now chimes just one tune, but every 30 minutes.

L: Colaba waterfront, South Mumbai
A: George Wittet, 1924
FF: This colonial arch evolved into a monument to independence when British troops passed through it on their final departure from India in 1948 – symbolising the end of British rule.

Sydney

'Sydney is rather like an arrogant lover. When it rains it can deny you its love and you can find it hard to relate to. It's not a place that's built to be rainy or cold. But when the sun comes out, it bats its eyelids, it's glamorous, beautiful, attractive, smart, and it's very hard to get away from its magnetic pull.'

Baz Luhrmann

Sydneysiders laugh up their board shorts when they remember that many of their forebears were transported here in the 18th century as a punishment. What with the sun, sand and sea, Blue Mountains to the west, Palm Beach to the north and Botany Bay to the south… that really showed those convicts. The harbour was described by Captain Arthur Phillip as 'the finest harbour in the world'.

There's little disputing that its greatest landmark is Jørn Utzon's audacious **Sydney Opera House**. With its enormous shell-like roof, the building looks like a ship in full sail, about to leave the harbour. Following arguments over the spiralling cost of the project, Utzon resigned but, using his drawings and models, the building was completed. Frank Gehry, a Pritzker Prize judge, commented: 'Utzon made a building well ahead of its time, far ahead of available technology, and he persevered through extraordinarily malicious publicity and negative criticism to build a building that changed the image of an entire country'. Gehry is no stranger to controversy himself; his recent brutalist University of Technology business centre has been dubbed the 'paper bag' owing to the crinkly look of its brown exterior. He responded by saying '98 per cent of everything that is built and designed today is pure shit. There's no sense of design, no respect for humanity or for anything else. They are damn buildings and that's it'.

Certainly many of the city's most important buildings were constructed with purpose overriding design. The modern city began as a penal colony and one of its oldest buildings is the **Hyde Park Barracks**, built by and for convicts. The Classical UNESCO World Heritage Site is cited as one of 'the best surviving examples of large-scale convict transportation and the colonial expansion of European powers through the presence and labour of convicts'. The barracks were designed by English-born Francis Greenway, himself an ex-convict who had been transported for the crime of forgery. He became Australia's first government architect and also designed Cadmans Cottage, made out of local sandstone.

Increased wealth and the gold rush of the 1850s saw a corresponding increase in decorative design, as illustrated by the high Victorian **Sydney Town Hall**, which was modelled on Philadelphia's Second Empire-style City Hall. It is known as the Wedding Cake Building thanks to its excessive ornamentation. The elaborate Romanesque **Queen Victoria Market**, with its glass roof and one large and 20 smaller domes, was actually built in a recession but was a way of employing a large number of craftsmen.

Another of the city's landmark buildings is the Roman Catholic **St Mary's Cathedral**. At over 46m (150ft), it's the largest church in Australia. The English geometric-decorated Gothic original, partly designed by Augustus Pugin, was destroyed by fire and rebuilt in 1928 by William Wardell using Sydney sandstone, Oamaru stone, marble, alabaster and Moruya granite.

But by the time the Great Depression took hold, there was a noticeable change in architectural style: designs were sparer with far less ornamentation. Designed by English firm, Dorman and Long, the single-span steel **Harbour Bridge** was a way of utilising otherwise unemployed labour and it took 1,400 men eight years to build. The 503m (1,650ft) span between Milsons Point and Dawes Point was built from each shore with underground cables holding the structures back until they were joined together in 1930.

After the Second World War the city removed building height restrictions and since then there has been a wealth of high-rises, including the **Sydney Tower** – the tallest structure in Sydney, and the third tallest in the southern hemisphere. High-speed elevators whizz visitors up to an eight-floor turret – the 'golden basket' – in just 40 seconds for 360-degree views of Sydney as far as the Blue Mountains. The Tower is robust enough to withstand strong winds and earthquakes, and is stabilised by 56 cables that, if laid end-to-end, would stretch from Sydney to New Zealand.

One of Australia's most important architects, Harry Seidler, was responsible for some of Sydney's most ground breaking designs, including **Australia Square Tower** – the world's tallest lightweight concrete building at the time of construction. Seidler had worked with structural engineer Pier Luigi Nervi on the tower, and throughout his career acknowledged the influence of other great modernists Walter Gropius, Marcel Breuer, Josef Albers and Oscar Niemeyer. The design for his Horizon Apartments, with their distinctive scalloped exterior, were created with pre-stressed concrete and finished in rendered concrete.

In the heart of the Central Business District lies one of Australia's cleverest and greenest projects; **1 Bligh Street** is the work of German architect Christoph Ingenhoven with Architectus. Its 'green' features include a basement sewage plant that recycles 90 per cent of the building's waste water, solar panels on the roof and air conditioning created by chilled beams.

It has a full double-skin facade with external louvres that automatically angle according to the sun's orientation, so conserving energy and cutting glare. The building was named the Best Tall Building in Asia and Australasia for 2012 in the Council on Tall Buildings and Urban Habitat's (CTBUH) Skyscraper Awards 2012 and also won the International Highrise Award in the same year. **One Central Park** is an apartment complex that, thanks to the vertical gardens on each floor, gives residents the feeling of living in a tree house. In 2014, it was chosen as the Best Tall Building in Asia and Australasia by CTBUH. At night, the building is lit up by Yann Kersale's LED art installation.

Another award-winning construction is Renzo Piano's first project in Australia, **Aurora Place**, which was also his first high-rise. The unusual shape that curves and twists has a facade made from white laminated glass that resembles a sail; this was Piano's deliberate way of creating a dialogue with the spinnakers of its more famous predecessor, the Sydney Opera House, down the road.

The challenge for Sydney, as with many cities, is how to build for the future without destroying the past. Sydney Living Museums curator Dr Caroline Butler-Bowden recognises that 'Sydney Harbour is dotted with overlooked landmarks that have long passed their use-by date' but believes that, rather than destroy to rebuild, it's important to find new love for otherwise mothballed landmarks of 20th-century industry, such as the once-bustling Walsh Bay Finger Wharves. Completed in 1915, the wharves were cutting edge in their day – instead of using steel, architect Henry Deane Walsh used plentiful supplies of hard wood – but following the introduction of container shipping, the wharves became obsolete. It looked as though the wharves would be destroyed but, following public protest, the entire area has been redeveloped, into a modern residential and cultural area providing sites for the Sydney Theatre Company, dance companies and a host of swanky bars and restaurants.

Hyde Park Barracks

Sydney Town Hall

One Central Park

Queen Victoria Market

Sydney Tower

Aurora Place

Australia Square Tower

1 Bligh Street

L: Queens Square, Macquarie Street
A: Francis Greenway, 1817–19
FF: Guided tours can be arranged, and during the summer Sydney Festival, jazz concerts are held in the grounds.

L: 483 George Street
A: J. H. Willson, 1869–89
FF: When it was installed in 1890, Sydney Town Hall's Grand Organ was the largest in the world and described as the 'finest organ ever built by an English organ builder'.

L: Broadway
A: Ateliers Jean Nouvel, PTW Architects Downtown, 2013
FF: The design includes a cantilevered section featuring a heliostat to provide light to the parkland below.

L: 455 George Street
A: George McRae, 1893–8
FF: The largest, central dome has a diameter of 20m (65.6ft) and consists of an inner glass dome and an exterior copper dome topped with a cupola.

L: 100 Market Street
A: Donald Crone, 1970
FF: The tower has a revolving buffet restaurant.

L: 88 Phillip Street
A: Renzo Piano, 2000
FF: On 2 June 2009, French urban climber Alain Robert scaled this building in protest against climate change.

L: 264 George Street
A: Harry Seidler, 1961–7
FF: Construction time for each floor was five days.

L: 1 Bligh Street
A: Architectus in collaboration with Ingenhoven Architects, 2011
FF: At its base, the tower is mostly open to the public, with a public meeting spot, a children's play area and open-air café seating.

St Mary's Cathedral

Sydney Opera House

Harbour Bridge

L: St Mary's Road
A: Augustus Pugin
(early version), 1821;
William Wardell (present
building), 1868
FF: The spires, reaching
more than 70m (229.6ft),
were added in 2000.

L: Bennelong Point
A: Jørn Utzon, 1973
FF: The shells are made from pre-cast concrete
sections that are clad with white glazed tiles.

L: Bradfield Highway
A: Dorman and Long, 1923–32
FF: BridgeClimb is a three-and-a-half-hour tour that includes a
two-hour walk to the top of the arch, 134m (439.6ft) above sea
level.

Beirut

'In Beirut, death's unremitting light shines bright for all to see, brighter than the Mediterranean sun, brighter than the night's Russian missiles, brighter than a baby's smile.'
Rabih Alameddine, *I, The Divine: A Novel in First Chapters*

The beauty of the capital city of Lebanon – once compared to that of Paris, thanks to French Mandate architecture, stylish bars and restaurants – has been devastated by a civil war that raged from 1975 to the early 1990s. There are plenty of examples of its toll on the city's architecture, but the now derelict **Barakat Building**, or 'Yellow House', is especially poignant. Designed by Youssef Aftimus during the French Mandate, the four-storey home of Nicholas Barakat combined the style and materials of east and west: sandstone walls, colonnaded verandas, Islamic arches and Art Deco floor patterns. Unfortunately its position along the Green Line that divided the city means that today it's a pockmarked symbol of Beirut's tragic past.

The city, which began more than 3,000 years ago, takes its name from the Phoenician word 'byrt', referring to the extant underground 'wells', and successive occupants have all left their mark on the city's culture, if not its architecture.

The **St George Greek Orthodox Church**, consecrated in 1764, sits on the Roman axis of the city's ancient Cardo Maximus, and excavation of the nearby area revealed many archaeological finds from the Greek, Roman, Byzantine, Medieval and Ottoman eras. One of the city's oldest buildings is the **Al-Omari Mosque**, once the 12th-century Byzantine Cathedral of St John built by the Crusaders, but transformed into a mosque by the Mamluks in 1291.

Joseph Philippe Karam, one of Lebanon's most famous architects, was responsible for some of Beirut's most radical buildings. He was influenced by the Bauhaus and International Style movements, as well as modernist Le Corbusier and, though his Beirut City Centre – a huge shopping complex – was never fully completed, his **Grand Theatre** cinema still exists. Known as 'the Egg', the brutalist concrete bunker was badly damaged during the civil war but, beloved by Beirutis, there are hopes of a future incarnation.

In spite of so much destruction, by 2009 the *New York Times* had voted Beirut its 'Number One destination to visit' and a multi-billion-dollar reconstruction project was under way, with buildings promised by the likes of Zaha Hadid, Herzog & de Meuron and Rafael Moneo. The project has encountered a fair bit of controversy – critics have accused it of tearing down rather than preserving, or simply ignoring the city's historic roots; the cosmopolitan **Saint-George Hotel**, inspired by the structuralist works of French designer Auguste Perret, was one of Beirut's most famous modernist buildings. Once a symbol of Beirut's golden age, the pink-stoned marina-front hotel was a beacon of glamour, frequented by the likes of Elizabeth Taylor, Catherine Deneuve and the Shah of Iran. The 1920s interior designed by Parisian designer Jean Royère is namechecked in Said Aburish's *Beirut Spy: International Intrigue at the St George Hotel Bar* as the place where Russian Agent Kim Philby met his third wife, Eleanor, shortly after arriving in the city. Already crumbling, the hotel suffered further damage in 2004 when a 4,000-pound bomb blast blew the front of the hotel clean off. The target of the blast was controversial business tycoon and Prime Minister Rafic Hariri, widely recognised as responsible for much of the restructuring of the city. Critics suggest that the hotel's sea view is being obscured by new builds.

Perhaps unsurprisingly, a recurring feature of some of Beirut's newest architecture is the strong reference to the spaces inhabited. Bernard Khoury's music club **B018** has been described as 'war architecture'. It's located at the 'Quarantaine', a place of quarantine during the French protectorate. The semi-industrial neighbourhood was home to more than 20,000 refugees until, in 1976, local militias moved in and completely demolished the area, killing up to 1,500 people. Khoury's

black metal and concrete 'spaceship' has an almost menacing aura about it; lying low on the ground it barely reveals an entrance to a subterranean bunker. But at night, mirrored plates that cover the club open up the space to the sky and reflect the movements of dancing clubbers within. Khoury has said that he rather likes the idea of beats and energy coming out of a dark past, bringing life to a dead zone.

Another example of a building integrating into its environment is Youssef Tohmé's **USJ Campus of Sport and Innovation**. Its exterior, with differently shaped windows, voids and moucharabieh-inspired perforations, references the shell-pocked buildings of the city's long conflict, while allowing light to enter the building and create an ever-changing interior, depending on the sun's position.

Beirut has also been known as the intellectual capital of the Arab world, thanks to an abundance of writers, artists, philosophers, political dissidents and filmmakers living there. One Beiruti architect determined to make the city a better place to live is Ghassan Maasri whose experimental 'Mansion' project was set up in a crumbling Ottoman-style family villa. It became a cultural centre where engaged Beirutis could meet and create, as well as question big architectural projects that might destroy Beirut's cultural landmarks. One of the artists, Tom Young, recently exhibited his work in another 19th-century Ottoman building known as the **Rose House**, where he made work that would 'capture the spirit and atmosphere of the space… [using] art as a way to bring life back into these empty spaces'.

It's just possible that New York firm SOMA has found an innovative way of combining the past with the future: **BoBo** is an 11-storey cantilevered glass construction that will house 13 luxury residences using a steel exoskeleton that protects the original 1920s house below. And for the future, Herzog & de Meuron's waterfront **Beirut Terraces** – a vertical village of glasshouses stacked irregularly on top of one another – are in line for the Best Sustainable Building award. The use of layers references the city's tumultuous history, while its garden terraces will provide an inside/outside feel and take advantage of the city views. Clearly, along with continuing controversy, there are some interesting projects ahead for Beirut.

St George Greek
Orthodox Church

BoBo

Grand Theatre

Barakat Building

Beirut
Terraces

L: Nejme Square
A: Unknown, 1764
FF: The interior of the cathedral is
decorated with ornate frescoes by
Ibrahim Youssef Saad.

L: Mar Mikeal
A: Michel Abboud, SOMA, 2015
FF: The ground floor will be given over
to retail space and an art gallery.

L: Cheikh Bechara Street
A: Joseph Philippe Karam, 1966
FF: Rumours abound that 'the Egg'
is about to be demolished. See it
while you can…

L: Damascus Road and
Independence Avenue
A: Youssef Aftimus, 1924–34
FF: There are plans to turn the
house into a museum and keep
the snipers' den within.

L: Minet El Hosn
A: Herzog & de Meuron,
2015
FF: The site is close to
a bombsite beside the
Saint-George Hotel.

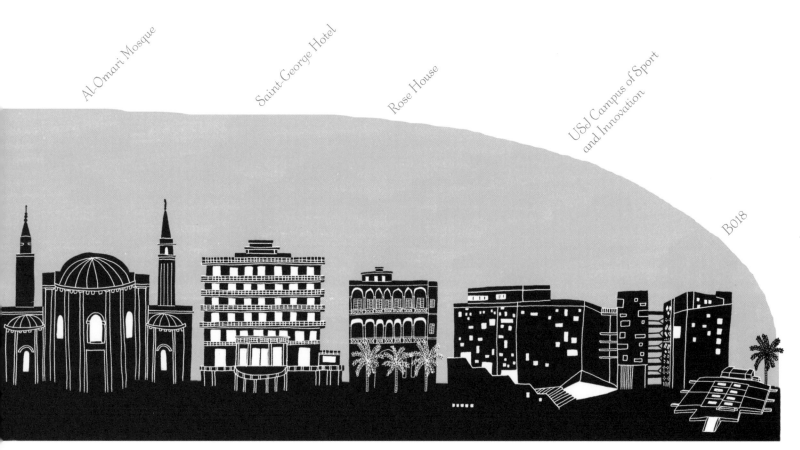

Al-Omari Mosque

Saint-George Hotel

Rose House

USJ Campus of Sport and Innovation

B018

L: Majidiye
A: Unknown, 12th century
FF: The interior sandstone walls are decorated with Mamluk and Ottoman inscriptions.

L: Aïn Mreisseh
A: Jacques Poirrier, André Lotte, Georges Bordes, Antoine Tabet, 1932
FF: Owner Fady Al-Khoury is determined to overcome obstacles and reopen the hotel in the future.

L: The Corniche, Al Manara
A: Mohammad Ardati, 1882
FF: The building is currently under restoration.

L: Rue de Damas BP
A: 109 Architects with Youssef Tohmé, 2011
FF: The stairs lead to a landscaped terrace with uninterrupted views of the city.

L: Karantina (La Quarantaine)
A: Bernard Khoury Architects, 2008
FF: You might bump into any number of international celebrities on the dancefloor, like Naomi Campbell or Dee Dee Bridgewater.

Havana

Sergeant Sarah Brown: *'You want to take me to dinner in Havana? Havana, Cuba?'*
Sky Masterson: *'Well, they eat in Cuba the same as we do.'*
Guys and Dolls (1955)

In the 1955 MGM musical *Guys and Dolls*, Marlon Brando's louche gambler Sky Masterson takes Jean Simmons' prim Salvation Army sergeant Sarah Brown to Havana for dinner – because he wants to take her to one of his favourite restaurants. The ensuing dinner scene shows the city as the exotic, heady paradise on America's doorstep that it was, and highlights its popularity with affluent Americans from all walks of life. By the 1950s gamblers, businessmen, actors, playboys and artists were all being drawn to a destination which, like Las Vegas and Miami, was marketing itself as a sun-filled haven of booze, gambling and debauchery. But unlike those newly emerging cities, Havana's landscape was shaped by a rich past.

During 400 years of colonialism, the city had amassed a fascinating collection of buildings influenced by its rulers – notably the Spanish. These are best seen in the shape of the Convento de Santa Clara, a pre-Baroque nunnery with beautiful cloisters and a great hall resembling an inverted ship, and the elegantly proportioned **Catedral de San Cristóbal**. With its two intriguingly asymmetrical towers and an elaborate Baroque facade designed by Italian architect Francesco Borromini, it's undoubtedly the best example of Cuban Baroque in the city.

At the beginning of the 20th century, and newly independent thanks to American aid, Havana was, along with Buenos Aires, one of the grandest and most important Latin American cities in the world. This was thanks largely to Havana's sugar and coffee production, and its role as one of the world's major ports. These industries had already paid for gas street lighting, introduced in 1848, a plethora of Spanish Baroque mansions, and world-class, French-influenced buildings such as the Aldama Palace, built in 1844.

By the 1920s, Cuban influences such as stained glass and *azulejo* tiles were giving the architecture a unique local flavour, and creating a panoply of interesting Art Nouveau and Art Deco buildings in the Vedado district – among them the neo-Italianate Renaissance villa Casa de la Amistad, on the grand avenue Paseo; and the twin-towered **Hotel Nacional de Cuba**, an eclectic mix of Hispanic-Moorish, neoclassical and neocolonial elements on a predominantly Art Deco structure. In the same year, the city saw its first high-rise block in the then whopping 12-storey Edificio Bacardi, whose classic Art Deco architecture, adorned with enamelled terracotta panels of naked nymphs by American artist Maxfield Parrish, also bore touches of Catalan modernism in its *azulejos* tile work and intricate ironwork. And Art Deco even became a defining feature in the Cementerio de Cristóbal Colón, when French glass designer René Lalique was called on to design the arresting Catalina Lasa and Juan Pedro Baró mausoleum. As the boom years continued, aided in no small part by the influx of US gangsters and 'businessmen' such as organised-crime king Meyer Lansky, drawn here by the opportunities offered by Prohibition back home in the US, buildings went up across the city that ranged from French neoclassical to Italian Renaissance and Art Deco to styles with a wide range of influences including, ironically, American.

That influence had begun decades earlier, with American architect Kenneth Murchison's elegantly proportioned four-storey **Havana Central railway station**. Its twin towers, terracotta medallions, mezzanine and broad waiting room clearly signposted a new modern style, and it became the first of more than two dozen buildings in Havana designed by New York architects. In 1932 Ricardo Mira's Art Deco **Lopez Serrano** apartment block clearly showed a debt to New York's Empire State Building in a stepped exterior, steel frame and Art Deco motifs, including zig zagged arches, intricate glasswork and flower friezes. In the old city, the **Capitolio** was reminiscent of a better-established American icon, apeing its Washington DC neoclassical namesake as a half-sized version complete with towering granite columns, a huge statue-flanked stairway leading to a grand entrance and a 91m (300ft)-high cupola.

By the 1950s the American influence had given way to a more bland International Style, with height the defining characteristic of many buildings. The sleek modernist Edificio Someillán had little to recommend it beyond its 32 floors, and the later, 39-storey **Edificio FOCSA** (at the time of its building it was the second largest reinforced concrete building in the world), illustrates the more prosaic excesses of the moneymen, with large apartments serviced by everything from a school and top-floor panoramic restaurant to a swimming pool and a bank. And close by, the 21-storey **Hotel Havana Riviera** was the largest purpose-built casino hotel in the world outside Las Vegas. Its futuristic design and a clever shape that gave each room a sea view literally illustrated the growing gap between rich and poor.

Fidel Castro and Che Guevara's rebellion took place in 1958, and on 1 January 1959, Castro's new government took its place in Havana.

The party was over, and a full trade embargo imposed by a jumpy America entering the Cold War led to the end of the building boom – but not before the completion of some still spectacular buildings, and one ingenious one.

The Plaza de la Revolución is Cuba's political heart and the core of Havana's modernist building. The National Theatre, Presidential Palace and the **Ministry of the Interior**, all built in 1958, are strong examples of the style, but it's the latter that stands out, notably for the enormous bronze wire sculpture of Che Guevara on the facade. Close by, the **Memorial to José Martí** honours Cuba's national hero with an arresting five-pointed star-shaped tower in Cuban marble.

The buildings of the Plaza were the last hurrah for architectural excellence in Cuba. With no steel for reinforced concrete, building in the city came to a virtual standstill; but Castro had ways to cope with such hurdles. By reappropriating the luxurious neoclassical Presidential Palace, he was able to create the **Museo de la Revolución**, devoted to the national rebellion of the Cuban people. And by utilising indigenous materials such as stone, cement and bricks, he was able to realise a grand plan for five national art schools that would physically illustrate the political ideology of Castro and Che's new socialist ideals – and be cheekily sited on the former ultra-exclusive Havana Country Club, where wide graceful domes, brick galleries and open piazzas on a human scale would foster freedom and openness.

While only two of the schools were ever completed, the unusual beauty of the **School of Ballet** – with its brick arches, vaulted ceilings and ceramic decoration in curved buildings that would not restrict dancers' movements as much as more rational spaces – is such that Norman Foster and Carlos Acosta's movement to restore it has gathered real pace. Let's hope that one day this laudable part of Castro's vision is realised.

Capitolio

Hotel Havana Riviera

Hotel Nacional de Cuba

Ministry of the Interior

School of Ballet

L: Prado 422
A: Raúl Otero and Eugenio Rayneri Piedra, 1926–9
FF: Directly beneath the dome lies an imitation 24-carat diamond set into the marble floor, from where all highway distances between Havana and the rest of Cuba are measured.

L: Paseo y Malecón
A: Igor Polevitzky, 1956
FF: Original owner and mobster Meyer Lansky chose Polevitzky to design his hotel because of his track record on some of Miami Modern's best buildings.

L: Calle O, esquina 21
A: McKim, Mead & White, 1930
FF: Al Capone, Ernest Hemingway, Frank Sinatra and Winston Churchill are just a few of the world-famous figures to have stayed here.

L: Plaza de la Revolución
A: Unknown, sculpture by Rafael Avila, 1958
FF: The metalwork sculpture on the building's facade was based on Alberto 'Korda' Gutierrez's famous photo of Che Guevara.

L: Reparto Cubanacan
A: Ricardo Porro, Roberto Gottardi and Vittorio Garrati, 1961
FF: A workman whose father had worked on Antoni Gaudí's buildings in Barcelona trained 80 workers to construct vaults and domes using bricks.

López Serrano

Museo de la Revolución

Catedral de San Cristóbal

Edificio FOCSA

Havana Central railway station

Memorial to José Martí

L: Calle 13 corner of L, Vedado
A: Ricardo Mira and Miguel Rosich, 1932
FF: Nip inside to see beautiful terrazzo floors and walls clad with red Moroccan marble.

L: Calle Refugio 1
A: Carlos Maruri and Paul Belau, 1920
FF: The interior design of the Palace is by Tiffany of New York, and includes a replica of the Palace of Versailles' Hall of Mirrors.

L: Corner of San Ignacio and Empedrado
A: Jesuits, begun 1748
FF: The building is mainly constructed of coral, and if you look carefully you can find marine fossils in the outer wall of the facade.

L: Calle 17, between M and N
A: Ernesto Gomez Sampera, 1956
FF: This remains the tallest building in Cuba, so for great views, head for the top-floor restaurant La Torre.

L: Calle Arsenal, esquina Egido
A: Kenneth Murchison, 1912
FF: The station was built on the site of the old Army Arsenal, and services a railway network established in 1873, making it one of the oldest in the world.

L: Plaza de la Revolución
A: Enrique Luis Varela, 1958
FF: The viewing platform at the top of the tower affords spectacular views of the city and island.

Helsinki

As anyone who's been there will know, Helsinki, the capital of Finland, has a distinct, esoteric identity shaped predominantly by a Baltic Sea location that's halfway between Sweden to its west and Russia to its east, and by centuries of rule by both. But while its inhabitants have continued to develop what was always a strongly nationalistic spirit in their youthful independence (2017 will mark Finland's centenary), to outsiders the city's identity is less clear-cut – as the drily knowing dialogue from *Die Hard* suggests.

The modern city was largely built by Russia and is closer geographically to St Petersburg than Stockholm, but its ancient relationship with Scandinavia is still a strong influence, resulting in a city that's an intriguing marriage of both Scandi and Stasi in many of its cultural aspects – not least its architecture.

It was the eastern influences that shaped the city's most famous site, the regal Senate Square. This early example of neoclassical architecture boasts four buildings designed by the German architect Carl Ludvig Engel and built between 1822 and 1852: **Helsinki Cathedral**, the Government Palace, the main building of the University of Helsinki and the National Library of Finland. The square's resemblance to St Petersburg is wholly intentional; Engel was a big fan of the style and the city. The cathedral is undoubtedly the centrepiece. Looking for all the world like a giant wedding cake, it is one of Finland's most famous buildings. In Helsinki, it fights things out in the fame stakes with the equally arresting **Uspenski Cathedral**. Sitting in red and gold glory on the old Helsinki headland district of Katajanokka, it looks even more Russian than the Cathedral, and even looks east towards St Petersburg, en route taking in the view of Suomenlinna fortress, a physical marker for Sweden, Finland and Russia's intertwined pasts, having belonged to all three in the past hundred years.

Where the cathedral has its neoclassical chums on Senate Square, the Uspenski is surrounded by a far more interesting array of buildings charting Helsinki's own growing identity, as the 19th century gave way to the modernity sweeping in from the west. Close by are some nice examples of the Finnish National Romantic movement's architecture, Jugendstil, and a key modernist site by the city's most famous inhabitant: Alvar Aalto. The Enso-Gutzeit HQ is the most controversial of Aalto's works in the city but by no means his most famous, or best. From a range of contenders, including the Rautatalo Office Building and the Otaniemi University campus, Aalto's **Finlandia Hall** is outstanding, its soaring white Carrara marble facade seemingly rearing out of the water like a collection of cubist icebergs on Töölö Bay.

Oddly, as though reflecting the city's duality, Helsinki's best buildings often come in pairs. Across the Mannerheimintie from Finlandia Hall sits the Finnish

National Museum. Adorned with literal impressions from the nationalistic epic saga, the Kalevala, it's one of the best examples of Jugendstil in the city. And just a kilometre away, two more excellent examples of the style sit at right angles to each other. Eliel Saarinen's **Central Station**, built in 1919, skilfully blends nationalistic symbolism with English Arts and Crafts ideas through materials such as sculpted pink granite, moulded copper and decorative steel and glass. Adjacent to it, the **Finnish National Theatre**, its local grey granite topped with red roof tiles, manages to look as old as the oral folklore and mythologies that Finnish Jugendstil drew on in the Kalevala, despite its youthful 110 years.

While the appeal of the pared-back style exhibited in the late-Jugendstil Central Station and the elegantly proportioned granite **Kallio Church** have endured, the folksiness of the style at its more whimsical isn't to everyone's taste. By the 1930s, civic and public architecture was in thrall to functionalism with the likes of the General Post Office, the Sokos Hotel Torni – a 14-storey tower that combines Jugendstil, Art Deco and functionalism in a fascinating mix – and the monolithic **Parliament House**, which employed Finnish craftsmen and materials such as red granite from Kalvola to create an appropriately dramatic piece of Nordic classicism decorated with 14 Corinthian columns.

The hulking machismo of such buildings, fuelled by Finland's rapid economic growth and industrialisation, reached its zenith in 1938 with the elegant white **Olympic Stadium**, whose plain facade gained a wooden wraparound to raise capacity from 50,000 to 70,000 in the 12 years between its build and its use. The wood signposted a new use of materials more suited to the mid-century modernism sweeping through neighbouring

Sweden, and a rash of arresting new buildings making inventive use of copper, wood and glass sprung up across the city.

Hewn out of granite, the Temppeliaukio Church is a wondrous mix of futuristic Ken Adam-style production design and natural beauty, its rough walls topped with a non-oxidised copper dome held aloft by 180 skylights and concrete beams. The result feels both ancient and modern, spiritual and functional, manmade and natural. In this, it marks the heart of Helsinki's character, and most of the city's architecture since has focused on material and craftsmanship, with nods to symbolism in sculptures such as the **Sibelius Monument**, whose 8.5m (28ft)-high hollow steel organ pipes are said to symbolise, among other things, waves, a birch forest and Sibelius compositions. The sculpture was thought to be too avant-garde for its time, but contemporary Helsinkilainens have tentatively embraced avant-garde in the shape of the **Kiasma Museum of Contemporary Art**. And a more recent building has managed to win the hearts of everyone; the distinctive wooden egg-cup that is the **Kamppi Chapel** may be tiny, but has a huge impact, despite – or perhaps because of – its siting next to a shopping centre on busy Narinkka Square.

The emphasis on natural materials and modern, contemplative spaces looks set to continue with the popularity of structures like the steamed wood Kupla lookout tower at the city's island zoo and the proposal for the new central library. Such an embracing of new ideas married with traditional materials and the celebration of age-old crafts suggests that, when its citizens celebrate their centenary in 2017, they will do so with a very clear sense of who they are and their place in the world. That's Helsinki, Finland.

Kamppi Chapel

Olympic Stadium

Kallio Church

Central Station

Uspenski Cathedral

Sibelius Monument

Finlandia Hall

L: Simonsgatan
A: Kimmo Lintula, Niko Sirola and Mikko Summanen, 2012
FF: Light enters via a void in the ceiling as the chapel has no windows.

L: Paavo Nurmen tie
A: Yrjö Lindegren and Toivo Jäntti, 1938
FF: The lift to the top of the 72m (236ft) tower offers terrific views across the Baltic.

L: Itäinen Papinkatu
A: Lars Sonck, 1912
FF: The seven German bells in the granite tower play a tune by Jean Sibelius at noon and 6 p.m.

L: Kaivokatu
A: Eliel Saarinen, 1919
FF: In 2013 the BBC declared this to be one of the world's most beautiful railway stations.

L: Kanavakatu
A: Aleksey Gornostaev, 1868
FF: The red bricks came from the Bomarsund fortress in Aland, which was destroyed during the Crimean War.

L: Sibeliuksen puisto, Mechelininkatu
A: Eila Hiltunen, 1967
FF: It is built of over 600 pipes and weighs 24 tons.

L: Mannerheimintie
A: Alvar Aalto, 1971
FF: Aalto designed every detail of the interiors, from lighting down to floors and furniture.

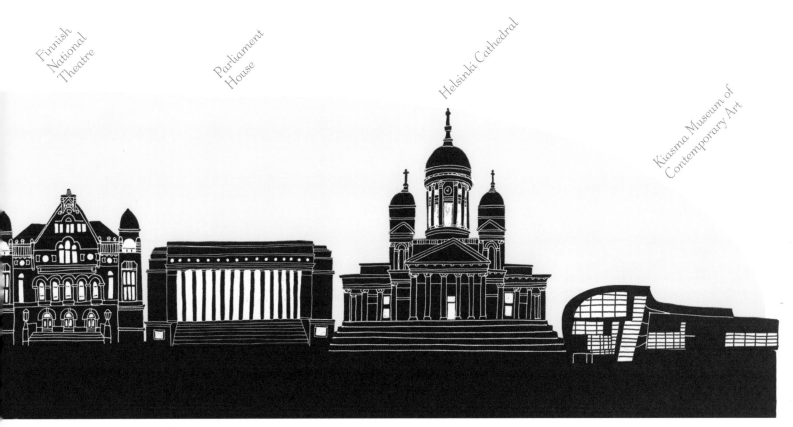

Finnish National Theatre

Parliament House

Helsinki Cathedral

Kiasma Museum of Contemporary Art

L: Läntinen Teatterikuja
A: Onni Tarjanne, 1902
FF: The theatre is the oldest Finnish-language theatre in Finland.

L: Mannerheimintie
A: Johan Sigfrid Sirén, 1931
FF: The five floors are linked by paternoster lifts, consisting of a chain of open compartments that move slowly in a loop without stopping.

L: Unioninkatu 29
A: Carl Ludvig Engel (completed by Ernst Lohrmann), 1852
FF: The statues of the apostles lining the roof are made of zinc and are copies of the sculptures on Copenhagen's Vor Frue Kirke.

L: Mannerheiminaukio
A: Steven Holl, 1998
FF: Kiasma was selected as the Museum of Contemporary Art site in a competition that drew 516 entries.

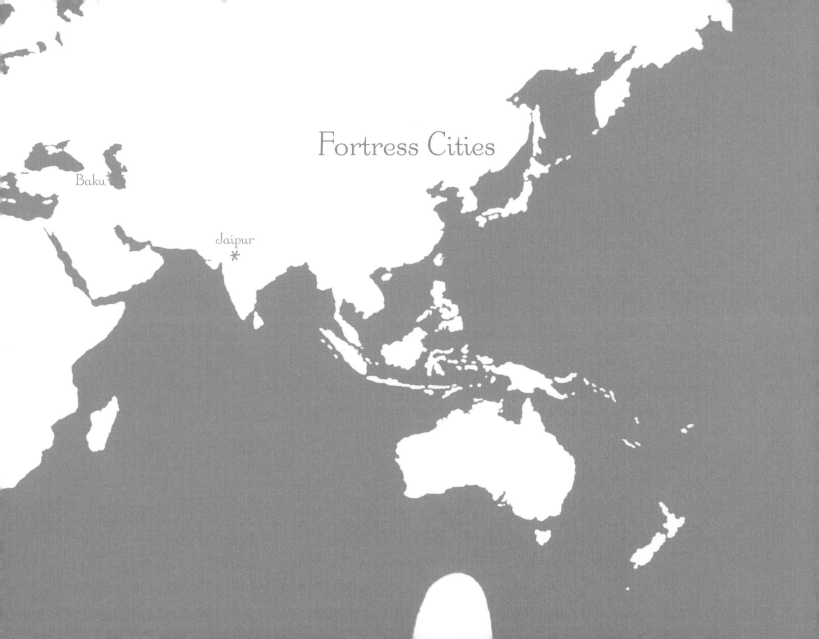

Fortress Cities

Baku

Jaipur

Marrakech

'It's the most lovely spot in the whole world.'
Winston Churchill to Franklin D. Roosevelt, 1943

As far back as the 7th century, camel caravans crossed the desert from Morocco to Mauritania and Sudan trading salt for gold and slaves. The routes were vital, busy and dangerous – a pound of salt was worth an ounce of gold – and the most successful traders were the Almoravids, a fiercely competitive Berber tribe. By the 11th century their empire stretched from the Maghreb in north-west Africa to the Al-Andalus of southern Spain, and when the nomadic Almoravids needed a permanent store for weapons and food they chose a strategic spot en route: it became known as Marra Kouch – 'Land of the Kouch-men', the dark-skinned warriors of Mauritania.

Fearing attack from rival Berbers (the Almohads), the Almoravids built 10km (6 miles) of 6m (19.6ft)-high walls made from the red soil that dominates the land. Today, aside from the red walls, their only surviving structure is the **Koubba El-Badiyin** dome, part of Sultan Ali Ben Youssef's 12th-century palace. On seeing the exquisite floral patterns and fine calligraphy when it was unearthed in 1948, a French art historian exclaimed that the 'art of Islam has never exceeded the splendour of this extraordinary dome'. The medina within the walls is a maze of hole-in-the-wall shops and stalls and inward-focused riads with internal courtyards open to the sky – a key feature of Islamic architecture, ensuring maximum family privacy.

The Almohads weren't kept out for long, taking the city in 1147, destroying most of the Almoravid structures and building their own using new techniques and styles; as well as mud brick and pisé, a dried mud strengthened with lime,

they used stone. **Bab Agnaou** is the limestone gate to the kasbah. The 'Gate of Gnawa', referring to the black slaves from sub-Saharan Africa sold in the market beyond the gate, features more 'masculine' geometric patterns than those favoured by the Almoravids. The nearby **Koutoubia Mosque** is one of the city's oldest buildings; the classic Moroccan-Andalucian architecture has been renovated many times but the trelliswork brick and green faience tiles of the minaret are original. The 13m (42.3ft)-tower is topped with three copper globes, originally believed to have been made from the gold donated by the sultan's mother as a penance for not keeping fast during Ramadan.

A successive Berber tribe of Marinids moved the capital to Fès, where their skill at creating intricate mosaics, known as *zellije*, flourished. Possibly inspired by Roman mosaics found at nearby Volubilis, artisans created their own non-representational designs in keeping with Islamic teachings. There are rumoured to be more than 360 mosaic shapes, once naturally coloured by ground lapis lazuli (blue), fresh mint (green), pomegranate skins or saffron (yellow) and poppies or paprika (red), but today more likely to be oxidised cobalt, copper, chromium and iron. The Marinids also introduced intricately carved stucco and woodwork, and the most beautiful example is the serene 14th-century **Ben Youssef**, expanded in 1564 by Saadian sultan Abdallah El-Ghalib. The Madrasa Saadians from Arabia took control in the 16th century and returned the capital to Marrakech. The Saadian **El Badi Palace**, built with money raised from successful campaigns in Portugal, used gold from the Niger and 50 tons of marble from Italy. It was stripped bare by the incoming Alaouites, who used the materials to create Moulay Ismail's palace in the new capital of Meknes. Today it is home to nesting storks and occasional cultural events, as well as being the temporary home of the Museum for Photography and Visual Arts.

The final resting place of the Saadian sultans was discovered by accident in 1917 by an inquisitive Frenchman who, having noticed the green pyramids in a poorer part of the town, tracked down the narrow entrance to a garden where the sultans were buried. A concerned guardian of the **Saadian Tombs** apparently begged the infidel 'not to make it mere show for your people to gaze at'. That didn't work so well; finely worked cedarwood and stucco have made them one of the most popular tourist sites in Marrakech.

The 19th-century **Bahia Palace** was built by powerful court vizier Ba Ahmed Ben Moussa, and lived up to its name, meaning 'brilliant' or 'incomparable', featuring arcades and pavilions, shady courtyards and orange groves, beautiful *zellije*, sculpted stucco and carved cedarwood ceilings. The vizier is thought to have been poisoned by the sultan's wife and certainly, after Ben Moussa's death, the palace was looted by the sultan Abdelaziz. Ba Ahmed's brother lived in what is now the Dar Is Said Museum, where evidence of artisan building and decorating skills can be found.

The story of Marrakech is also that of clever garden design. When the Almoravids moved here from the desert in the 11th century they brought their revolutionary water technology with them; *khettaras* – long baked-mud irrigation pipes that used a system of hydraulics – brought water from the Ourika Valley to irrigate private and public gardens. It's said that when the El Badi Palace was completed, the people were as impressed by its sunken gardens and hundreds of fountains as the palace itself. The Almohads expanded the water system using *seguias* – open-air canals – to bring water from the High Atlas. The

increased water supply meant they too could establish wonderful gardens like the Menara to the west of the city.

When Morocco became a French protectorate in 1912, French governor Lyautey commissioned Henri Prost, a pioneer of French urbanism, to redesign the city, and the modern, geometric Guéliz area was the result. With the Koutoubia Mosque as a focal point, he designed a great road from his *ville nouvelle* which is now the Avenue Mohammed V. It was in Guéliz that artist Jacques Majorelle came to open his studio and, together with his brother, create the beautiful **Majorelle Garden**. He gave his name to the garden and the rich cobalt blue colour now found on so many Marrakchi walls, window frames, doors and gates. Today the garden houses a museum of Berber culture.

Prost was also responsible for the building of the glamorous La Mamounia hotel in the 18th-century gardens of al-Mamoun. Elegantly combining Art Deco and Marrakchi design, the hotel was soon frequented by the rich and famous: Winston Churchill came here to paint watercolours, Doris Day sang 'Que Sera, Sera' in room 414, and Nicole Kidman and Gwyneth Paltrow are more recent visitors. In an extensive refurbishment in 2009, Jacques Garcia retained the Majorelle blue ceilings, carved stucco arches and intricate *zellije*, and added even more fountains.

In 2014 King Mohammed VI announced the 'Marrakech City of Permanent Renewal' programme, which will doubtless be well represented by David Chipperfield's **Museum for Photography and Visual Arts**, slated for completion in 2016. Destined to be the largest gallery in North Africa, the low-rise sandstone cube will be set in the 12th-century Menara Gardens, and promises to link old architectural practices with modern. One thing is certain: however modern it becomes, the city is likely to remain stubbornly low-rise and red – Mohammed V insisted that no building rise above five storeys and must be some shade of terracotta red.

Majorelle Garden

El Badi Palace

Museum for Photography and Visual Arts

Koubba El-Badiyin

Koutoubia Mosque

L: Off Avenue Yacoub el Mansour
A: French artists Jacques and Louis Majorelle, 1920s
FF: See Yves Saint Laurent's collection of local arts and antiques in the Berber Museum.

L: Ksibat Nhass
A: Almohads, 1593
FF: The colonnades were made from Italian marble believed to have been exchanged for their equivalent weight in sugar.

L: Menara Gardens
A: David Chipperfield Architects, 2016
FF: The gallery is controversial as the locals are not comfortable with having their photograph taken.

L: Kaat Benahid
A: Almoravids, 12th century
FF: The foundation inscription — 'I was created for science and prayer, by the prince of the believers, descendant of the prophet, Abdallah, most glorious of all Caliphs. Pray for him when you enter the door, so that you may fulfil your highest hopes' — is the oldest inscription in cursive Maghrebi script in North Africa.

L: Avenue Mohammed V
A: Caliph Yaqub al-Mansur, 1184–99
FF: The mosque was the model for the Giralda Tower in Spain.

Ben Youssef

Saadian Tombs

Bahia Palace

Bab Agnaou

L: Rue Souk el Khemis
A: Almohads, 1570
FF: It's the largest madrasa in
North Africa.

L: Rue de La Kasbah
A: Unknown, 16th century
FF: The mausoleum comprises
the interments of about 60
members of the Saadi Dynasty.

L: 5 Rue Riad Zitoun el Jdid
A: Unknown, 19th century
FF: The current king still uses the
palace for functions but many
of the rooms can be visited,
including the royal harem where
24 concubines lived.

L: Rue Moulay Ismail
A: Almohad sultan Abu Yusuf Yaqub
al-Mansur, 12th century
FF: Three panels have Qur'an
inscriptions in Maghrebi script –
foliated Kufic letters.

Prague

'Your time is up! Havel to the castle!'
The 800,000-strong crowds who gathered in Prague's squares to bear witness to
Czechoslovakia's Velvet Revolution, November 1989

Visitors to 21st-century Prague might be forgiven for thinking we'd made a mistake in including the city in the fortress category of this book, and yet from the 13th century until as recently as the early 19th, what was then the city – the four independent towns of Old Town, New Town, Lesser Town and Hradcany – boasted stone fortifications as high as 10m (25ft). By the 19th century nearly all of them had gone, to be replaced by roads and river embankments.

But it's not just in their physical absence that modern Prague's walls are forgotten; the city is simply not one we associate with battlements, despite the castle that looms over it. What we associate most with Prague is popular protest and dissent in a long history of revolutions and uprisings against everything from church corruption to political ideologies; most memorably of course in the Velvet Revolution that led to Václav Havel becoming the first democratically elected president of the Czechoslovak Republic in 41 years on 29 December 1989.

Unlike previous leaders, and despite the chants of the crowds who supported him, **Prague Castle** was not an obvious choice of home for the newly elected Havel, who sited his office in it but chose to live elsewhere. It's easy to see its appeal to less self-effacing leaders though. Offering spectacular views of the city below, the castle complex, begun as a simple

wooden fortress in the 9th century, grew to become one of the largest in the world, with an area of almost 70,000m². Within it lies the city's most iconic sight, the Gothic **St Vitus Cathedral**, built over 800 years and boasting a Gothic and Renaissance Great Tower that dominates the city's skyline, topped with a Baroque bell tower housing the 16th-century, 15,120kg bell known as Sigismund.

A more complete Baroque work lies nearby in the complex in the shape of the Basilica St George, but the church towers that most visitors will note as they wander the city belong to the **Church of Our Lady before Týn**, whose twin towers are the epitome of late 14th-century Gothic styling, when it was built near the Old Town Square as a church for the people and became a popular meeting spot for the anti-establishment Hussites. An equally arresting but less obvious Gothic outline is that of the **Old-New Synagogue**, built a century earlier and the oldest synagogue in Europe. In its long history it has been a place of refuge for the city's ancient Jewish population, walled up in a ghetto until the late 18th century and almost entirely wiped out by the Nazis in the 20th.

Prague's public buildings, both secular and religious, have seen more turbulence than most, even as late as the 20th century. The medieval **Old Town Hall**, for example, has a 12th-century dungeon whose underground passages came in very handy when it became the headquarters of the Resistance during the city's uprising against the Nazis in 1945. And some of the city's buildings have seen more traditional resistance. The **Church of the Most Sacred Heart of Our Lord**, built in 1932 by pioneering Slovenian architect Josip Plečnik, is one of the city's most interesting pieces of modern architecture – its unique structure, materials and styling quite unlike anything else you'll see – but sadly, it didn't impress the locals at the time of its building and many still view it as an eyesore.

Yet despite their largely traditional approach to architecture, the citizens of Prague have embraced a handful of modern buildings in a city which has a surprising number of them, across a range of styles. Le Corbusier, for example, was initially nonplussed by, but then much taken with, the glass-walled low-slung functionalism of Josef Fuchs' **Veletržní Palace**, a trade fair palace that now houses the National Gallery collection of 19th-, 20th- and 21st-century art. The box-like structure was a pared-down version of cubism, applied to the built environment. Czech architects Josef Gočár, Vlastislav Hofman, Josef Chochol and Pavel Janák created a number of notable cubist buildings in the city, with the **House of the Black Madonna** by Gočár standing out for its clean lines and his Czechoslovak Legion Bank of 1924 illustrating the short-lived idea of rondocubism, which utilised rounder forms and is seen at its most arresting in the Adria Palace on Jungmannova.

But the modern building the locals have done the biggest volte-face with is far more modern than any of these. The sinuous, flowing **Dancing House**, designed in 1992 by Croatian architect Vlado Milunić and Frank Gehry, is much loved now, but at the time of its completion in 1996 opinions were as

divided as one would expect in this city of passionate cultural engagement. A large part of its detractors were particularly dismayed by its siting among the city's more classically traditional buildings, including the much-loved **National Theatre**. Conceived as a national monument to the performing arts, the original building of 1881 hosted just 12 concerts before being very badly damaged in a fire that destroyed the stage, auditorium and copper dome. Such was the strength of feeling about the building though that within two months the money to rebuild it had been raised by public donations, and the newly reconstructed theatre reopened on 18 November 1883.

The theatre was the last gasp of the neo-Renaissance style, a revival of the Renaissance-era architecture brought to the city by Italian craftsmen and draughtsmen in the 16th century. Of the few remaining examples of their skills, the restored **Schwarzenberg Palace** stands out for its *sgraffito* wall decoration.

With the 20th century came a new style, secessionism. As the Czech version of Art Nouveau, the standout example is the **Municipal House**, built on the site of the old Royal Court Palace as a mixed-use building with the 1,500-seat performance hall of the Prague Symphony Orchestra at its heart. Next door to it, the 65m (213ft)-high Gothic Powder Gate has borne witness to centuries of tumultuous events, among them religious riots in the 15th century and the city's most important historical event of recent history: on 28 October 1989 Czechoslovakia's independence was proclaimed here. If ever a building were the right one to witness such a metaphorical tearing down of walls, it is the 15th-century gate, built to replace one of the original Old Town gates and one of the few remaining reminders of Prague's once-fortified state.

Veletržni Palace

House of the Black Madonna

Church of the Most
Sacred Heart of Our Lord

Dancing House

Old Town Hall

Prague Castle/
St Vitus Cathedral

L: Dukelských Hrdinu 530/47
A: Oldřich Tyl and Josef Fuchs, 1920s
FF: The trade fair palace was meant to be demolished after a fire in 1970, but was given a new lease of life when it was chosen by the National Gallery to house its collections of modern and contemporary art.

L: Ovocný trh 19
A: Josef Gočár, 1911–12
FF: Taking its name from the Black Madonna located high up on it, this cubist building was originally a department store, then the Centre of Czech Art & Culture, before being opened in 2003 as the Museum of Czech Cubism.

L: Jiřího z Poděbrad
A: Josip Plečnik, 1929–32
FF: The glazed bricks and artificial granite of the church's facade make it stand out so clearly that it can be seen from as far away as Prague Castle.

L: Jiráskovo náměstí 1981–6
A: Frank Gehry, Vlado Milunić, 1992
FF: The building's nickname, Fred and Ginger, after Fred Astaire and Ginger Rogers, derives from the graceful form the building creates on the banks of the Vltava River.

L: Staroměstské náměstí 1/3
A: Unknown, 14th–15th centuries
FF: The Old Town Hall's most famous building is the tower, whose 15th-century clock tells the time and planetary movements, and features the 12 apostles, who appear when the clock strikes the hour.

L: Prague 11908
A: Jože Plečnik, Benedikt Rejt, Bořek Šípek, St Vitus: 1344–1929
FF: The guards' uniforms were designed by Theodor Pištěk, who won an Oscar for his costume designs for the film *Amadeus*, much of which was shot in Prague.

Church of Our
Lady before Týn

Schwarzenberg
Palace

National Theatre

Municipal House

Old-New
Synagogue

L: Staroměstské náměstí
A: Matthias of Arras, Peter Parler,
14th–15th centuries
FF: Buried in a marble tomb here is
the Danish astronomer Tycho Brahe,
famous for his false nose.

L: Hradčanské náměstí 2
A: Agostino Galli, 1545–76
FF: The interior of this Florentine palace features
four ceiling paintings dating from 1580.

L: Národní 2
A: Josef Zítek, 1878, Josef Schulz, 1883
FF: After its near destruction in a fire,
the theatre reopened on 18 November
1883 with a performance of Bedřich
Smetana's opera *Libuše,* composed for
this occasion.

L: Náměstí Republiky 5
A: Antonín Balšánek and Osvald Polívka,
1905–12
FF: The interior of the building features
murals by Alfons Mucha, the famed Czech
Art Nouveau painter and decorative artist,
and a huge mural above the main entrance
by Karel Špillar.

L: Maiselova 18
A: Unknown, 1270
FF: It's said that the
body of the Golem lies
in the synagogue's
attic, should it ever
be needed to defend
the Jewish community
again.

Baku

'The Black City throughout centuries will turn White, clean, there will be grown flowers, and it will come to be a beautiful sight of Azerbaijan...'

Heydar Aliyev, President of Azerbaijan

Way back in the 6th century Baku was a little desert village, sitting on the Absheron peninsula jutting out into the Caspian Sea. Once part of the Persian Empire, Azerbaijan was a bizarre land of mud volcanoes, salt lakes, burning mountains and Stone Age petroglyphs carved into the rock faces of cave dwellings. The word 'Azerbaijan' comes from the Persian word for fire – 'Azar', and the Land of Fire is where the Zoroastrian fire-worshipping cult developed, with temples being erected around burning gas vents. Today Azerbaijan supplies half of the world's oil, but the centuries-old civilisation can still be found in the music, the way of life and the architecture.

Bringing the past together with the present was something that architects HOK considered when constructing the iconic **Flame Towers**. Barry Hughes, HOK's vice-president, believes that every building 'starts with a single germ of an idea', and the design team realised that the towers could be a symbol of the fire-worshipping Zoroastrians as well as reference the booming economy based on the country's natural gas. The three towers are covered with LED screens that display the movement of fire that is visible from all over the city.

The old walled city Içeri Sehear, today a UNESCO World Heritage Site, dates at least as far back as the 12th century and within it are two of Azerbaijan's oldest structures. The mysterious **Maiden Tower**, which may date back to the 7th century, is almost circular but appears to have a tail and is thought to represent the Zoroastrian symbol for fire. Its purpose is unknown, though it may have been built to protect Azeri women from attacks on the city. The **Palace of the Shirvanshahs** was commissioned by Sheikh Ibrahim I, one of the Shahs who ruled Shirvan in northern Azerbaijan from the 16th to 6th century BC and is a fine example of Azeri architecture. The palace itself has internal and external apartments laid out over two storeys, with more rooms on the second floor, where the Shahs lived, than the first, where supporting staff lived.

Between the Palace and the Maiden Tower lies the **Muhammad Mosque**, constructed in 1078 and one of the oldest in Azerbaijan. The nearby **Sinig-Gala Minaret**, known as the 'Broken Tower', was damaged by the army of Peter the Great in 1743 and never repaired, as a reminder of the attack.

Azerbaijan's fortunes changed when its unlimited natural resources were discovered in the 19th century. Prospectors flocked from every corner of the country and the sleepy little town was transformed into a boomtown. Local landowner, Isa Bey Hajinski, was one of those who discovered oil on his land and commissioned an extravagant five-storey residence (the **Hajinski Mansion**) with such eclectic styling that it looks like two separate buildings. It is rumoured that the architect was siphoning off materials to build his own property (now the American Embassy).

The Soviet era between 1920 and 1991 saw much of the oil boom architecture repurposed for more 'fitting' pursuits; today's **State Philharmonic Hall** was originally built in 1910 to entertain rich gamblers, and the architect was clearly influenced by Monte Carlo casinos, hence plenty of rococo and a gilt roof. With gambling hardly a suitable activity during the Russian Civil War, the club was then used for rallies and later for Azerbaijani classical music. It closed in 1995, was renovated in 2002 and reopened in 2004. In 1969, the Republic's governor, Heydar Aliyev, awarded Baku mayor Alish Lambaranski the job of guiding construction. Lambaranski oversaw a host of important Soviet buildings including the **Heydar Aliyev Palace** (previously Lenin Palace), one of Baku's main performance venues and a fine example of Soviet architecture. It was considered as a possible location for the 2012 Eurovision Song Contest before the **Crystal Hall** was built.

The **Azeri TV Tower**, started in 1979 by order of the Ministry of Communications of the USSR, is the tallest structure in Azerbaijan and the tallest reinforced concrete building in the Caucasus. Made entirely of concrete, it has a revolving restaurant on the 62nd floor and, on occasion, sections of the tower are lit in different colours to represent the Azerbaijani flag to help celebrate national holidays.

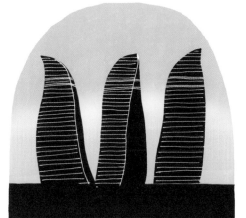

The futuristic **International Mugham Center** was built in 2008 as a showcase for the extraordinary Azeri music known as *mugham*, a complex art form combining classical poetry and musical improvisation, featuring a male or female singer and using traditional instruments. In 2003 the music gained UNESCO status as a masterpiece of 'Oral and Intangible Cultural Heritage of Humanity'.

Another venue playing a role in the cultural and intellectual life of the city is the curvaceous **Heydar Aliyev Center** designed by Iraqi–British architect Zaha Hadid. Far removed from the angular boxy architecture so typical of the Soviet era, the arts complex is a flowing, undulating construction. In apparent tribute to historical Islamic architecture there are no sharp angles, and continuous calligraphic and ornamental patterns flow from carpets to walls. The centre was awarded Design of the Year 2014 by London's Design Museum.

Baku's appearance on the world stage was secured by its hosting of the Eurovision Song Contest in 2012. The circular Crystal Hall has the appearance of a glowing gemstone, thanks to thousands of interactive lights that can respond to events occurring within the building. The arena will probably be used for the handball and indoor volleyball events in the first European Games to be hosted here in 2015.

Looking ahead, it's intended that the European Grand Prix will weave through the city's medieval streets in 2016. There's also a bid to host the 2020 Olympic Games and, presumably in the interests of making the best first impression, Turkish design studio Autoban was invited to design the newest terminal at Heydar Aliyev International Airport. Inspired by Azerbaijan hospitality, Autoban created cosy cocoons to house cafés and bars. Each cocoon is clad in diamond-shaped wood shingles, creating shells around the different-sized forms.

The National Leader of Azerbaijan, Heydar Aliyev, has initiated a scheme to develop the city further by revitalising the 'Black City', so-called thanks to its creation during the oil boom. An area of 221 hectares has been designated to create a brand new 'White City' intended to attract local and foreign investment for residential and commercial buildings.

Finally, at a whopping 1,050m (3,445ft), the Azerbaijan Tower will be the tallest building in the world (the Burj Al Khalifa is a mere 829m [2,720ft]). Work starts in 2015 and is expected to be completed in 2019.

State Philharmonic Hall

Azeri TV Tower

Heydar Aliyev Palace

International Mugham Center

Muhammad Mosque and Sınıq-Qala Minaret

Crystal Hall

HEYDƏR ƏLİYEV SARAYI

L: Istiglaliyyat Street 2
A: Gabriel Ter-Mikelov, 1910
FF: Open-air shows are staged during the warmer months.

L: Sabayil
A: Unknown, 1996
FF: Views from the revolving restaurant at 175m (574ft) are spectacular.

L: Prospect Bülbül 35
A: Alish Lemberanski, 1972
FF: As well as musicals and dance shows, some big jazz musicians play here.

L: Boulevard Park
A: Unknown, 2008
FF: The buildings are made of Baku stone and are said to symbolise the traditions and history of *mugham*: the glass and metal express modernity, while the wooden parts represent folklore.

L: Kiçik Qala
A: Mohammad Abu Bakr, 1078
FF: Nearby is the former house of Vagif Mustafazadeh, the father of *mugham* jazz. It's now a museum.

L: National Flag Square
A: GMP International, 2012
FF: The building's facade is covered with 9,500 LED lights, which bring the structure to life after dark.

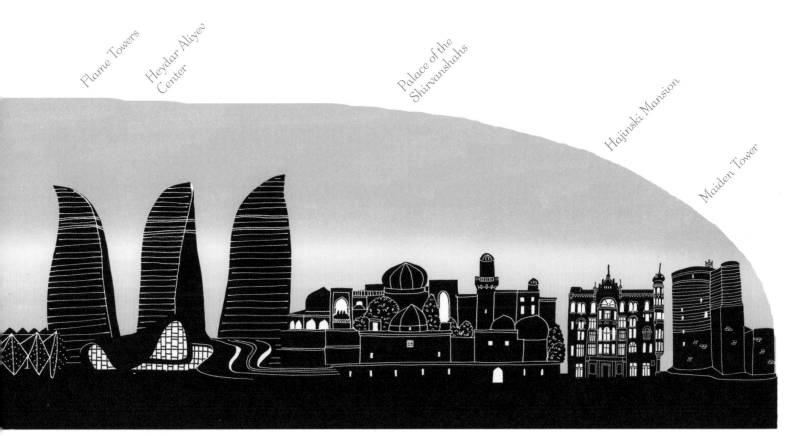

Flame Towers

Heydar Aliyev Center

Palace of the Shirvanshahs

Hajinski Mansion

Maiden Tower

L: Mehdi Hüseyn Street
A: HOK, 2007
FF: All three towers have different functions: residence, hotel and office.

L: 1 Heydar Aliyev prospect
A: Zaha Hadid, 2012
FF: The entrances are represented by folds in a continuous surface; spaces can be connected or allowed to remain separate and private.

L: 46 Boyuk Gala Street
A: Unknown, 15th century
FF: One of the mausoleums is said to have been built for the sufi mystic Seyid Yahya Bakuvi, hired as the tutor for the ruler Khalilullah I's children.

L: Neftchilar 105
A: Unknown Italian, 1912
FF: The building is now occupied by a Tom Ford fashion store.

L: Neftchilar Avenue
A: Unknown, 7th century
FF: A first floor display shows early maps and photos of the city.

Carcassonne

'Carcassonne is a unique example of a double fortification. The older part dates from late antiquity, the more recent part from the 13th century. The first without doubt inspired the second. The projection of the towers from the wall, and the fact that they therefore commanded it, made possible a more flexible system of defence.'

John Julius Norwich, *The World Atlas of Architecture*

On a hill above the river Aude in south-west France lies the fortified medieval city of Carcassonne. Recognising its strategic position, Neolithic settlers had created a proto-fort (oppidum) here as far back as 600 BC. The Romans occupied the hilltop around 100 BC, building up fortifications on concrete foundations that they then topped with rubble core and faced with fashioned stone.

Though the fortifications were strong, they were no match for the forces of Pope Innocent III, who had initiated a 20-year military campaign – the Albigensian Crusade – to rid the Languedoc region of Catharism, a dualist faith that posited that there were two principles: a good creator god and an evil adversary. Carcassonne's hereditary count, Raymond-Roger Trencavel, was no Cathar himself, but he also didn't persecute them as the Papacy would have liked and, in 1209, the city was sacked; Raymond-Roger wound up in a dungeon in his own castle, where he died, possibly from dysentery or perhaps poisoning. The **Château Comtal** – a 'fortress within a fortress' – was built by Trencavel's ancestors in the 11th century and boasts turrets, a curtain wall, a barbican and now an architecture museum. It also affords access to part of the Cité ramparts.

But it was the threat from the Crown of Aragon in north-eastern Spain that resulted in the largest European fortress ever built, with the addition of a second wall, with 17 towers and barbicans. These outer ramparts, which run for three kilometres, along with the crenellated turrets and towers that give the city its fairy-tale appearance, were built by King Louis IX. One of the towers housed the Catholic Inquisition – the very first – that was set up by the Papacy in a more robust attempt to stamp out the Cathar 'heresy' that continued to sweep the region. Today, the 'Inquisition Tower' houses a Torture Museum, which creepily exhibits some of the original implements of torture.

Following a rebellion in the 13th century, Louis (later known as Saint Louis), turfed the locals out of the fortified town and they set up in Basse Ville (lower town), today known as Bastide St Louis, and the commercial heart of the city. The **Pont Vieux bridge**, which spans the Aude river and was once the only link between the two parts of the city, dates back to the Middle Ages.

The **walls of the city** were punctuated with regular horseshoe defences, such as **Porte Narbonnaise**. Added by Louis' son Philip, the Gothic twin-towered bastion, which features traceried windows, is so-called because it faces towards the nearby town of Narbonne. The city's fortifications were now so solid that they were never breached during the Hundred Years War (1337 to 1453) between France and England.

Carcassonne was the first fortress to use hoardings during times of siege; temporary wooden ramparts were fitted to the original structure to protect defenders of the wall, and to allow them to hurl projectiles from saftey. Though the city's walls were never breached, the town was ravaged by a great fire in 1355 during a thwarted attack by Edward, Prince of Wales, known as the Black Prince. A survivor of the fire was the **Maison du Sénéchal** (purportedly the house of the nobleman in charge of the castle's domestic affairs), said to be the oldest house in the Basse Ville. The windows and Medieval ogival door on the ground floor are the oldest part of the building, while the first-floor windows date from the 14th century, and the columns that decorate a well in the interior courtyard date from the 16th century.

During Napoleon's Ancien Regime, Carcassonne was struck off a list of official fortifications and began to fall into disrepair. Following the French Revolution, the town was used as an arsenal, and then as a source for stone, and by 1849 the French government decided that the city fortifications were in such bad shape that they might as well be demolished. Thankfully the decision was strongly opposed, especially by historians and archaeologists, and Eugène-Emmanuel Viollet-le-Duc was called in to undertake the restoration.

Viollet-le-Duc, a French architect who was responsible for restoring the Notre Dame Cathedral in Paris, was, at the time, already involved in the refashioning of the 11th-century Gothic **Basilica of St Nazaire** – with a six-bayed nave, barrel-vaulting and some fine stained-glass windows that are more than 700 years old. Viollet-le-Duc began his life's work in remodelling the city in 1853 and continued until his death.

The city has evolved over the years. A good example of this is the **Théâtre Jean-Deschamps**, an open-air theatre that was built in 1908 on the site of an old cloister. The semi-circular auditorium, faced with a medieval wall on two sides, can accommodate around 5,000 spectators and hosts the annual Festival des Deux Cités. In 2006 the name changed to Jean-Deschamps Theatre in memory of the French actor and director.

Viollet-le-Duc believed that architecture should be a direct expression of current materials, technology and needs, but his Gothic remodelling didn't always go down so well with the purists, who even suggested that the use of slate in the roofs was inauthentic. John Ruskin decried Viollet-le-Duc's embellishments as 'a destruction out of which no remnants can be gathered: a destruction accompanied with false description of the thing destroyed'. But times and attitudes change, and today Viollet-le-Duc is considered to be the father of modern restoration and, in spite of the criticisms, the restored citadel was added to UNESCO's list of World Heritage Sites in 1997.

Porte Narbonnaise

Maison du Sénéchal

City Walls

Basilica of St Nazaire

L: Cité de Carcassonne
A: Unknown, 1280
FF: The gateway provides the only entrance to the Cité by road. A drawbridge was added in the 19th century by Viollet-le-Duc.

L: 70 Rue Aimé Ramond
A: Unknown, 14th century
FF: It is unlikely that the Sénéchal actually lived here; he was more likely to have resided in the castle.

L: Cité de Carcassonne
A: Various, 1st–14th centuries, Eugène-Emmanuel Viollet-le-Duc led the restoration project in the 19th century
FF: The area between the walls known as the *lices* or 'lists' is where medieval jousting once took place.

L: Place Auguste-Pierre Pont
A: Unknown, 11th century
FF: Mass is held every Sunday at 11 a.m.

Château Comtal

Théâtre Jean-Deschamps

Pont Vieux bridge

L: 1 rue Viollet-le-Duc
A: Unknown, 12th century
FF: The château houses a museum of architecture and admission is free.

L: Place Saint-Nazaire
A: Unknown, 1908
FF: The summer Festival des Deux Cités is one of France's largest arts festivals.

L: Bastide St Louis
A: Unknown, 15th century
FF: Until the 19th century it was the only link between the Baside St Louis and the Cité de Carcassonne.

Genoa

'There lies all Genoa, in beautiful confusion, with its many churches, monasteries, and convents, pointing up into the sunny sky.'

Charles Dickens, *Pictures from Italy*

The second largest port in the Mediterranean takes its name from the Latin 'Janua', meaning 'gate', and from the 7th century BC it was attacked, destroyed and rebuilt by, in no particular order, Arabs, Byzantines, Carthaginians, Etruscans, Franks, Goths, Lombards, Romans and Saracens. The need for defensive walls was paramount. The first Roman walls were probably destroyed by the Lombards, but the city reinforced its defences many times, right up to the 17th century. One of the earliest surviving gates within the city walls is the twin-battlement towered **Porta Soprana** (meaning 'door raised above street level'), built in 1155. Close by is the **Christopher Columbus House Museum** – an 18th-century reconstruction of the medieval original – where he reputedly lived before setting off on his sea voyages.

During the 9th and 10th centuries, Italian ports were under constant attack from Spanish Muslim raiding parties, but by the 11th century, Genoa was on the offensive and success at sea saw her become an independent maritime republic, along with Amalfi, Pisa and Venice. By the 13th century Genoa was the most important naval power in the western Mediterranean and the medieval city within its walls was the largest in Europe; its narrow cobble-stoned alleyways, known as *caruggi*, still lead from the port up to Piazza de Ferrari, now the city's main square.

During the Middle Ages, the city was ruled by doges, who made their home in the imposing **Palazzo Ducale**. Only the left wing remains of the 13th-century palace, with later alterations including a tower built by the Fieschi family, restoration by Andrea Ceresola in the 16th century and, following a fire in 1777, the Simone Cantoni neoclassical rebuild that can be seen today.

Founded in the 9th century and remodelled in the 12th, the Romanesque **Cattedrale di San Lorenzo** got a Gothic makeover in the 14th century and gained its 'zebra' exterior of grey-and-white striped marble. Dedicated to Saint Lawrence, the cathedral was paid for with money raised by successful crusades. It was built on an earlier church dedicated to the 12 apostles and further excavations revealed Roman walls and pavements as well as sarcophagi, suggesting it was built on an ancient burial site. In 1550, Perugian architect Galeazzo Alessi reconstructed the nave and aisles, the dome and the apse.

By the 13th century, the Genoese, along with the other maritime republics, were looking for a sea route to the Orient. Venetian Marco Polo spent years sailing the globe, travelling to the court of Kublai Khan, the Mongol ruler of China, as well as Persia, Sumatra, Ceylon, southern India and Iran. In 1295 he returned to Venice only to be captured, in battle, by the Genoese and imprisoned in **Palazzo San Giorgio**; the palace built by Guglielmo Boccanegra, uncle of Simone Boccanegra, the first Doge of Genoa, was now a prison.

The 13th-century palace had originally been built using materials taken from the demolished Venetian embassy in Constantinople, which were donated by Byzantine Emperor Michael VIII in thanks for Genoese help against the Latin Empire. The exterior has a fresco showing St George slaying a dragon. While imprisoned, Marco Polo revealed his wild adventures to fellow inmate Rustichello da Pisa, who, perhaps embellishing them somewhat, spread 'Travels of Marco Polo' all over Europe. Columbus certainly studied them before setting off on his own adventures.

By the 15th century Genoa had control of most of the trade routes in the eastern Mediterranean, enabling the wealthy to put their names behind what is likely to be the oldest bank in the world. The Bank of Saint George, founded in 1407, had its headquarters in the same Palazzo San Giorgio where Marco Polo had been held more than 100 years earlier. Powerful Genoese bankers financed many of Spain's early expeditions across the Atlantic, including that of Columbus.

The city became a republic in 1522 and increased wealth can be seen in the Renaissance and Baroque palaces on the *Strade Nuove* ('New Streets'). Built between the 16th and 18th centuries, many of the elegant stuccoed palaces were listed on the *Palazzi dei Rolli* – a register of dwellings whose aristocratic owners offered hospitality to kings and other important personages on state visits. Peter Paul Rubens was so impressed by the palaces that, in 1550, he published a collection of designs that were so detailed they were used in the reconstruction of those palaces that had suffered bomb damage during the Second World War. A staggering 46 (out of 163) are UNESCO World Heritage Sites and three are now galleries: Palazzo Tursi, now the City Hall, holds one of Paganini's violins as well as, reputedly, Christopher Columbus's bones.

The 17th/18th-century **Palazzo Spinola** is one of the city's finest. There are stunning *trompe l'oeil* frescoes (a Genoese speciality) and a gallery of

mirrors designed by French architect and designer, Charles de Wailly, who went on to design the Château de Fontainebleau. In 1959 it became the city's National Gallery and holds exquisite collections of furniture, porcelain, textiles and silverware, as well as artwork belonging to its previous owners.

Charles Dickens came to Genoa in 1844 and stayed at **Villa Pallavicino** in the Castelletto area. The palace, which was designed by Galeazzo Alessi for the banker and Spanish fleet ship-owner Tobia Pallavicino, would have been outside the city walls until the 17th-century 'New Walls' were erected. Castelletto (meaning 'small castle') takes its name from a now-demolished 10th-century fort that overlooks the whole Genoese area. According to Dickens's biographer and friend, John Forster, Dickens was inspired by the church bells heard from his villa: 'All Genoa lay beneath him, and up from it, with some sudden set of the wind, came in one fell sound the clang and clash of all its steeples, pouring into his ears, again and again, in a tuneless, grating, discordant, jerking, hideous vibration that made his ideas "spin round and round till they lost themselves in a whirl of vexation and giddiness, and dropped down dead".' (*The Chimes*, 1844.)

Pritzker prize-winning architect, Renzo Piano, was born in Genoa. He has been a key figure in reshaping the Porto Antico that was so vital to the city's fortunes. He designed **Il Bigo** – the panoramic lift that resembles the cranes of the old docks – for the 500th anniversary of the 'discovery' of America (Genoa's other famous son), and he also designed a huge metal and glass **biosphere** – 'Piano's Bubble' – that sits above the water and is filled with exotic plants and butterflies.

As Goodwill Ambassador of UNESCO for Architecture, Renzo Piano has been credited with redefining modern and postmodern architecture. 'When people ask me what the city of the future will look like, I tell them: 'I hope like the one of the past'.'

Biosphere

Villa Pallavicino

Palazzo Ducale

Porta Soprana

L: Porto Antico
A: Renzo Piano, 2001
FF: Thanks to a sophisticated 'system of sails', the tropical environment is protected from the direct irradiation of the sun.

L: Via San Bartolomeo degli Armeni, Castelletto
A: Galeazzo Alessi, 16th century
FF: The gardens are terraced with ponds that give them the name Peschiere ('fishponds').

L: Piazza Giacomo Matteotti, 9
A: Unknown, 1251–75; Simone Cantoni, 18th century
FF: Today the palace hosts regular art and photographic exhibitions, as well as the Pesto World Championship.

L: Via di Porta Soprana
A: Unknown, 12th century
FF: You can head up into the towers to admire the view.

Palazzo
San Giorgio

Christopher Columbus
House Museum

Palazzo Spinola

Cattedrale di
San Lorenzo

Il Bigo

L: Via della Mercanzia, 2
A: Unknown, 1260
FF: The frescoes on the
western facade (discovered
during renovations) are the
work of Lazzaro Tavarone.

L: Via di Porta Soprana
A: Unknown, 15th century
FF: Next door is a pretty
ruin – the Chiostro di
Sant'Andrea (cloister of
St Andrew).

L: Piazza di Pellicceria, 1
A: Unknown, 17th–18th centuries
FF: The roof garden offers
wonderful views over the city.

L: Piazza di San Lorenzo
A: Unknown, 9th–16th centuries
FF: In the crypt's Museo del Tesoro
there is a silver chest that is said
to contain the ashes of St John,
which are carried around the city
on 24 June.

L: Porto Antico
A: Renzo Piano, 1992
FF: The lift elevates passengers up 40m (130ft)
and rotates 360 degrees, giving a spectacular
view of the city, along with commentary.

Dubrovnik

'If you want to see paradise on earth, come to Dubrovnik.'
George Bernard Shaw

When Dubrovnik's city walls were first conceived as a defence more than a thousand years ago, then realised in their present form during the 14th and 15th centuries, their creators always knew that their little city would need greater protection from the landmass behind them than the sea in front of them. As the walls were strengthened against the threat of attacks from the Venetians and the Turks in the 15th century, what the rulers of Ragusa, as the town was then called, could never have imagined was what would happen 500 years on. With modern long-range weaponry, the Serbs and Montenegrins mounted such a ferocious attack from **Mt Srdj**, the towering mass that sits behind the little city, when the countries clashed in the 1990s, that they did more damage to Dubrovnik than 1,000 years of wars, occupations and earthquakes had managed to do. This despite the city having been declared a UNESCO World Heritage Site in 1979.

But the builders of Dubrovnik's city walls would have been proud of the fact that despite 111 direct hits, the shellings failed to breach any of the 1,940m (6,365ft) of walls that encircle most of the old city, which is hardly surprising, given their thickness of between 1–3m (3.3–9.8ft) in the sea-facing walls, and between 4–6m (13–19.6ft) in the Srdj-facing ones. And just to be on the safe side, the walls were fortified by four impressive forts, including the stolid mass of **St John's Fortress**. Its extraordinary scale is down to the fact

that it was originally two structures, Dock Fort and Fort Gundulić, unified by local architect Paskoje Miličević, who spent five decades strengthening and fortifying the walls during the 16th century.

Miličević worked on the harbour fortifications as well as completing the cylindrical Bokar and **Minčeta** towers. This latter, begun by Florentine architect/sculptor Michelozzo di Bartolomeo Michelozzi, and added to by Zagreb architect Juraj Dalmatinac, is the highest point of the fortifications, and affords great views over not just the wall, with its 12 square towers and five bastions, but also the two huge fortresses supplementing the city's defences, Revelin and the 11th-century **Lovrijenac**. The 4–12m (13.1–39.3ft) walls of this latter site, majestically sited on its own 37m (121ft)-high rock, have most recently been breached by a totally unexpected army; *Game of Thrones* fans from around the world flock here to visit the location of King's Landing.

What they see in their mind's eye is not so different to what the 14th-century citizens of Ragusa would have seen in reality, though the tiny maritime republic was a much more egalitarian society than the fictional King's Landing; Ragusa elected a Senate annually, banned slavery in 1416, gave its citizens clean water and even had an old people's home. The clean water was fed from a well 12km away into the impressive **Onofrio's**

When the 1667 earthquake destroyed much of the city, the fountain, badly damaged and permanently losing its top, continued to work as a city reservoir, and did so for another 332 years. Close to it, the 1528 **Church of St Saviour** proved equally resistant to seismic disruption, being one of the very few buildings in the city to remain almost intact – perhaps because it was built in thanks for the city's survival of an earthquake 147 years earlier.

Nearby, the 14th-century Romanesque **Franciscan Monastery** was less fortunate, so badly damaged all that's left of its original church is a portal decorated with a beautiful pietà, sculpted by local sculptors Petar and Leonard Andrijić in 1498. But it did manage to retain some original features, including a pharmacy that has been in continuous operation since 1317, and a beautiful Romanesque cloister with ornate double columns, lush planting and a pretty 15th-century fountain by Onofrio. Its lovely three-tiered tower dominates the western part of the city, and is matched to the east by the **Dominican Monastery**'s equally elegant bell tower – a late 18th-century addition to the 13/14th-century monastery. Still, the late Gothic cloisters are original, as is the unusually simple Gothic/Renaissance

styling of the facade and the large, single-naved monastery church.

Continuing along the harbour front, you'd be forgiven for thinking Ragusa's former customs house and mint, the **Sponza Palace**, was another casualty of the earthquake, but its architectural mix has real charm; its gracious columns and porticoed front, topped with late Gothic mullioned windows and Renaissance-style windows above them, combine to create a rare example of the Adriatic's dominant style in the 16th century. Adjacent to the palace, the Clock Tower was first recorded in 1444, and while a diminutive 31m (102ft), is a source of pride to locals, not least for the daily performance put on by Maro and Baro, the two replica bronze figures who strike the ancient bronze bell.

Next door to the Palace lies one of the city's, if not the Adriatic's, grandest civic buildings, the **Rector's Palace**. Home to Ragusa's Senate meetings, it's remarkable this building is here at all. Having survived fire, an explosion, two earthquakes and the Serbian attack, its amalgamation of Gothic, Renaissance and Baroque makes it a standout piece of architecture.

South of it, you'd expect the **Assumption Cathedral** to be the city's most imposing religious site, but it has little of note beyond its dominant cupola and an impressive interior space featuring some colourful marble altars. More arresting, both inside and out, is the **Jesuit Church**, also called St Ignatius, whose tower dominates the Dubrovnik skyline. Its dramatic setting is reached by an equally dramatic flight of stairs built by Roman Pietro Passalaqua in 1770. From here, looking out across the town to the rebuilt cable car bobbing its way up to Mt Srdj, it's hard to imagine the terrible damage the city so recently sustained, but a closer look at the old town's terracotta rooftops reveals the extent of the damage to the city – almost 70 per cent of the city's total. The solid city walls, by contrast, stand tall and firm, looking for all the world like they'll still be there in another thousand years.

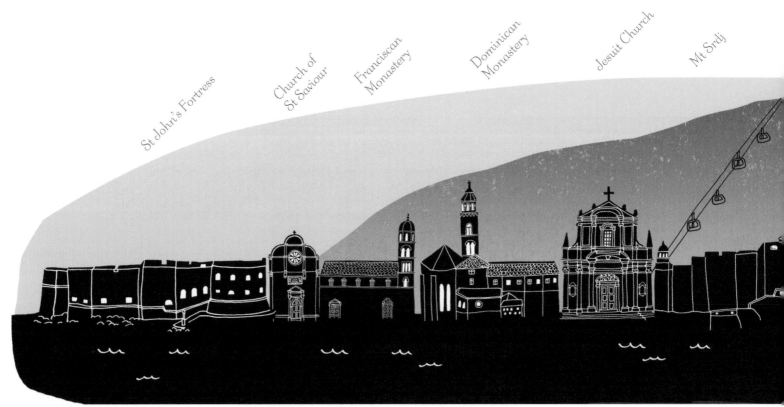

St John's Fortress

Church of St Saviour

Franciscan Monastery

Dominican Monastery

Jesuit Church

Mt Srdj

L: South-eastern side of the old city port
A: Unknown, 1346–1557
FF: Heavy chains were stretched between the fort and the Kase jetty to block entry to the port.

L: Ulica od Puca 8
A: Petar Andrijić, 1528
FF: Candlelit concerts are held here regularly.

L: Stradun 2
A: Mihoje Brajkov, 1360, Leonard and Petar Petrovic, 1498–9
FF: The monastery actually has two cloisters, but one is for private use only and not accessible to the public.

L: Sv Dominika 4
A: Various, incl. Bonino of Milan, Massa di Bartolomeo Božitko Bogdanovic, Paskoje Mili čević and Checo of Monopoli, 14th–15th centuries
FF: The monastery houses a fine collection of late 15th-century artworks by painters of the Venetian school, including *Annunciation* by Nikola Božidarevic and *Triptych of St. Nicholas* by Mihajlo Hamzic.

L: Gundulic Square
A: Iganzio Pozzo, 1725
FF: The church belfry houses the oldest bell in Dubrovnik, cast in 1355.

L: N/A (Cable car, Petra Kresimira IV bb)
A: N/A
FF: The cable car to the top of the mountain was built in 1969, destroyed in 1991 and rebuilt in 2010. On a clear day, you can see up to 60km away.

City walls and Minčeta tower

Assumption Cathedral

Sponza Palace

Rector's Palace

Onofrio's Fountains

Lovrijenac

L: N/A
A: Michelozzo di Bartolomeo Michelozzi, Juraj Dalmatinac, Paskoje Miličević, 13th–17th centuries
FF: Michelozzo di Bartolomeo Michelozzi was more famous as a sculptor than a builder, and collaborated on artworks with Donatello.

L: Opcina Dubrovnik
A: Andrea Bufalini, 1671–1713
FF: The current cathedral replaces a 12th-century one supposedly funded by a gift from England's King Richard I, the Lionheart, who was saved from a shipwreck here on his way back from Palestine in 1192.

L: Opcina Dubrovnik
A: Paskoje Miličević, 1516-1522
FF: Just inside the entrance is the Memorial Room of the Defenders of Dubrovnik, 300 photographs of those who died defending the city during the seige of Dubrovnik in 1991–2.

L: Pred Dvorum 3
A: Onofrio della Cava, Michelozzo di Bartolomeo Michelozzi, 16th century
FF: On the 16th-century Baroque staircase, look out for the sculpted hands that keep the handrail in place.

L: Poljana Paska Miličevića
A: Onofrio della Cava, 1438
FF: Originally the fountain was decorated, but it was heavily damaged in the 1667 earthquake and only 16 carved masks remain, with water gushing from their mouths into a drainage pool.

L: West entrance to the old city
A: Various, incl. I. K. Zanchi, 14th–17th centuries
FF: The three terraces of the fort make a wonderfully spooky backdrop for Dubrovnik's Summer Festival, when *Hamlet* is staged here complete with ghosts on the battlements.

Jaipur

'A vision of daring and dainty loveliness... Aladdin's magician could have called into existence no more marvellous abode.'
Poet and journalist Sir Edwin Arnold, on the Hawa Mahal

The Rajasthan capital of Jaipur could have gone into the Visionary section of this book, given its genesis as one man's vision of how a city should and could be built. But we've included it in Fortress cities because that man, Jai Singh II, planned his city with the protective walls that stand to this day, punctuated by ten remaining gates and once defended by impressive forts, including the Nahargarh fort that looms over the city. Within the walls, Maharaja Jai Singh II and feted Bengali Brahmin architect Vidyadhar Bhattacharya built a city based on various classical Indian architectural principles, including *vastu shastra* and *shilpa shastra* – an ancient Hindu treatise on architecture in which blocks are contained within a grid structure set around a central square and divided by broad avenues, and began its construction in 1727.

Contained within the blocks are stunning palaces, temples, huge townhouses built for the city's aristocracy and one block that is the go-to site for all visitors to the Pink City – the City Palace. This comprises a handful of outstanding buildings, including **Chandra Mahal** and **Mubarak Mahal**, built in a richly decorated architectural hotchpotch of Rajput, Mughal and European styles, and accessed via ornate gateways like the triple-arched Tripolia Gate, lavishly decorated with Mughal murals, fretwork and mirrors and reserved for the royals who still live in part of the Chandra Mahal. This seven-storey building is a star of the complex, despite its corner location, with each floor decorated in a different style and the whole towering above the surrounding structures. But in the centre of the palace, the sandstone and Dolomite marble Mubarak Mahal holds pride of place, its exterior of delicate filigreed fretwork and slender arches matched inside by some of the most opulent textiles in Rajasthan in its role as the city's textiles and costume museum.

Nearby, one building outdoes even the palace's splendour. The red and pink pyramid-shaped **Hawa Mahal**, or Palace of the Winds, is the most intricate building in the city, yet is something of a sham. For behind its 953 latticed windows, or *jharokhas*, the seemingly imposing, peculiarly Baroque structure built of lime and mortar is just one room deep, and doesn't even have a solid back wall. Still, for the Maharaja's wives, courtesans and servants concealed behind its windows, the building afforded a fantastic view of the daily life they were unable to take part in, and, in the distance, the **Ishwar Lat** or Sargasuli tower, a lovely eight-sided minaret built 50 years earlier by Ishwari Singh to mark a victory in battle with his stepbrother Madho Singh I.

Closer to hand, the women peeping out of the Hawa Mahal would likely have been bemused by the far more radical shapes of the **Jantar Mantar** observatory. Here, 16 bizarre sets of measuring instruments and tools made of stone, marble, bronze and brass attest to the lifelong fascination Jai Singh II held for astronomy; this is the largest of five observatories he built in north India and includes huge sundials, compasses and even an invention of Singh's comprised of two concave marble spheres meant to determine local time and the sun's path. Sadly, the Maharaja's enthusiasm wasn't matched by his observational skills; by 1800 the observatory had fallen into disuse, but is now a UNESCO World Heritage Site, the only one in the city.

While the undoubted highlights of Jaipur stem from Jai Singh II's careful planning of the old walled city, there are some more modern buildings beyond the walls, largely developed by Maharaja Ram Singh II during the early 19th century, that are equally interesting and well thought out – and some not so. Atop Moti Doongri, for example, is an imposing building that looks for all the world like a Scottish castle, complete with turrets and fortifications. This privately owned hilltop palace, converted from a fort by 20th-century Maharaja Man Singh II, literally surrounds one of the city's most important temples, the Moti Doongri Ganesh temple, carved out of rock by Seth Jai Ram Paliwal in 1761 – no mean feat when you consider its span of 2km. Below it at the bottom of the hill, the **Lakshmi Narayan Temple** is far less bashful, happy to dominate the skyline with its bright white marble facade and trio of domes, under which are housed impressive carvings of Vishnu, Narayan and Lakshmi, and various mythological and religious scenes and images.

But perhaps the most arresting building outside the walls is something very different. The **Government Central Museum**, also known as Albert Hall, was commissioned by Ram Singh II to honour the visit of the Prince of Wales, Edward Albert in 1876, when its foundation stone was laid. With its styling an ornate hybrid of traditional Indian and European Gothic Revival known as Indo-Saracenic, or Indo-Gothic, and housing spectacular examples of Rajasthan arts and crafts, the museum was an immediate hit on its opening in 1887. Its popularity has given rise to a number of other cultural institutions in the city, most recently the **Jawahar Kala Kendra** arts centre, known as the JKK, which draws on the walled city's grid structure with eight blocks set around a central open performance square. In its themes, forms, aims and content, the centre marries old and new Jaipur respectfully and elegantly – even its oranges and pinks affectionately reference one of Jaipur's most visible attributes; the pink paintwork and stonework that give the city its nickname. But whether Jaipur will stay in the pink remains to be seen; a more recent building, the World Trade Park retail and leisure mall, may look like a space age sci-fi version of Jantar Mantar, but its thrusting, macho glass and steel bombast clearly turns its back on the Pink City.

Maharaja Jai Singh II is probably turning in his very beautiful grave, but hopefully taking solace from knowing it's surely the loveliest of the marble *chhatris* or domed kiosks that are home to the remains of the city's rulers at the **Royal Gaitor Tombs**. Set between modern Jaipur and Jai Singh's original location for his city, Amer, where the Amer Fort looms over the town, it's a fitting tribute and spot for a visionary, enlightened leader, whose city looks as arresting today as it did when he conceived it 200 years ago.

Jantar Mantar

Government Central Museum

Ishwar Lat

Hawa Mahal

L: Chandni Chowk
A: Jai Singh II, 1728–34
FF: A large set of astronomical instruments make up the observatory, including the 27m (88ft) high Samrat Yantra, the world's largest sundial, and a metal astrolabe inscribed with a diagram of the cosmos, recorded by Guinness World Records as the world's largest astrolabe.

L: Ram Niwas Bagh
A: Sir Samuel Swinton Jacob, 1876–86
FF: The Albert Hall, as the museum was originally called, was inspired by the Victoria & Albert Museum in London, and contains one of the world's largest and most colourful Persian garden carpets, dating from 1632.

L: Aatish Market, J. D. A. Market
A: Ganesh Khovan, 1749
FF: Local legend has it that the tower's real purpose was not to mark a war victory, but as a covert viewing spot for the Maharaja, who had fallen in love with the daughter of General Hargobind Natani in the house opposite.

L: Hawa Mahal Road, Badi Choupad
A: Lal Chand Ustad, 1799
FF: The protruding balconies and screened windows of the building were constructed in such a way as to maximise any breezes for the women concealed behind them as they watched processions and daily life in the lively bazaar below.

Mubarak Mahal

Lakshmi Narayan Temple

Royal Gaitor Tombs

Chandra Mahal

Jawahar Kala Kendra

L: Jalebi Chowk, near Jantar Mantar, Tripolia Bazaar
A: Lala Indra Sahai, Lala Chiman Lal and Sir Samuel Swinton Jacob, 1900
FF: The Mubarak Mahal was built as a guest house, hence its name, which translates as 'Welcome Palace'. Guests have included the Prince of Wales, and Lord and Lady Mountbatten, who stayed here in 1922.

L: Below the Moti Doongri Hill
A: Unknown, 1988
FF: The temple is built on land formerly owned by the royal family and sold for a nominal sum to the industrialist Birla family, hence its more common name of Birla Mandir. It glows at night.

L: Foot of Nahargarh fort, northern edge of city centre
A: Unknown, various dates
FF: The mausoleum of Jai Singh II was built by his son Iswari Singh, who would go on to take his own life by ingesting poison and having a cobra bite him. Many of his wives followed suit, with the remaining 21 self-immolating on his funeral pyre.

L: Jalebi Chowk, near Jantar Mantar, Tripolia Bazar
A: Vidyadhar Bhattacharya, 1729–32
FF: The miniseries The Far Pavilions, based on a novel written by M. M. Kaye, was shot here and in the rest of the City Palace.

L: Jawaharlal Nehru Marg
A: Charles Correa, 1986–91
FF: The centre houses museums, two art galleries, an amphitheatre and a closed auditorium, along with a library, small hostel and art studio.

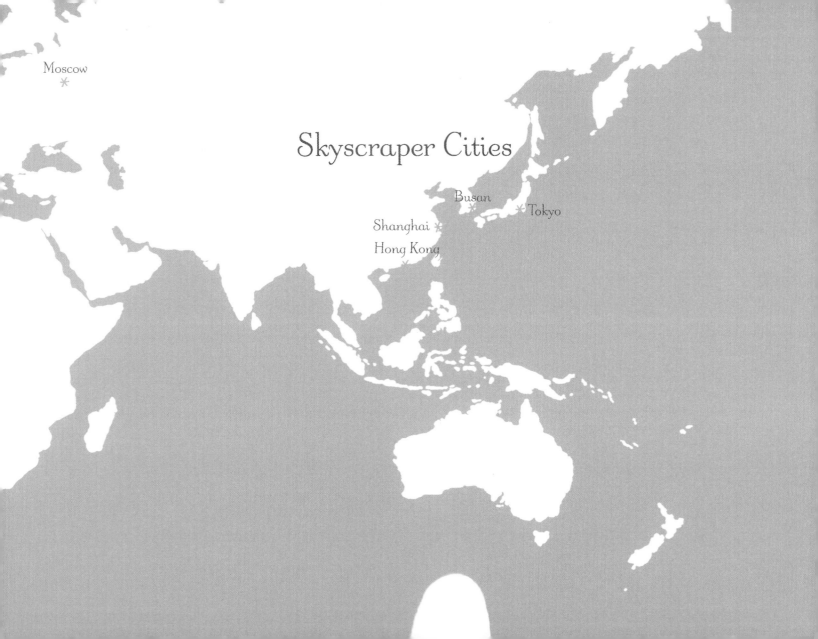

Skyscraper Cities

Moscow

Busan

Tokyo

Shanghai

Hong Kong

Hong Kong

'The business community is a very small group of elites in Hong Kong who control the destiny of the economy. If we ignore their interests, Hong Kong capitalism will stop [working].'
Wang Zhenmin, dean of the Tsinghua University School of Law in Beijing, in a speech at the Foreign Correspondents' Club, Hong Kong, 2014

There is something both terrifying and exhilarating, hopeful and hopeless, monstrous and marvellous about the skyline of Hong Kong. A semi-autonomous city with one of the biggest income divides in the world, its schizophrenic status is reflected compellingly in its mix of architecture. Staggeringly tall buildings literally dwarf the activities of the 7.2 million people who live in and among them in one of the most densely populated cities on the planet, creating an uneasy domination of the built environment over the needs and welfare of the people in it. Nowhere is this more apparent than in the city's tallest building, the 485m (1,591ft) **International Commerce Centre** in West Kowloon. Standing almost twice as tall as the surrounding buildings, depending on your viewpoint it's either monstrous or magnificent, and is matched by its counterpart across Victoria Harbour on Hong Kong Island, the 415m (1,361ft) Two International Finance Centre. In a strikingly arrogant display that acts as a metaphor for the capitalism driving the city, the rounded tower sits bang in the middle of the view of Victoria Peak behind it. Luckily, a much more arresting building is still visible on that peak. **Peak Tower**, designed by British architect Terry Farrell, acts as the terminal building for the Peak tram, and while its odd wok shape may seem quite arbitrary, Farrell designed it to follow the contours of the hills behind it, and restricted its

height so that it would not obscure them. It's this kind of mix that sums up the city; on the one hand, big businesses paying little or no mind to the surroundings or harmony of a space; on the other, social organisations more attuned to the aesthetics and appeal of a city making an effort to commission buildings that complement it – it's perhaps no surprise that the Peak Tower's owner is the Hongkong and Shanghai Hotels group.

Another recent building clearly hopes to emulate the singularity of Farrell's; unsurprisingly, it's by Zaha Hadid. The **Jockey Club Innovation Tower** opened in 2014 to house the 1,800 students and staff of both the Hong Kong Polytechnic University (PolyU) School of Design, and the Jockey Club Design Institute for Social Innovation. At just 76m (250ft), it stands out for its flowing, organic shape filled with light, and opening out into numerous interior and exterior courtyards that act as communal spaces. There couldn't be a more hopeful harbinger of a more dynamic and visually eclectic future for the city.

The current plethora of identikit skyscrapers leaves much to be desired, barring a handful of outstanding examples – among them Norman Foster's **HSBC Building** and its near neighbour the **Bank of China Tower**. The former was the world's most expensive building on its completion in 1985, and still stands out for its elegant steel and glass construction, and an air conditioning system that uses sea water as its coolant. The latter has struggled to overcome some very negative feng shui associations – among them accusations of its meat-cleaver shape and jagged asymmetric panels deliberately pointing negativity at the HSBC building and the heart of Hong Kong beyond. However, it's undoubtedly one of the city's most recognisable modern buildings. **Central Plaza** is another, notable for its 102m (334ft)-tall rooftop mast which changes colour every 15 minutes, and a triangular floor plan that allows the vast majority of the offices to have harbour views. These three epitomise modern Hong Kong, but a small clutch of older buildings attest to a more interesting architectural heritage.

If any one building could be said to sum up Hong Kong's status as a world centre of commerce, it's **Jardine House**, a trading house currently in its third incarnation. Owner Jardine Matheson was one of the original Hong Kong trading houses in Imperial China, having established a foothold in the city in 1842. This period, following on from the Treaty of Nanking, was one of rapid development as traders poured into the city to create not only a building boom, but arguably lay the foundations for a get-rich-quick attitude that defined, and continues to define, the city. While hundreds of offices and warehouses went up around Central's waterfront, and grand Victorian and Edwardian colonial architecture – such as the neoclassical red-brick and granite Former French Mission building and the Georgian-style Government House – dominated what would become known as Government Hill, a general hospital for Hong Kong's citizens, the Tung Wah Hospital, would not appear until 1870.

As lawlessness, corruption and violence flourished, so did poverty and overcrowding; by the time the Republic of China was established in 1911,

Hong Kong was well on the way to a huge housing shortage. With limited space, the solution, of course, was to build housing estates – on a vast scale. In 1965, Mei Foo Sun Chuen in Kowloon became the city's first private housing estate, its 99 towers accommodating some 70,000–80,000 people in 13,500 apartments. Now that figure seems almost quaint; the Kin Ming Estate, completed in 2003, houses 22,000 in just ten blocks, but more interesting by far is Aedas' **Mongkok Residence**, built in one of the world's most densely populated neighbourhoods, an area where hundreds of stolid soaring tower blocks house 130,000 people per square kilometre. Aedas' building references the post-war habit of adding illegal balconies to these apartments, and its modern reinterpretation of the habit, a graceful facade of irregular protrusions above a living wall base, has resulted in an elegant building that stands out for its innovative style and as a successful contemporary interpretation of traditional architecture.

The earlier **Peninsular Hotel**'s tower extension went even further, building an elegant addition to the 1928 original to show how modern design could nicely complement older structures, and One Peking Road's slender frame and curved sail shape illustrate how a tower can still have delicacy and grace. And even more interesting modern designs are making their way into the crowded city. The **Hong Kong Design Institute** by CAAU is an arresting glazed box held aloft by four white lattice-steel towers, the sense of space created by the grass podium below offering a welcome respite from the crowds of tower blocks surrounding it. And when Herzog & de Meuron's new museum of visual culture, M+, is completed in 2018, it will surely add still greater depth to a cityscape that for too long has been dominated by the the pure bombast of the city's business interests.

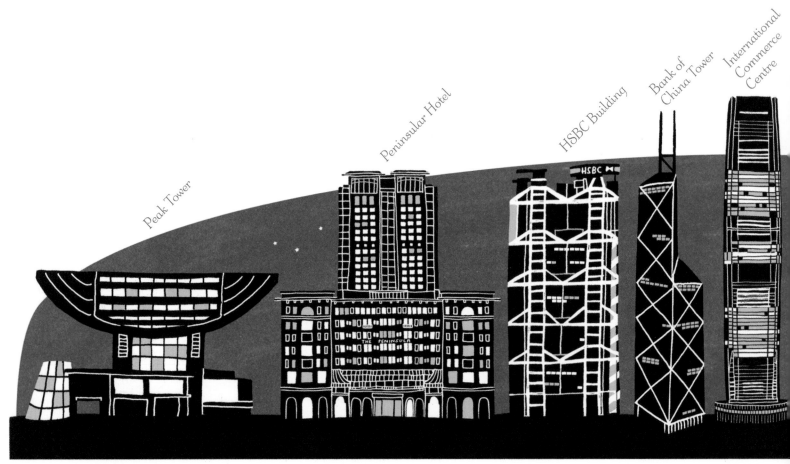

Peak Tower

Peninsular Hotel

HSBC Building

Bank of China Tower

International Commerce Centre

L: 128 Peak Road, The Peak, Hong Kong Island
A: Terry Farrell, 1997
FF: The tower's top-floor viewing terrace is called Sky Terrace 428 because it's 428m (1,404ft) above sea level.

L: Salisbury Road, Tsimshatsui, Kowloon
A: Rocco Design Architects, 1994
FF: The tower is topped with a helipad, one of only two private rooftop helipads in the territory.

L: 1 Queen's Road, Central, Hong Kong Island
A: Norman Foster, 1985
FF: The tower replaced Hong Kong's first skyscraper, a 1935 granite building that featured centralised air conditioning, lifts and two large bronze lions, Stephen and Stitt, that are still in place. Stephen's left flank shows shrapnel damage from the Pacific War.

L: 1 Garden Road, Central, Hong Kong Island
A: I. M. Pei and Partners, 1990
FF: A digitally modified image of the building was used as the Starfleet Communications Research Center in the TV series *Star Trek: Voyager*.

L: 1 Austin Road West, West Kowloon
A: Kohn Pedersen Fox Associates, 2010
FF: In 2003 the world's largest advert – for the *FT*, Cathay Pacific and HSBC – was displayed on the ICC's facade; it was 230m (754ft) long.

Central Plaza

Jardine House

Mongkok Residence

Jockey Club Innovation Tower

Hong Kong Design Institute

L: 18 Harbour Road, Wan Chai, Hong Kong Island
A: DLN Architects & Engineers, 1992
FF: The world's highest church is located here, in the pyramidal atrium.

L: 1 Connaught Place, Hong Kong Island
A: Palmer and Turner, 1973
FF: Its nickname is the 'House of a thousand arseholes', partly for its 1,700+ round windows, and partly for the financial traders contained within it.

L: 78–88 Sai Yee Street, Mongkok, Yau Tsim Mong District, Kowloon
A: Aedas, 2013
FF: The balconies of the building were inspired by the illegal iron balconies people used to build on their post-war apartments in this densely populated high-rise neighbourhood.

L: The Hong Kong Polytechnic University, Hung Hom, Kowloon
A: Zaha Hadid, 2014
FF: Public spaces in the college include a design museum, permanent and temporary exhibition galleries and a communal viewing lounge.

L: 3 King Ling Road, Tseung Kwan O, Kowloon
A: CAAU, 2011
FF: The four 'pillars of education' house the classrooms, while the glass box they hold up, called the 'aerial city', provides services and quieter spaces for the students.

Buenos Aires

'And the city, now, is like a map
Of my humiliations and failures;
From this door, I have seen the twilights
And at this marble pillar I have waited in vain.'
Jorge Luis Borges, 'Buenos Aires'

Porteño Borges was one of Latin America's most famous writers and he occasionally used architecture as a way of expressing his ideas: *The Library of Babel* was a mythical tower of interconnecting hexagonal rooms holding a collection of books that no one could understand. Inspired by his home city of Buenos Aires, Borges claimed to prefer the 'literary possibilities of the disreputable, humble suburbs' to the gentrified city streets, so one can only imagine what he would have made of the towers that have been racing up – 19 of them over 120m (394ft) tall – since the city's financial meltdown in 2001.

Home to writers, artists, despots and dictators, the city has seen plenty of booms and busts as well as civic unrest, and there is no more politically charged place in Buenos Aires than its Plaza de Mayo, also known as the 'Plaza de Protestas'. The city's main square since the 1590s, it became known as 'May Square' when the Spanish were finally ousted on 25 May 1810. It's where the *descaminados* ('shirtless ones'), the loyal impoverished followers of the Péróns, gathered in the 1940s; it was bombed by its own military in an attempted coup in 1955 and, until 2006, the Madres de Plaza de Mayo walked around the central **Pirámide de Mayo** to protest the disappearance of their loved ones during the military dictatorship from 1976 to 1982. The pyramid is the oldest monument in the city and is topped by *Liberty*, the work of the French sculptor Joseph Dubourdieu.

Thanks to its colourful and often controversial history, the city's architecture is a melting pot of styles. The neoclassical **Catedral Metropolitana** in the corner of the square is the sixth church built on this site – the cornerstone of the first was laid by the city's founder, Spanish conquistador, Juan de Garay, in 1580 – and its high Baroque interior holds a rococo main altar and the tomb of General José de San Martin, hero of the struggle for South American independence.

Following the country's rejection of the Spanish, architects were keen to adopt design ideas from elsewhere in Europe, but seemingly always with a little something extra. Danish architect Morten F. Rönnow created the **Edificio Otto Wulff** in Jugendstil, the German version of Art Nouveau. There's a bit of Renaissance and Gothic thrown in too, along with a few eclectic touches such as the human figures, resembling Greek caryatids, supporting the roof.

Italian architect Mario Palanti's high Renaissance **Palacio Barolo** was inspired by Dante's *Divine Comedy*: the 100m (328ft)-tall building (a metre for every canto) is divided into three sections, with the basement and ground floor, inlaid with fire-like designs, representing hell, the central floor for purgatory and the highest floors, with wonderful views over the city, representing heaven. When it was built in 1923, the Art Nouveau masterpiece was the tallest in South America.

It was superceded by **Edificio Kavanagh**, a spectacular Art Deco apartment block funded by an Irish millionairess. The slim and pared-back building combined modernist and rationalist approaches as well as state-of-the-art technologies including air conditioning. According to legend, a romance between a Kavanagh girl and the son of the aristocratic Anchorena family was disapproved of, so Kavanagh took her revenge by building her tower between the Anchorena's palace and their church, making it a condition of the build that it should be tall enough to obscure the Anchorena's view of the church. Mission accomplished.

Built the same year, **El Obelisco** was erected to mark several major events, including the declaration of the city as a capital and as the site of the demolished San Nicolás church where the national flag was first flown. Today it's a symbol of the city but the modernist structure wasn't immediately popular and its height was the subject of much controversy, seen as overtly phallic by the city's feminists, who called for it to be chopped in half.

In spite of a financial crash in 2001, Buenos Aires has been rapidly rebuilding. East of Plaza de Mayo is the dockland area of Puerto Madero. Once a skyline of 19th-century red-brick buildings and warehouses, the

area fell into decline but today the quayside is awash with skyscrapers; chichi bars and restaurants are interspersed with high-rise apartments and commercial developments such as the **Colección de Arte Amalia Lacroze de Fortabat**. The glass and concrete gallery shaped like a claw is named after one of the richest women in Argentina, with an art collection to match that of Peggy Guggenheim's. The dockside redevelopment, with some of the highest property prices in Latin America, ironically references the downtrodden and oppressed – if only in its street names, such as 'Azucena Villaflor', founder of the mothers of Plaza de Mayo and 'Encarnación Ezcurra', the wife of 19th-century *caudillo* (military leader) Juan Manuel de Rosas. Another cultural behemoth is the 15,000sq m (161,000sq ft) cultural centre **Usina del Arte** – a former power plant reincarnated in the style of a Florentine palace – in down-and-out La Boca.

The dockland area is also home to **El Faro**, two of the tallest buildings in Argentina until 2008, when they were surpassed by the Mulieris Torre Norte, then Mulieris Torre Sur and now the Le Parc Figueroa Alcorta, but not for long... there are already another three high-rises proposed or under construction, with the Alvear Tower due to top out at 235m (770ft). Borges claimed that while he loved his country, he never understood it. Parts of the city he would have recognised have disappeared under the wrecking ball, including his favourite café, but the National Library where he worked as director and which inspired his short story still exists.

Usina del Arte

Edificio Otto Wulff

Edificio Kavanagh

El Faro

L: Avenida Don Pedro de Mendoza y
Agustin R. Caffarena
A: Juan Chiogna, 1916
FF: There is a rich programme of dance,
art and theatre.

L: Avenida Belgrano 601
A: Morten F. Rönnow, 1914
FF: The different faces of the caryatids
correspond to the workers who worked
on the building, including its architect.

L: Florida 1065
A: Gregorio Sánchez, Ernesto Lagos and
Luis María de la Torre, 1936
FF: In 1994 the Kavanagh Building was
declared a Historic Civil Engineering
Landmark by the American Society of
Civil Engineers.

L: Puerto Madero
A: Gerardo Dujovne, Silvia
Hirsh, 2003–5
FF: The two skyscrapers are
linked and intertwined together
by four sky bridges.

El Obelisco

Palacio Barolo

Catedral Metropolitana

Pirámide de Mayo

Colección de Arte Amalia
Lacroze de Fortabat

L: Avenida 9 de Julio,
y Avenida Corrientes
A: Alberto Prebisch,
1936
FF: The phallic spike
was covered in an
enormous red condom
on World AIDS Day
in 2005.

L: Avenida de Mayo 1370
A: Mario Palanti, 1923
FF: The nearby Hotel
Castelar, opened in 1928,
is also by Mario Palanti.

L: Avenida Rivadavia, y San Martin
A: Unknown, 16th–19th centuries
FF: Joseph Dubourdieu's Greco-Roman
frontispiece depicts the reunion of Joseph and
his brothers in Egypt as well as the battle
of Pavón in 1861, when Buenos Aires troops
defeated *caudillo* Justo José Urquiza.

L: Plaza de Mayo
A: Pedro Vicente Cañete
and Juan Gaspar Hernández,
1811
FF: The white headscarf painted
on the tiles around the pyramid
is the symbol of the mothers who
circled the pyramid protesting
the disappearance of their
children.

L: Olga Cossettini 141
A: Rafael Viñoly, 2008
FF: The roof has a system of mobile
aluminium awnings that open and close
according to the sun's position.

New York

'I would give the greatest sunset in the world for one sight of New York's skyline.
Particularly when one can't see the details. Just the shapes. The shapes and the thought that made them.
The sky over New York and the will of man made visible. What other religion do we need?'
Ayn Rand, *The Fountainhead*

New York City has been and still is, more than any other metropolis in the world, symbolised by its skyline. The city came of age at the same time as the skyscraper – the ultimate totem of modernity – and its architecture in the decades that followed has created veritable forests of steel and glass on the island of Manhattan. New York's skyline wasn't always a homage to modernity of course; go back 150 years and the tallest buildings in the city were its churches – the visual symbols of aspiration before the religion of Capitalism took over. Broadway's Gothic Revival **Trinity Church** was, at 85m (278ft), the city's tallest building until 1890, when it lost the crown to the nearby (later demolished) New York World Building. From then on, the only way was up for most new architecture – a direction insisted upon by Manhattan's island geography, which also accounts for New York's many bridges. **Brooklyn Bridge**, built in 1883, is the perfect symbol of the brave new era of technological and economic innovation that was taking hold here in the late 19th century; upon completion the structure was the world's longest suspension bridge by a good distance. Three years later, the city gained another key landmark; the **Statue of Liberty** – a gift from France to celebrate US independence – evolved to become a symbol of freedom and a beacon of hope for the thousands of immigrants who were flooding into New York at this time.

The new technologies that allowed the city's first skyscrapers to be built in the late 1800s continued to develop in the early 1900s. Steel skeletons allowed new heights to be reached by buildings, while the invention of the elevator made them practical. Most early skyscrapers were built in the classical Beaux Arts architectural style prevalent at the time, with Midtown's **Flatiron Building** perhaps the most famous skyscraper to grace this style. The office building's palazzo-like terracotta facade gives it a European quality also found in another skyscraper of this era: Broadway's **Woolworth Building**, which was dubbed the 'cathedral of commerce' upon completion in 1913, in reference to both its Gothic cathedral-like crown and its function as the retail giant's headquarters.

With its record-breaking height of 241m (790ft), the Woolworth led directly to the 1916 zoning code, which sought to address concerns about modern buildings blocking out light and airflow on the city's streets; a concern that would unwittingly usher in a new style of skyscraper. One of the main features of the zoning code was its requirement for 'setbacks' in skyscrapers – tapered tops that allowed light to reach the streets. This stepped-back form fused perfectly with the Art Deco aesthetics emerging in the 1920s. A new vertical building style, referred to as 'Skyscraper Style', was born, which became truly emblematic of New York City. The building that most fully embodies this style is the **Chrysler Building**. Completed in 1930, the Chrysler is especially celebrated for its beautiful Art Deco building top – a glittering chrome crown that was also the secret behind it emerging victorious in the infamous 'race for the skies' of the late 1920s. (The Chrysler team added the tower at the last minute, when the team behind 40 Wall Street thought victory was already in the bag.) The building boom of the time meant that the Chrysler's 'world's tallest building' status was, however, short-lived. Eleven months later, the crown was passed to the 102-storey, 380m (1,246ft) – not including its antenna – **Empire State Building**, which remained the world's tallest building until the construction of the Twin Towers in the 1970s. But the bold, romantic symbolism that the Empire State embodied during construction was soon inverted. As E. B. White eloquently put it, the Empire State reached 'the highest point in the sky at the lowest moment of the Depression', and its lack of tenants saw it dubbed 'the Empty State' not long after completion. The slump would continue until the 1950s, when a new architectural vision, the International Style, arrived courtesy of a new wave of immigrants fleeing war-torn Europe. Influenced by the European Bauhaus school, it symbolised New York's renewed confidence and innovation after the Second World War, but as Columbia University's Andrew Dolkart commented, the style in the US, 'instead of being a vision for a socialist future, becomes a vision for a corporate future'. Mies van der Rohe's **Seagram Building**, built in 1958, is perhaps the most accomplished of the International Style skyscrapers, its floor-to-ceiling windows and narrow bronze-clad form evoking an exciting new era. But while the Seagram and nearby Lever House were complex,

radical new buildings designed according to principles of harmony and transcendence, their form was easy to debase, and dozens of banal glass slabs followed in their wake.

It wouldn't be until the 1990s that innovation would be focused on the dynamism of New York once again. Building tops, homogenously flat during the 1950s, '60s and '70s, became distinct again, and building design reflected new concerns, such as green design and the harmonising of the old and the new. Times Square's 48-storey **Condé Nast Building**, completed in 2000, is one of the heroes of this era; the building's green design incorporates recycling chutes, and its cutting-edge insulation system means it rarely needs to be heated or cooled. Its antenna-laden top references early skyscrapers while its multifaceted facade is lively and dynamic on its Times Square side, and more serious and sober on its business district side. Norman Foster's glass-and-steel **Hearst Tower** is another eco-friendly notable, innovatively fusing two very different architectural styles as the new building seamlessly emerges from the 1920s Art Deco Hearst Corporation Building. Nine years' later – and 14 years after 9/11 – the New York skyline saw the completion of its latest 'tallest building': **One World Trade Center**, the Twin Towers' replacement and part memorial. Though slated by architectural critics as a diluted version of its original plan, One World Trade Center has been unanimously celebrated for one key innovation: its elevator, which, through digital screens installed on all sides, takes visitors through a changing panorama of 500 years of New York's history as it ascends – from Native American village to early skyscrapers to the present-day forest of iron, glass and steel.

Statue of Liberty

Brooklyn Bridge

Trinity Church

Flatiron Building

Seagram Building

Condé Nast Building

L: Liberty Island
A: Frédéric Auguste Bartholdi, 1886
FF: Lady Liberty is maintained by the National Park Service, whose employees have been caring for her since 1933.

L: Across the East River that links Manhattan (Civic Center area) to Brooklyn (Dumbo area)
A: John Augustus Roebling, 1883
FF: It's sometimes possible to see peregrine falcons overhead; the birds like nesting in high places, and the Brooklyn Bridge is a favourite location.

L: 75 Broadway, Manhattan
A: Richard Upjohn, 1846
FF: The church has three bronze doors that were a gift from William Waldorf Astor in memory of his father John Jacob Astor III. New York's history is depicted in the panels of the south door.

L: 175 Fifth Avenue, Manhattan
A: Daniel Burnham, 1902
FF: The Flatiron's notable triangular form was dictated by its oddly shaped ground space resembling the outline of a clothes iron – hence the name.

L: 375 Park Avenue, Manhattan
A: Ludwig Mies van der Rohe, 1958
FF: The Seagram's design got around the 1916 zoning code that required 'setbacks', by occupying just 25 per cent of the building lot and creating a plaza in the remaining 75 per cent to allow for more light and airflow.

L: 4 Times Square, Manhattan
A: Bruce Fowle (Fox & Fowle), 2000
FF: The building's air delivery system provides 50 per cent more fresh air than industry codes specify.

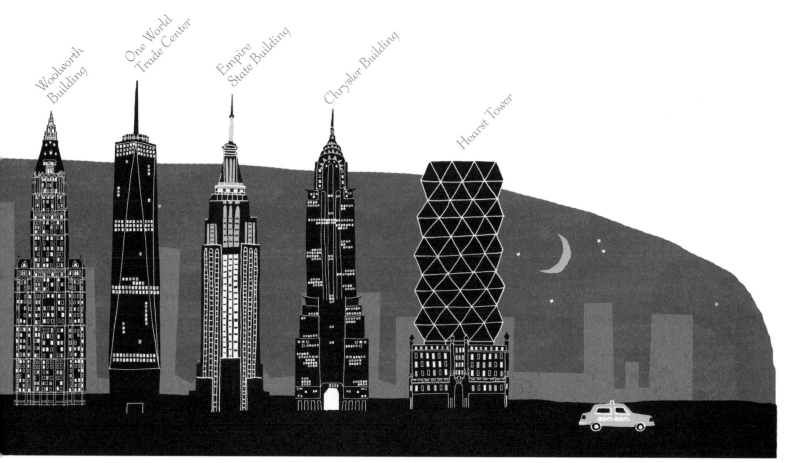

Woolworth Building

One World Trade Center

Empire State Building

Chrysler Building

Hearst Tower

L: 233 Broadway, Manhattan
A: Cass Gilbert, 1913
FF: The building's cathedral-like marble lobby has an ornate vaulted ceiling, stained glass and mosaics.

L: 285 Fulton Street, Manhattan
A: Daniel Libeskind, David Childs, 2014
FF: Referred to as the 'Freedom Tower' during construction, but formally changed in 2009 stating it was easier for people to identify with.

L: 350 Fifth Avenue, Manhattan
A: William Lamb, 1931
FF: From the building's 86th- and 102nd-floor observatories you can see five states in good weather: New York, New Jersey, Pennsylvania, Connecticut and Massachusetts.

L: 405 Lexington Avenue, Manhattan
A: William Van Alen, 1930
FF: Symbolic corner ornamentation on the building's exterior includes Chrysler radiator caps on the 31st floor and steel eagle heads on the 61st floor.

L: 300 W 57th Street or 959 8th Avenue
A: Norman Foster (Foster + Partners), 2006
FF: The Hearst Building was originally built in 1928 as the proposed base for a skyscraper for the William Randolph Hearst media empire, but work was halted by the Depression; it's now a designated landmark.

Shanghai

'The fifth city of the earth, the megalopolis of continental Asia, inheritor of ancient Baghdad, of pre-war Constantinople, of 19th-century London, of 20th-century Manhattan.'
Fortune magazine, 1935

Shanghai-born filmmaker Wong Kar-wai moved, with his parents, to Hong Kong just before the Cultural Revolution. His Palme D'Or-nominated *In the Mood for Love* – a tale of two Shanghainese emigrés – is saturated with the language, music and images of the protagonists' home city: narrow alleyways, cramped tenements and sounds of Shanghai music from the 1930s and 1940s. Wong's original Chinese title *Hua Yang Nian Hua* ('Age of Bloom'), a reference to the fleeting nature of time, might be a metaphor for Shanghai itself; the city has been almost constantly occupied by foreign nations from the 1840s until its liberation from the Japanese in 1945, and its architecture reflects them all, from the neoclassical lines of the British-designed Shanghai Club and Paul Veysseyre's Streamline Moderne that fills the French Concession, to the onion-domed Russian Orthodox churches.

Shanghai was once walled to protect its inhabitants from Japanese raiding parties as well as foreigners, who were considered uncivilised, but, though the walls stayed up until the 1911 revolution, relations changed in the 19th century when the British became trading partners. To pay for Chinese tea, silks and porcelain, the British introduced Indian opium – stronger than the Chinese product – with disastrous results. Attempts by

the Qing dynasty to close down the industry resulted in the First Opium War, and the British gaining a concession in Shanghai not subject to Chinese laws. The Americans and the French soon followed, and so began the city's ascent (or descent, according to one's perspective), earning it the nickname 'Paris of the East' or 'Whore of the Orient', depending on whether you were considering its artistic and intellectual prowess, or its reputation for vice and decadence.

By the 1920s and 1930s, Shanghai was a boomtown – a heady mix of opium and gambling dens, brothels, jazz music and dancing in nightclubs that never closed. A mob boss called Du Yuesheng, known as 'Big Ears', ran much of it and, understandably, he did his utmost to protect his empire, even allying himself to the Kuomintang, the ruling Nationalist party, in its battles against the city's Communists.

The most elaborate and possibly most expensive dance hall of its age was the Art Deco **Paramount Ballroom**, and its Chinese name 'Gate of 100 Pleasures' suggested that jazz and dancing weren't the only activities on offer here. The roaring nightlife of Shanghai came to an abrupt end when the Communists took over in 1949, with many of the bourgeoisie fleeing to Hong Kong. The Paramount eventually reopened as the Red Capitol

Cinema, showing propaganda films, but slowly began to fall apart, and it wasn't until a Taiwanese businessman came to the rescue in 2001 that the dance hall came to life again, but this time it was strictly for dancing…

The **Shanghai Race Club** was another symbol of Shanghai's 'fun city' status. The sumptuous neoclassical clubhouse, with its marble staircases, oak parquet floors and teak-panelled rooms, even had a four-faced clock once called 'Big Bertie' or 'Little Ben'. The club housed the Shanghai Museum of Art up until 2012, when it moved to the site of the 2010 World Expo. The area enclosed by the old racetrack is now the People's Park and the People's Square.

In 2003 the **Tomorrow Square** development totally dwarfed the old racecourse clubhouse, piercing the skyline like a rocket. The **Park Hotel**, which overlooks People's Park, was the 'first high building of the Far East' and the tallest building in China until the 1980s. The Art Deco masterpiece was built in 1934 by Hungarian architect László Hudec, who was inspired by the American Radiator Building, and it's said that watching it being built inspired I. M. Pei to take up architecture. Close by is the glass-fronted **Museum of Contemporary Art**, a reworking of the abandoned People's Park greenhouse, which opened in 2005 and has featured works by Ai Weiwei. Another clever bit of repurposing is that of the kitschy pink **Oriental Pearl Tower**, a radio and TV tower that houses the city's History Museum; today it boasts a super-cool 20-room hotel and a revolving restaurant.

Sadly, repurposing isn't as common as razing to the ground and starting from scratch; much of the old *shikumen* – the indigenous alleyway housing that was once home to the city's middle classes – has disappeared. The first Expo to be held in China took place here in 2010 and cost an eye-watering $25 billion – double the amount spent on the Olympics – with much of it

spent on new infrastructure built on the marshland straddling the Huangpu. The metro network rapidly expanded from two lines to 14, and by 2012, Shanghai had more than 5,000 buildings over 100m (328ft) tall.

The **Urban Planning Exhibition Center**, established in 2000, was created to showcase the city's continuing architectural development and features a huge scale model of the city, with existing and approved buildings, to show how it will look in the future. The museum also looks back at the past using multimedia displays and dioramas. The modernist building, clad in white aluminium panels, is reminiscent of a pagoda, thanks to its membrane roof that floats out beyond the building.

Shanghai's old colonial Bund area faces off the new Lujiazui, where most of the super-tall skyscrapers line up, across the Huangpu River. The landmark **Jin Mao Tower**, a postmodern, pagoda-style construction, was the tallest building in China up until 2007 and today houses the Grand Hyatt Hotel, where the Cloud 9 and Sky Lounge bars (87th and 88th floors) are some of the highest watering holes in the world. It's also home to the highest pool in the world, and features some groundbreaking technology that protects the building from high winds and earthquakes.

In 2008 it was overtaken by the **Shanghai World Financial Center**, then the world's second tallest building; today it's number seven. But onwards and upwards: Jin Mao and the Shanghai World Financial Centre are soon to be joined by the **Shanghai Tower** – nine cylindrical towers stacked one on top of the other, twisting as they rise, to reach 121 floors. Each of the nine towers will have its own atrium with restaurants, cafés and gardens. Once complete, in 2015, the tower will be the tallest building in Asia and the second tallest building in the world, after Dubai's 828m (2,716.5ft) Burj Khalifa.

Museum of Contemporary Art

Paramount Ballroom

Shanghai World Financial Center

Shanghai Tower

Jin Mao Tower

L: People's Square, 231 Nanjing West Road
A: Samuel Kung Foundation, 2005
FF: The rooftop patio and bar offer spectacular views across the water lily-covered lake.

L: 218 Yuyuan Road
A: S. J. Young, 1933
FF: On the dance floor, professional dance partners take your hand to transport you back into another era of jitterbugging jams.

L: 100 Century Avenue
A: Kohn Pedersen Fox, 2008
FF: Said to represent China's present, where the Jin Mao Tower represents the past and the Shanghai Tower is the future.

L: Lujiazui, Pudong
A: Gensler, 2015
FF: Each zone has its own gardens, cafés and restaurants as well as 360-degree views of the city.

L: 88 Century Avenue
A: Skidmore, Owings & Merrill, 1999
FF: Have a drink in the highest bar in the world… so far.

Tomorrow Square

Shanghai Race Club

Park Hotel

Oriental Pearl Tower

Urban Planning Exhibition Center

L: 399 Nanjing West Road
A: John Portman & Associates, 2003
FF: Don't miss the beautiful marquetry in the cocktail bar before taking a swim in the indoor or outdoor pool.

L: 335 Nanjing West Road
A: Moorhead & Halse, 1933–4
FF: The China Art Museum moved to the Expo China Pavilion in 2010.

L: 170 Nanjing West Road
A: László Hudec, 1931–4
FF: The Art Deco lobby was lovingly restored by American architect Christopher Choa in 2001.

L: 1 Shiji Dadao
A: Jiang Huan Chen, Lin Benlin, and Zhang Xiulin, 1994
FF: The tower houses a 20-room hotel between the spheres and a revolving restaurant.

L: 100 Renmin Avenue
A: Ling Benli of the East China Architecture Design & Research Institute (ECADI), 2000
FF: The building was designed to complement the Grand Theatre at the other end of the People's Square.

Tokyo

'The contrast between that which preceded the funeral car and that which followed it was striking indeed. Before it went old Japan; after it came new Japan.'
New York Times on the funeral of Emperor Meiji in 1912

From 10,000 to 300 BC the land that would become known as Edo was marshy and good for hunting but not much else. It was still little more than a hamlet when shogun Ieyasu Tokugawa arrived in 1590. He took up residence in Edo Castle, the world's largest, which boasted defence walls that stretched out for 16km (10 miles), and the Tokugawa shogunate ruled for the next 240 years. During that period a seclusion policy was established to ensure that Japanese culture remained pure and untouched by outside influence. It wasn't until 1868, when the last shogun was overthrown and Emperor Meiji came to power, that the nation rapidly changed from a feudal state and was set on its path to becoming one of the most successful industrial nations in the world.

Little remains of the Edo period – thanks to a succession of fires, earthquakes and wars, and an unstoppable urge to tear down anything more than a few decades old – but there are a few scraps of fortification around the Imperial Palace, which was built on part of the Edo Castle site. Many traditional shrines are reconstructions of earlier incarnations, such as the wooden **Hongan-ji Temple** that, having burnt down nine times, was finally rebuilt in stone by architect Ito Chuta, whose design was clearly influenced by temples in south Asia. The **Sanmon Gate** is a rare survivor and the oldest wooden structure in Japan; it's the main entrance to the Buddhist Zojo-ji Temple that was used by Tokugawa and each of its three sections represents the stages required to enter Nirvana.

The seismic activity of the region had, until recently, precluded the building of anything of any height, with the exception of the communications and observation **Tokyo Tower**. The second tallest structure in Japan is easily the most recognisable structure in the city and its lattice metalwork is based on the Eiffel Tower.

Kenzo Tange was the first modern Japanese architect to gain worldwide recognition. He combined Japanese sensibilities with Western elements and, like Le Corbusier, he was a big fan of reinforced concrete, using it in most of his works. His aerodynamic **Yoyogi National Gymnasium** was designed for the 1964 Tokyo Olympics and the swimming area was notable for the largest suspended roof in the world, made from welded steel slung between two reinforced concrete masts; in spite of its modernity and state-of-the-art technology, the shape is reminiscent of the roof of a Shinto shrine. Tange also designed **St Mary's Cathedral**, a towering concrete building clad in stainless steel that, in spite of its apparent abstract design, has a glass roof shaped like a cross.

In the 1960s, a new generation of architects known as the Metabolists emerged. They were influenced by Kenzo Tange and set out their principles and ideas for urban architecture in their manifesto *Metabolism: Proposals for a New Urbanism*. New construction techniques allowed for taller, more exciting buildings to be made and Kisho Kurokawa's **Nakagin Capsule Tower** is thought to best encapsulate the Metabolist ideals. Kurokawa created a mega-structure of reinforced concrete within which the elevators, stairs and bridges are housed, with prefabricated capsules, resembling washing machines, that could be attached as and when necessary. The randomness of their positioning would create a continually evolving structure. He called it 'housing for the Homo-movens: people in motion'. Sadly it's fallen into disrepair and may soon be demolished.

Tange's student, Fumihiko Maki, was a founder member of the Metabolist Group and his iconic **Spiral Building** managed to combine commercial considerations with art and form: the fragmentary cubist composition is thought to resemble the layered spaces that exist in traditional Japanese architecture and gardens. It is thought that Maki's Spiral helped ensure that the tree-lined Omotesando area became an architectural mecca for fashion. Tadao Ando's Omotesando Hills is an enormous urban regeneration project

that was completed in 2005. Controversially many Bauhaus buildings were destroyed in its construction, but in an area where commerce talks…

In spite of Japan's economy nose-diving in the 1990s, exciting building projects were still being commissioned. Kenzo Tange's twin-towered **Tokyo Metropolitan Government Building No. 1** is a thoroughly modern complex of three structures that manages to resemble a computer chip and a Gothic cathedral at the same time. It was the tallest building in Tokyo until the **Midtown Tower** was completed in 2006. Like Roppongi Hills, the 25-acre Midtown complex is thought to be loosely based on Le Corbusier's vertical city proposition. Skidmore, Owings and Merrill referenced a Japanese rock garden so there is plenty of bamboo and light wood, with walkways resembling tatami mats, and cherry trees in the open spaces. The 54-storey tower, currently Japan's tallest office building, houses numerous companies, including the Ritz-Carlton. Across town, Roppongi Hills, the brainchild of property magnate Mori Minoru, is a mini-city in itself: shops, hotels and restaurants as well as the fifth tallest tower in Japan – **Mori Tower**.

Three of the Metabolists' leading proponents, Koh Kitayama, Yoshiharu Tsukamoto and Ryue Nishizawa, examined architecture as 'icon' in *Tokyo Metabolizing* (2010). Kitayama cites **Prada's flagship store** as an example of brands meshing consumerism with culture; it manages to be both a stunning five-sided construction of irregular green, diamond-shaped glass panels, as well as a store that sells every line that Prada produces.

In 2011, Tokyo's neo-futuristic digital broadcasting tower, **SkyTree**, entered the *Guinness Book of Records* as the tallest tower in the world and, to date, it's the second tallest after Dubai's Burj Khalifa. But in spite of the continuing modernism, there are often hints at the past; the height of 634m (2,080ft) was settled on because '634' in old Japanese numbers is *mu-sa-shi*, and would remind Japanese people of Musashi Province of the past, that used to cover Tokyo, Saitama and part of Kanagawa Prefecture.

At over 2,000m (6,561ft), the tallest building in the world, by more than a mile, may never be built as its foundations could not support its weight, but the hypothetical Shimizu Mega-City Pyramid was designed to be more than 14 times higher than the Great Pyramid at Giza, and, to help with Tokyo's lack of space, would house 1,000,000 people. It is intended that, once the super-light and strong material has been invented, the building designed by Dante Bini and David Dimitric can go ahead.

Yoyogi National Gymnasium

Nakagin Capsule Tower

Tokyo Tower

St Mary's Cathedral

Tokyo Metropolitan Government Building No.1

Mori Tower

L: Yoyogi Park, 2-1-1 Jinnan, Shibuya
A: Kenzo Tange, 1963
FF: It's still in use and will host the handball competitions at the 2020 Summer Olympics.

L: 16-10, Ginza 8-chome, Chuo-ku
A: Kisho Kurokawa, 1972
FF: Visit it soon as the building is slated for demolition and redevelopment.

L: 4-2-8 Shibakoen
A: Tachu Naito, 1958
FF: It's 13m (43ft) taller than the Paris version.

L: 3-15-16 Sekiguchi, Bunkyo-ku
A: Kenzo Tange, 1964
FF: The sloping walls inside are sometimes lit in red or blue giving the austere concrete interior a warm glow.

L: 2-1-1 Nishi-Shinjuku
A: Kenzo Tange, 1991
FF: There are two observation decks for great views.

L: 6-10-1 Roppongi, Minato
A: Kohn Pedersen Fox, The Jerde Partnership, 2003
FF: The Mori Arts Centre, including the Mori Museum, occupies floors 49–54.

Sky Tree

Midtown Tower

Sanmon Gate

Spiral Building

Prada's flagship store

Hongan-ji Temple

L: 1 Chome-1-2
Oshiage, Sumida
A: Nikken Sekkei,
2012
FF: The LED lights
are illuminated
daily in patterns
known as *Iki*
(chic stylish),
sky blue and
Miyabi (elegance
refinement),
purple.

L: 6 Akasaka
A: Skidmore, Owings &
Merrill, 2007
FF: The 'Diamonds are
Forever' martinis at the
Ritz-Carlton (served over
a one-carat diamond,
£1,000) are probably the
drink *du jour* in the Ritz-
Carlton Suite (Japan's
most expensive, $26,500
a night).

L: 4-7-35 Shiba-Koen Minato-ku
A: Unknown, 1605
FF: A mausoleum in the temple
grounds contains the tombs of six
Tokugawa shoguns.

L: 5-6-23 Minami-
Aoyama
A: Fumihiko Maki,
1985
FF: The spiral ramp
that encircles the rear
gallery space and
climbs to the second
floor appears to float.

L: 5-2-6 Minami-Aoyama,
Minato-ku
A: Herzog & de Meuron,
2003
FF: At the touch of a
button, the glass walls
in the changing rooms
become opaque.

L: 3-15-1 Tsukiji
A: Ito Chuta, 1931–4
FF: The temple is a pilgrimage site as it
holds some artifacts of Prince Shotoku,
Shinran Shonin and Shonyo Shonin.

Chicago

Standing in the prow of one of the Chicago Architecture Foundation tour boats, floating along the city's waterways to take in what is undoubtedly one of the most spectacular skylines in the world, it's impossible not to agree with Norman Mailer's assertion in 1968 that while 'New York is one of the capitals of the world and Los Angeles is a constellation of plastic… Chicago is a great American city. Perhaps it is the last of the great American cities.' Given that the city can lay claim to three of the five tallest buildings in the US, Mailer's statement, almost 50 years on, stands firm, but things weren't always so positive. Little more than a century ago, the city named for the plentiful wild garlic fields it was once famous for (a derivation of the Native American word *shikaakwa* or 'stinking onion') was a heaving mess of impoverished immigrants scrabbling in the dirt to rebuild a city destroyed in the Great Chicago Fire of 1871.

The fire had razed to the ground a wood-built city whose strategic position on Lake Michigan, linking the Great Lakes and the Mississippi basin, had, everyone thought, assured its future as a major centre of transportation, shipping and commerce. But what might have felt like the death knell for the city was in fact a clarion call to modernity, as the old was literally cleared away to make way for a new style of architecture that would radically alter the shape of the city – and the skylines of cities around the globe.

By the end of the century, glass and steel examples in the influential Chicago School of architecture style were beginning to appear that made much of advances in technology, among them William Le Baron Jenney's Home Insurance Building, whose soaring ten floors made it what's considered to be the world's first skyscraper. And when the world's first Ferris wheel was built, it was in Chicago, as part of a 1893 World Fair that showcased architecture, art and industrial know-how. A copy of the wheel can be seen today at Navy Pier on Lake Michigan.

Where Le Baron Jenney's early innovative ideas in engineering were rooted in experimentation with form and function, another key figure of the era would forge a different but equally influential path. Working in a troubled city where philanthropists like the activist, social scientist and Nobel Peace Prize winner Jane Addams were driving forces, Frank Lloyd Wright determined to create buildings that strived to preserve human dignity and reflect American democratic values. His Prairie style of low-slung airy architecture favoured open space and natural materials, and **Robie House**, with its movable room partitions creating flexible interiors, is considered one of a handful of groundbreaking designs that changed America. Yet as an example of domestic architecture, its scale is distinctly at odds with the prevailing machismo of 1920s boomtown design, as illustrated by the likes of the **Wrigley Building**. By the time it was built, skyscrapers housing manufacturing businesses were going up so fast that the HQ of the world's most famous chewing gum company had to be built north of the Chicago River; still, as the city's first air-conditioned building, it could look snootily over the river back to its Loop-based competitors.

Through ups and downs including the Great Depression and a subway project that would provide years of work to thousands of men, Chicago's skyline continued to grow and evolve through elegant but sometimes socially divisive buildings, such as the Art Deco **Bank of America Building** and the **Chicago Board of Trade** building, one of the first commercial buildings to have electric light – and the astonishing price tag of $2 million. Such growth and expansion were drawing not only manufacturing, business and industry. The moneymen and middle classes needed culture, and found it in speakeasies where jazz musicians like Louis Armstrong, Ella Fitzgerald and Bessie Smith played, and gangsters during Prohibition flourished – Al Capone even held shares in the city's Uptown Green Mill Cocktail Lounge, favouring a booth where he could best see who came in and out. Today the lounge still offers Chicagoans an opportunity to hear modern jazz.

The 1960s saw a second Chicago School emerging, this time influenced by the work of Ludwig Mies van der Rohe, whose steel and glass masterpiece **S. R. Crown Hall** is the home of Illinois Institute of Technology. The spare and sleek horizontal planes of this single-storey building emphasised the importance of the open space, revealing the

materials being used; but against this backdrop of innovation and cultural progress, the city continued to suffer great poverty and inequality. Martin Luther King Jr's Chicago Freedom Movement set out to improve housing, education and transport for black residents, and in 1966 he held a civil rights rally in Soldier Field, designed in 1919 as a memorial to American soldiers killed in battle. Nowadays the site is home to the NFL's Chicago Bears, who've played at the distinctive stadium since 1971.

Through such changes, Chicago's obsession with building further skywards continued apace, and Fazlur Khan's groundbreaking structural system of framed tubes is the basis on which most buildings over 40 storeys have been built ever since. His 110-storey **Willis Tower** and 100-storey **John Hancock Center** are among the top 50 tallest buildings in the world, dwarfing William W. Boyington's **Water Tower**, one of the few buildings to survive the Great Fire.

Set against the tower's mad neo-Gothic styling, described by Oscar Wilde in 1882 as 'a castellated monstrosity with pepperboxes stuck all over it', wonderfully quirky buildings like Helmut Jahn's **James R. Thompson Center** pay homage to an architectural heritage that exemplifies the modern city and celebrates a short but spectacular history. Today, what Chicago's buildings lack in antiquity they make up for in originality. Sure, the city still loves super-tall constructions – witness the 96-storey **Trump Tower** – but more democratic projects sit happily alongside them. Popular with residents and commercial interests alike, Frank Gehry's enormous Millennium Park, with its host of public amenities and one of the largest green roofs in the world, points the way forward for a place that will hopefully endure as *the* great American city.

S. R. Crown Hall (now Illinois Institute of Technology)

Water Tower

Trump Tower

Willis Tower (known as Sears Tower until 2009)

Wrigley Building

L: 3360 South State Street
A: Ludwig Mies Van Der Rohe, 1950–6
FF: Visitors can explore the building by attending a lecture, exhibit or music recital.

L: 806 North Michigan Avenue
A: William W. Boyington, 1867–69
FF: It has been a tourist information office since the 1970s.

L: 401 North Wabash Avenue
A: Skidmore, Owings & Merrill (Adrian Smith), 2005–9
FF: The restaurant's Swarovski crystal chandelier was created with more than 19,000 crystals.

L: 233 South Wacker Drive
A: Skidmore, Owings & Merrill (Fazlur Khan & Bruce Graham), 1970–4
FF: Don't miss the outdoor viewing platforms on the 103rd floor, called, appropriately, 'The Ledge'.

L: 400–410 North Michigan Avenue
A: Graham, Anderson, Probst and White, 1919–25
FF: The skywalk connecting the two towers was added in 1931.

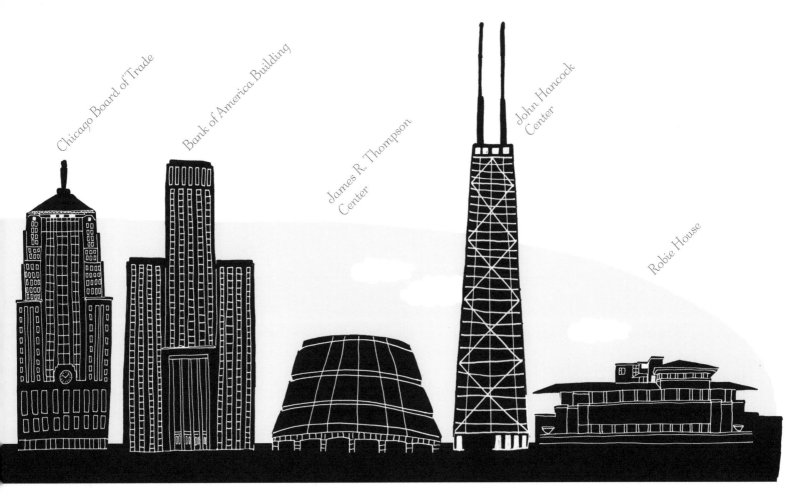

Chicago Board of Trade

Bank of America Building

James R. Thompson Center

John Hancock Center

Robie House

L: 141 West Jackson Boulevard
A: Holabird and Root, 1929–30
FF: Look out for John Storr's aluminium sculpture of Ceres, the Roman goddess of agriculture – 9m (30ft) tall, weighing over 3 tons.

L: 135 South LaSalle Street
A: Graham, Anderson, Probst and White, 1931–4
FF: Keep an eye out for the mail chutes in the shape of the building.

L: 100 West Randolph Street
A: Helmut Jahn, 1979–85
FF: Consider that, whatever you think of the baby pink/blue décor or the 'melting' décor, it cost a whopping $173 million.

L: 875 North Michigan Avenue
A: Skidmore, Owings & Merrill (Fazlur Khan and Bruce Graham), 1965–9
FF: Take a skate in the sky: the 94th-floor observatory has a small ice-skating rink in it.

L: 5757 South Woodlawn Avenue
A: Frank Lloyd Wright, 1908–10
FF: The Smart Museum of Art at the University of Chicago has the original dining room table and chairs on display.

Moscow

'The most beautiful thing in Tokyo is McDonald's. The most beautiful thing in Stockholm is McDonald's. The most beautiful thing in Florence is McDonald's. Peking and Moscow don't have anything beautiful yet.'

Andy Warhol, *The Philosophy of Andy Warhol (From A to B and Back Again)*

Andy Warhol's derision of Moscow was rather glib, but more notable critics have been even more forceful in their disdain for the city. Le Corbusier, in a long and complex relationship with Moscow, wrote off Soviet society as incapable and unprepared to appreciate modern architecture, and called for the wholesale levelling and rebuilding of the city from scratch. Frank Lloyd Wright, asked for his opinion on Alexey Shchusev's Stalinist-era Hotel Moskva in 1937, said 'It is the ugliest thing I have ever seen.' And travel guide *Time Out* was moved to describe the 1960s Brezhnev-era siting of the Hotel Rossiya as 'one of the greatest crimes against aesthetics ever perpetrated by the Soviet state'.

Moscow's skyline and built environment have never been great beauties, or particularly valued; more than 1,000 historically important buildings have been destroyed in the past 20 years. But things are changing. Old buildings are being restored and preservation orders being placed on significant sites, including the iconic **Shabolovka Radio Tower**, described by Norman Foster as 'a structure of dazzling brilliance and great historical importance'. As towers go it's contributed to what little architectural identity the city has; it's heartening then that of the new skyscrapers and superstructures on the city's skyline, there are significant designs that promise to develop that identity further.

Chief among these is **Capital City Towers**, twin towers composed of a series of stacked offset cubes in a vast mixed development known as the Moscow International Business Center (IBC). By its completion date of 2020, the IBC will contain some of Europe's tallest buildings, including the 373m (1,224ft) Federation Towers, the 352m (1,155ft) OKO Apartment Tower, the 338.8m (1,112ft) Mercury City Tower and the 308m (1,011ft) Eurasia Tower.

In the IBC, Moscow is continuing not one but two 20th-century preoccupations. With the Russian Revolution of 1917 came the desire for utilitarian centres for living that chimed with constructivism's central desire to change humanity through architecture. The **Zuyev Workers' Club**, built for the Union of Communal Services workers, epitomised the avant-garde. With its large glass cylinder bisected by concrete horizontal planes, the design was meant to represent the spirit of the revolution and the mechanical age, and still stands as a stunning example of the style.

Architects like Konstantin Melnikov were using the elementary geometries of constructivism to create more idiosyncratic spaces, including a decidedly bourgeois single-family dwelling, the Melnikov house and studio – ironically designated a national monument in 1987. But Melnikov's five workers' clubs – including the Rusakov, Svoboda Club and Frunze –

are more in keeping with the social tenets of the time while displaying the same architectural coda of constructivism that drew the likes of Le Corbusier to build in the city. The latter's **Tsentrosoyuz Building**, built for the Central Union of Consumer Co-operatives, was a troubled project that suffered from the sudden unpopularity of avant-garde design, but it has the distinction of being the only Le Corbusier building in the whole of Russia.

By the mid-1930s a new type of socialist realism was shaping the city, led by Stalin's desire to marry classicism with a Soviet mark – and improve on the skyscrapers of the US. Again, the idea was vast buildings that saw to all their users' needs, as exemplified by the Seven Sisters. Built in a range of styles, and utilising the skills and technological know-how picked up by Soviet architects in New York during the 1920s and 1930s, these seven skyscrapers, which include the **Kotelnicheskaya Apartments** and the main building of the **Moscow State University**, still stand as grandiose testaments to one man's ego. Another 'sister', conceived by Stalin as a cathedral to the USSR, was never built; had it been, the 400m (1,312ft)-high Palace of the Soviets would have dwarfed all the city's current towers.

Most of the city's best-loved towers predate those of the sisters by centuries, and are not cathedrals to the state, but to the church. The bulk of them reside in the Kremlin's Cathedral Square, where the gold domes of the **Ivan the Great Bell Tower** loom over four cathedrals, including the Cathedral of the Assumption. It has long been considered Russia's main church, but the city's landmark church is in Red Square, where the ten multicoloured roofs and domes of the **Cathedral of St Basil the Blessed** are Moscow's defining tourist sight. Two kilometres west along the river, the gold-topped white monolith that is the Cathedral of Christ the Saviour gives St Basil's a

run for its money, as the tallest Orthodox Christian church in the world, but it's the **Ascension Church** in Kolomenskoye Park that made the UNESCO World Heritage Site list in 1994.

Whether any of Moscow's more recent buildings will be similarly lauded in the future remains to be seen, but the city is certainly constructing some unusual contenders, though perhaps none as striking as the VDNKh's **Monument to the Conquerors of Space** would have been to visitors in 1966. Of all the pavilions and monuments that make up the VDNKh, or Exhibition of Achievements of the People's Economy, it's the 110m (361ft)-high titanium obelisk of a rocket that perhaps best sums up the old Soviet Union and its ambitions at the height of the Cold War. The new Russia is more down to earth, but shares some old ideas. Vladimir Plotkin's Aeroflot HQ reflects the airline's 1923 logo, and tower blocks like the **Mosfilmovskaya Complex**, with its two structures of a 214m (702ft)-high tower and a smaller 130m (427ft)-high building, ape the old idea of housing Muscovites in huge buildings, but whether they will have the longevity of the decaying yet still beautiful 1928 **Narkomfin Building** remains to be seen.

Built as the ultimate avant-garde communal housing block for the workers at the People's Commissariat of Finance in the heyday of Soviet social radicalism, with kitchens replaced by communal dining rooms, the Narkomfin has come full circle, housing an array of residents who have created their own unique community, and in some cases their own apartments, virtually rebuilding parts of the structure to create affordable living spaces. The building is being renovated and only time will tell if any form of communal dining will be reinstated; Andy Warhol would probably have voted for a McDonald's.

Capital City Towers

Ascension Church

Zuyev Workers' Club

Moscow State University

Ivan the Great Bell Tower

Shabolovka Radio Tower

Monument to the Conquerors of Space

L: 1 Presnenskaya Emb. 8
A: NBBJ, 2010
FF: The complex architectural
form is inspired by *Corner
Counter Relief* by Vladimir
Tatlin, often heralded
as the father of Russian
constructivism.

L: Kolomenskoye Park
A: Prince Vasili III, 1532
FF: The church was built to
commemorate the birth of Ivan
the Terrible.

L: 18 Lesnaya Street
A: Ilya Golosov, 1926–8
FF: The club still functions
as a social club, with two
theatres.

L: Mokhovaya Street
A: Lev Vladimirovitch Rudnev, 1953
FF: The star surrounded by ears of
wheat at the top of the spire weighs
12 tons, and is 9m (30ft) in diameter.

L: Kremlin Complex
A: Bon Fryazin, Petrok
Maly, 1505–10
FF: The tower rests on
brick walls that are
5m (16.4ft) thick at
the base.

L: Shabolovka
Street
A: Vladimir
Shukhov, 1920–22
FF: Alexander
Rodchenko
immortalised the
tower in a famous
photo for the cover
of *Radioslushatel*
in 1929.

L: VDNKh, nr Prospekt
Mira
A: A. N. Kolchin and
M. O. Barsch (architects);
A. P. Faidysh-Krandievsky
(sculptor), 1964
FF: A statue of rocket
scientist and
astronautics pioneer
Konstantin Tsiolkovsky
stands in front of the
obelisk.

Cathedral of
St Basil the Blessed

Kotelnicheskaya
Apartments

Narkomfin Building

Mosfilmovskaya Complex

Tsentrosoyuz Building

L: Red Square
A: Commissioned by Ivan IV,
architects unknown, 1555–61
FF: Basil's domes are believed
to be the earliest use of the
onion dome, or *lukovitsa* in
Russia.

L: Kotelnicheskaya
Embankment
A: Dmitry Chechylin and
Andrei Rostkovsky, 1952
FF: This was the first
building to top 150m
(492ft) in Moscow.

L: 25 Novinsky Boulevard
A: Moisei Ginzburg and Ignaty Milnis,
1928–32
FF: Despite the presence of a canteen,
many residents partitioned their
spaces to create a tiny kitchen.

L: Mosfilmovskaya Street
A: Sergey Skuratov, 2011
FF: The height of the main
tower is emphasised by
eight shades of tiling on the
facade, from white at the
top to dark limestone at the
bottom.

L: 39 Myasnitskaya Street
A: Le Corbusier with Nicolai Kolli,
1929–33
FF: The ground floor was initially
planned to be exposed to the exterior
so that it would be filled with light.

London

'I don't know what London's coming to – the higher the buildings the lower the morals.'
Noël Coward, *Collected Sketches and Lyrics*

London is a mess. A sprawling, wild, nonsensical mess that, over 2,000 years, has been almost totally destroyed by fire, randomly damaged by bombs and systematically assaulted by terrible civic planning. But it remains one of the greatest cities in the world and its skyline tells the story better than any historian could hope to. And with every new building comes new controversies, as Londoners have a love-hate relationship with almost every building of any interest, stretching back as far as the modern city itself.

The golden-capped **Monument**, a simple Doric column 62m (204ft) tall, lies 62m (204ft) from Pudding Lane, where the Great Fire of London is thought to have started in 1666. London was a city made almost entirely of wood and the fire that raged for three days destroyed more than 13,000 houses and 89 churches, including the 'Old' St Paul's. The Monument was designed by Sir Christopher Wren and, in 1677, was the tallest construction in London. It bore three Latin inscriptions, one of which described how the fire started and was eventually extinguished. Anti-Catholic sentiments ran high back then and, in 1681, some additional words were added: 'But Popish frenzy, which wrought such horrors, is not yet quenched'.

Just as controversial was what is now regarded as Wren's finest work – his 17th-century replacement of **St Paul's Cathedral** which, at over 100m (328ft), took 'the tallest building' award and held it until 1962. This perfect example of Baroque has two towers topped by golden pineapples – a symbol of peace, prosperity and hospitality. While the cathedral is a city favourite today, the design was roundly criticised at the time by a largely Anglican populace who disliked the fancy Catholic dome with its golden cross.

The city's church spires have now been largely overshadowed by the spires of commercial enterprises, the latest of which is **The Shard**. At 310m (1,017ft), Renzo Piano's design currently holds the crown as the tallest building in Europe and is at once loathed and loved. Architects hail it as inspirational for its cutting-edge engineering – the steel tip has to withstand winds of up to 100mph – and critics deride it for its cost, its size and the fact that it detracts from the rest of the City. But, crassness aside, tourists love it for the four-storey observation deck that rewards them with unparalleled views of the city.

Today's skyscrapers are symbolic of money and prestige. The Shard is the pinnacle of a 'race to the top' that began back in the 1980s when commercial buildings such as the **Lloyd's Building** were designed to be looked at. Richard Rogers' stainless steel masterpiece revealed every heating duct, air conditioning vent and stairwell, and even had the glass lifts travelling up the outside of the building. Rogers' 'inside-out' building, once criticised for its uncompromising functionality, is one of the most visited architectural sites of the annual Open House weekend.

Some of Rogers' ideas are almost standard in architectural terms today: the Heron Tower features external bracing with transparent lifts whizzing up to the 38th floor where visitors can have dinner, drinks and 360-degree views of London. The first tower to offer all this was the then-monikered **Post Office Tower** – a transmission tower built in 1962 to hold VHF aerials which was, at 191m (627ft), the tallest building in London. Billy Butlin's revolving restaurant 'Top of the Tower', on the 34th floor was a fabulous feature that has sadly never been repeated.

But before commercial towers came into existence, skyscrapers had a more urgent purpose – to house the population. Bombs had devastated post-war London and the Barbican Centre was to become a symbol of how London could, phoenix-like, rise again. Chamberlin, Powell & Bon designed Europe's largest reconstruction project and, like so many modernists, were hugely inspired by Le Corbusier's Unité d'Habitation in Marseille. Another committed modernist, Ernö Goldfinger, had a similarly utopian vision. His 32-storey concrete **Trellick Tower** was social housing that would aid urban living, with rooms offering plenty of light, space and clever detailing. A clubroom, nursery school, a doctor's surgery and three communal launderettes were all housed in a separate tower linked by a walkway. Today it's Grade II* listed and a desirable address.

Cities also build to celebrate: the millennium saw a rush of building projects that, as usual, garnered mixed reactions, but the Millennium Wheel (now the **London Eye**) was loved from the get-go and, though only expected to last a year, became another London favourite, not least for the wonderful views it affords of the city's skyline.

The identity of a city is etched on its buildings, providing instant links to the past. More importantly for a commercial capital, they can also be money-makers – one of the City's oldest structures and most iconic tourist attractions is the **Tower of London**. Today it's home to the Crown Jewels

but it was once a royal residence, a branch of the Royal Mint and, most famously, a prison renowned for torture, executions and imprisonment, including those of Anne Boleyn, Guy Fawkes and, rather improbably, East End gangsters Ronnie and Reggie Kray. Dating back to William the Conqueror, the White Tower was, at 27m (89ft), the very first 'tall' building in London. Charles Barry's neo-Gothic **Palace of Westminster** is another popular attraction and symbolic of the country's democracy, but on New Year's Eve it's the north tower that is the focus of attention. Augustus Pugin designed the famous clock tower that houses '**Big Ben**', writing: 'I never worked so hard in my life for Mr Barry for tomorrow I render all the designs for finishing his bell tower and it is beautiful'. It was his last work.

Thankfully, in recognition of past great design, there's also the desire to protect and repurpose. Built in the 1930s, Giles Gilbert Scott's **Battersea Power Station** – the largest brick building in Europe – is an Art Deco masterpiece. Neglected for decades, the chimney stacks of the decommissioned coal-fired power station, once white, now smoke-choked, are in the process of being cleaned and brought back to life – albeit as a hotel – and it looks set to create thousands of jobs, open up the land along the Thames and reinvigorate the area.

Like a palimpsest, London continually recreates itself, and today Greater London has more skyscrapers than any other metropolitan area in the European Union, with 17 skyscrapers at least 150m (492ft) tall: Number One Canada Square, 'London's tallest' in 1990, is currently number two, but even The Shard won't hold the title for long. The clock ticks on… bulldoze, rebuild, regenerate, with the accolades and brickbats that inevitably follow. The sky's the limit.

Trellick Tower

BT Tower (formerly Post Office Tower)

Big Ben, Palace of Westminster

Lloyd's Building

The Shard

L: 7 Golborne Rd
A: Ernö Goldfinger, 1972
FF: It's possible to visit during London's annual late September Open House weekend.

L: 60 Cleveland Street
A: Ministry of Public Buildings and Works, 1962
FF: The restaurant was rumoured to be reopening for the Olympics but it didn't and there has been no further word on it.

L: City of Westminster
A: Charles Barry, 1840s
FF: The clock's mechanism is regulated by adding pennies for weight, and the four clock faces are each 7m (23ft) across.

L: 1 Lime Street
A: Richard Rogers, 1986
FF: The Committee Room on the 11th floor contains an original 18th-century dining room designed by Robert Adam.

L: 32 London Bridge Street
A: Renzo Piano, 2012
FF: The Sky Boutique on the 68th floor is the highest shop in London.

L: St Paul's Churchyard
A: Christopher Wren, 1675–1708
FF: The geometric staircase in the South West Bell Tower appears in a number of films including *The Madness of King George* (1994), *Harry Potter and the Prisoner of Azkaban* (2004) and *Sherlock Holmes* (2009).

L: Nine Elms, Battersea
A: Giles Gilbert Scott, 1933
FF: The redevelopment is slated to include a snaking building by Norman Foster and a leaning design by Frank Gehry.

L: Jubilee Gardens, South Bank
A: Marks Barfield Architects, 2000
FF: On a clear day, from the top, you can see around 40 km (25 miles) – as far as Windsor Castle.

L: Tower Hill
A: Founded by William the Conqueror, 1078
FF: Many believe that the Tower of London is haunted by, among others, the ghosts of Anne Boleyn, Lady Jane Grey and the murdered 'Princes in the Tower'.

L: Fish Street Hill
A: Christopher Wren, Robert Hooke, 1677
FF: During the last refurbishment, a 360-degree panoramic camera was installed at the top of the Monument which runs 24 hours a day, and updates every minute.

Busan

'The future of architecture has no gravity, no columns, just buildings hanging in the sky.'
Wolf D. Prix, designer of the Busan Cinema Center

Seoul may be the beating heart of South Korea, but Busan, with just four million inhabitants in the metropolitan city, could be said to be its real soul. This is in part due to the city's status as South Korea's playground, with its seaside setting making it the go-to destination for holidaymakers; as many as 500,000 people cram onto the city's Haeundae beaches during summer, creating a sense of playfulness and fun that characterises and humanises the city in a way that, of all Korea's cities, is unique to Busan. The result is a vibrant metropolis that's also aesthetically appealing – not least for a dramatic mountain backdrop fronted by rolling foothills leading down to the sea, and despite the growing number of skyscrapers that increasingly dominate but still don't define or engulf the city.

In part, the skyscrapers have grown to accommodate the holidaymakers, but Busan's real power emerged during the 20th century, first under colonial rule by Japan, when the city, then called Pusan, developed as a major port for shipping resources from Korea to Japan, then during the Korean War of 1950–3, when it was declared South Korea's temporary capital and accommodated huge numbers of refugees. By 2002, the newly named Busan was the third largest container port in the world, after Hong Kong and Singapore. And less than ten years later, it had two 300m (985ft)

skyscraper residential complexes, the 300m **Doosan Haeundae We've the Zenith Tower complex** of 2011 just beating the 298m **Haeundae Udong Hyundai I'Park** in height. The former, looking like a surreal cluster of pipes or wind instruments, beats the latter in appeal, too, its three towers offering a harmonious whole whose design supposedly references flowers, the curves of Haeundae beach's waves in front of the complex and the peak of Mt Jang behind it. By contrast, the I'Park, comprised of three curved and tapering residential towers and a mixed-use tower with hotel, retail space and offices, calls to mind the somewhat more alarming feel of a clutch of foil scalpel blades; not, according to its architect Studio Daniel Libeskind, a reference to its cutting-edge modernity, but 'a homage to traditional Korean architecture, which often derives its forms from natural beauty – the curl of an ocean wave, the unique composition of a flower petal, or the wind-filled sails of a ship'.

The Busan International Finance Center Project (BIFC) takes the idea of the curl but squares it off in its **Landmark Tower**, which matches the I'Park in height and stands out in the city by dint of towering above the remaining seven buildings that make up the complex – among them a culture and experience zone, an entertainment centre and two banks. If any one building sums up 21st-century Busan it is, for the time being, this one, a multi-functional modern complex which embodies the idea of Busan as a world centre of marine finance. By contrast, two towers that have a very different aesthetic, even a retro feel to them, are the **World Business Center (WBC) Palace Towers**, a pair of residential towers that rise up alongside each other in the fast-developing business district of Centum City. In a dull sea of dull towers they stand out by virtue of their vertically stepped facias, but they're nothing compared to what they were meant to be; the original award-winning design for World Business Center Busan (WBCB) by American practice Asymptote was meant to soar up 560m (1,837ft) before it was cancelled.

Amid all this construction and economic boom, Busan's cultural history is slowly being swallowed up, but one building, the **Beomeo-sa Temple**, exists as a moving testament to the country's Buddhist past. Founded in AD 678, the Daeungjeon complex comprises a range of serene pagodas from the 17th and 18th centuries that look far older than their 300 years, perhaps because many of them are renovations of originals dating back much further; in the case of Iljumun, the three-storey pagoda with four pillars, all the way back to the 9th century. It's an expressive building, but not the most moving in the city. That accolade goes to the circular **Chunghon Tower** in Jungang Park, dedicated to the memories of the service personnel who died in the Korean War. Their location on top of Daecheong Mountain is as well thought out as the rather beautiful tower; during the war, the slopes of the mountain sheltered many of the refugees who had flocked here from the north. Their views of the city they had escaped to would have been sweeping ones that took in the entire city, and it's still a great spot from which to appreciate the changing skyline. Why anyone bothers to opt

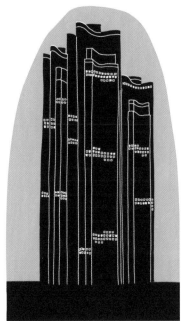

instead for the tourist-attracting **Busan Observation Tower** is a mystery, especially as both sites feature an elevator to whisk less able visitors up to their lofty viewing points.

From either, one curiosity stands out in the crowded landscape. The **Busan Cinema Center** is arguably one of the city's most unusual pieces of architecture, looking like some alien spaceship among the towering skyscrapers around it. Built to house and celebrate the city's popular annual film festival, it's comprised of three main buildings – Cine Mountain, BIFF Hill and Double Cone – around a huge central open-air space seating 4,000, as well as smaller screen spaces, lecture halls and other facilities. It's hard to imagine a more idiosyncratic building in the city will exist in the near future, with the current architectural trend more focused on elevation than imagination, but perhaps one building will encompass both. The **Busan Lotte Town Tower**, currently under construction, breaks the 500m (1,640ft) mark and is vying to be the 10th tallest building in the world. When it's completed, it will contain the usual mix of cultural, retail and business spaces, but its design, based on a standing ship in reference to the city's harbour, is anything but usual. Which is perhaps fitting for a city whose most arresting high-rise buildings are not skyscrapers at all, but a cluster of brightly coloured houses on a hillside overlooking the towers below; the **Gamcheon Culture Village**, built overlooking the sea on the hills that rise above Busan. Here, in a once-dilapidated neighbourhood dating back to the war, an imaginative Ministry of Culture, Sports and Tourism project called 'Dreaming of Busan Machu Picchu' led to the creation of an artists' village that has become the go-to destination in Busan, with galleries, installations and sculptures providing an attraction that's worlds away from the skyscrapers below – it blends old and new Busan beautifully.

Gamcheon Culture Village

Busan Cinema Center

Busan Lotte Town Tower

Haeundae Udong Hyundai I'Park

L: Gamcheon-dong, Saha-gu
A: N/A
FF: The village has a range of Western nicknames, including 'Lego village' and 'Santorini of the East', after the Greek village of the same name.

L: 120, Suyeonggangbyeon-daero, Haeundae-gu
A: Coop Himmelb(l)au, 2011
FF: The larger of the centre's two roofs holds the Guinness World Record for the world's longest cantilevered roof, stretching almost 90m (295ft) from its single-pillared support, the Double Cone. It looks particularly impressive at night, when its underside is illuminated by a changing LED display of colours.

L: Jungangdong 7(chil)-ga, Jung-gu
A: Skidmore, Owings & Merrill, 2009–19
FF: The tower is meant to resemble a standing ship, referencing the city's status as the largest port in Korea.

L: Haeundae Udong 1408
A: Studio Daniel Libeskind, 2011–13
FF: In 2013, the tallest of the four towers was completed at an elevation of 298m (978ft), making it the tallest residential tower in Asia.

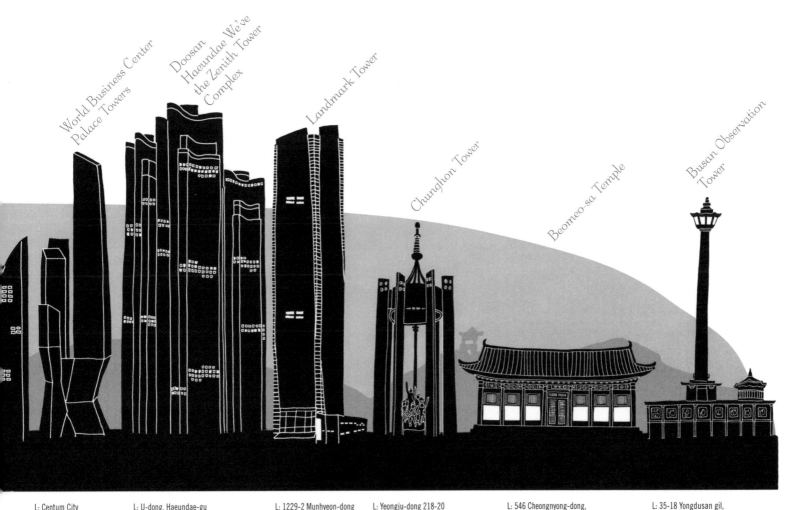

World Business Center
Palace Towers

Doosan
Haeundae We've
the Zenith Tower
Complex

Landmark Tower

Chunghon Tower

Beomeo-sa Temple

Busan Observation
Tower

L: Centum City
A: WonWoo Architects, 2008–11
FF: At 265m (869ft), the two Palace Towers are among the top ten tallest buildings in Busan.

L: U-dong, Haeundae-gu
A: De Stefano & Partners, 2007–11
FF: The complex houses a wine club, a soundproof music practice room and family cinema, hobby rooms and reading rooms.

L: 1229-2 Munhyeon-dong Nam-gu
A: Unknown, 2010–14
FF: At the time of writing the tower was the third tallest in the city.

L: Yeongju-dong 218-20
A: Unknown, 1970
FF: The tower's base features the names of fallen soldiers and military personnel on the inside, and is also known as the 'Tower to the Loyal Dead'.

L: 546 Cheongnyong-dong, Geumjeong-gu
A: Unknown, 17th–18th centuries
FF: The temple complex includes seven royal palace wings, pavilions, three gates and 11 hermitages.

L: 35-18 Yongdusan gil, Gwangbok-dong, Jung-gu
A: Unknown, 1973
FF: The 118m (387ft) tower offers good views of the city's port, even from its hilltop base in Yongdusan Park, which can be accessed via an escalator. The tower itself has two elevators to a café and viewing platform.

Sacred Cities

Jerusalem

Mecca

Varanasi

Lhasa

Kyoto

Jerusalem

'The view of Jerusalem is the history of the world; it is more, it is the history of earth and of heaven.'

Benjamin Disraeli

Someone who had never visited Jerusalem might expect its mash-up of architecture created by and for the three great monotheistic religions of Judaism, Christianity and Islam to create a landscape that's as inharmonious and confused as the social history of the city.

Yet modern Jerusalem, a city sacred to more than a third of the world's population, is a winning mix, possibly because of its torrid 5,000-year history. Visitors to the Tower of David Museum, set in the citadel near the Jaffa Gate entrance to the Old City, can discover the complexities of that history before climbing the tower to see the new city laid out before them. It's a great spot, offering far-reaching views that take in a much more recent tower: the Art Deco **YMCA Tower**, designed by Arthur Loomis Harmon of US firm Shreve, Lamb and Harmon – perhaps better known for New York's Empire State Building. Harmon designed the entire building as a metaphor for peace, and so its décor, structure and even gardens share Abrahamic symbolism from all three of the city's religions, while its entrance plaza is planted with 12 cypress trees to recall the 12 tribes of Israel, the 12 disciples of Jesus and the 12 friends and supporters of Muhammad.

Standing proudly above the city's mass as a modern beacon of hope, the YMCA tower is open to all, unlike many of the city's more well-known buildings. But those elder statesmen hold their own in historical and architectural stature, notably in, on and around the Old City. For followers of Islam, Temple Mount's 7th-century **Dome of the Rock** (Qubbat As-Sakhrah) and Al-Aqsa Mosque, set on a plaza above the Old City, offer a wonderful example of early Islamic architecture, with the striking octagonal plan and 18m (60ft) timber-framed double dome, lined with coloured and gilded stucco and covered in Persian tiles (now Turkish replicas) added by Suleiman I in the 16th century, demonstrating core Byzantine motifs. Through history, bitter conflict has surrounded the Rock, and it was no surprise that during the Crusades it was commandeered as a Christian shrine, with Al-Aqsa becoming the royal palace of the Crusader kings, then the headquarters of the Knights Templar in 1118. Nowadays, the key Christian building in the city, the **Church of the Holy Sepulchre**, has its own share of conflict, with Greek Orthodox, Armenian Apostolic, Roman Catholics, Coptic Orthodox, Ethiopian Orthodox and Syriac Orthodox protecting strictly regulated times and places of worship. Physically, the church is equally segmented, and an architecturally confused counterpoint to the wonders of nearby Temple Mount – surprisingly, given its status as the holiest Christian site in the world. Dating back to the 4th century, the existing church dates predominantly from 12th century, the original having been destroyed in 1009. Ninety years later the Crusaders set about enlarging the site and restoring the large blue dome directly over the supposed tomb of Christ.

If the church shows little physical elegance, other key Christian sites offer plenty for modern Christian architecture fans to admire – and occasionally scratch their heads over. The seven gilded domes and fanciful turrets of **St Mary Magdalene Church**, for example, offer a perplexing slice of Russia incongruously perched on the Mount of Olives, where another Russian Orthodox church, the Church of the Ascension, offers a foreign take on local design with a 64m (210ft) square tower topped by a pointed belfry. More appealingly simple than both is the **Church of St Anne**. Built in the 12th century by the Crusaders, its unusually asymmetrical design, unadorned facade and elegant proportions create a harmonious whole that offers a beautiful example of Romanesque architecture. And in the beguiling walled compound that is the Armenian quarter of the Old City, the ancient cathedral of St James, some of it dating back to AD 420, offers another Christian spot whose design is equally arresting in its proportions and simplicity.

The Old City, and in particular its Jewish Quarter, have been attracting pilgrims from across the globe since the Ottoman era, with the Western or Wailing Wall drawing millions to Judaism's holiest place to mourn the destruction of the Temple that they believe housed the Ark of the Covenant. But architecturally, the more interesting Jewish sites lie in structures like the **Belz Synagogue** and the **Givat Ram Synagogue**. Located in the hilltop Kiryat Belz neighbourhood, the squat yet harmonious Belz building is strikingly faithful to the 1843 original it was modelled on, and dominates the city skyline; its vast interior comfortably holds 10,000 worshippers, making it the largest synagogue in Israel. By contrast, the Givat Ram, or Rabbi Dr Israel Goldstein, synagogue holds just 100 and is just 3.7m (12ft 3in) high, but its ethereal, organic form, evoking something natural but in flux, eloquently captures Jerusalem

as a paradox of both the timeless and ephemeral, and an interesting stepping stone to the modern, wider city of Jerusalem.

The attempt to create a society for so many diverse groups has resulted in some fascinating buildings – chief among them the **Ramot Polin Apartments**. Built as one of a wide range of housing developments in the region after the Seven Day War in 1967, the 720 apartments were composed of an avant-garde modular system of dodecahedrons that resembled a chemical formula or honeycomb, and drew both praise and criticism for a development that might be visually and technically innovative, but in practice proved virtually uninhabitable. More successful by far in terms of marrying prosaic everyday workability with lofty aims and aesthetics has been the **Supreme Court**, a low-slung building that manages to capture something monumental, feeling both timeless and futuristic.

A different kind of futurism lies behind the John F. Kennedy Memorial **Yad Kennedy**, a poignant white sculptural piece that resembles an 18m (60ft)-felled tree, built in part with donations from American Jewish communities. Set in a forest, the slim white columns and everlasting flame are a sad reminder of a more hopeful time. And from the same era, the **Bank of Israel** headquarters offers its own take on the space age. Looking like a modern church organ or a squat, alien ship, the exterior is a paean to the International Style, yet inside it tumbles with plants and vegetation, humanising the space for workers and visitors alike. More recent additions to the city's landscape, in the shape of Santiago Calatrava's Bridge of Strings and the Israel Museum, point towards a continuation of this humanisation, but perhaps the real hope for the future lies in buildings like the **Orthodox School** in Remle. Here, centred around a courtyard, a beautiful white building of gentle slopes, interesting planes and pools of cool shade creates a space that feels like a physical representation of harmony and hope.

Bank of Israel

Givat Ram Synagogue

Ramot Polin Apartments

Orthodox School

St Mary Magdalene Church

Dome of the Rock

L: Giv'at Ram, 2 Kaplan Street
A: Arieh Sharon, 1974
FF: Arieh Sharon has said his 'first lesson in architecture was given to me by a bee… who are among nature's most successful architects and engineers'.

L: Elyashar Street, Edmond J. Safra (Givat Ram) Campus, Hebrew University
A: Heinrich Heinz Rau and David Resnick, 1957
FF: In 1975 the synagogue featured in a series of Israeli postage stamps dedicated to architecture in Israel.

L: Ramot, Haroe
A: Zvi Hecker, 1972–5
FF: The 720 apartments were originally cast in concrete and covered in Jerusalem stone.

L: Jerusalem, Israel
A: Dan and Hila Israelevitz Architects, 2010
FF: The school was planned in response to the shortage of classrooms for the Christian community in the city, and is now a much-loved cultural icon in the local area.

L: Mount of Olives
A: Tsar Alexander III, 1888
FF: The church houses the remains of the Grand Duchess Elizabeth Feodorovna, killed in the Russian Revolution of 1917, and the body of her niece Princess Alice of Greece, who protected Jews during the Nazi occupation of Greece.

L: Temple Mount
A: Caliph Abd al-Malik, AD 687–691
FF: The dome enshrines the Rock (al-Sakhra), from which Muhammad is said to have ascended to heaven, and is the oldest Islamic monument in the world.

Church of the Holy Sepulchre

YMCA Tower

Yad Kennedy

Belz Synagogue

Supreme Court

Church of St Anne

L: Suq Khan e-Zeit and Christian Quarter Road
A: Constantine the Great, AD 326–335; unknown, 12th century
FF: The original church was built on a site believed to encompass both Golgotha, or Calvary, where Jesus was crucified, and the tomb (sepulchre) where he was buried.

L: 26 King David Street
A: Arthur Loomis Harmon, 1933
FF: Three inscriptions revealed at the building's dedication in 1933 read 'The Lord our God the Lord is One' in Hebrew, 'I am the Way' in Aramaic and 'There is no God but God' in Arabic.

L: Aminadav Forest, Jerusalem
A: David Resnick, 1966
FF: The 51 white columns that make up the John F. Kennedy Memorial represent the 50 states of the United States, plus the District of Columbia.

L: 2 Dover Shalom Street
A: Isaac Blatt, 2000
FF: Nine 5.5m (18ft)-high chandeliers each contain over 200,000 pieces of Czech crystal.

L: Sha'arei Mishpat 1, Western Jerusalem
A: Ada Karmi-Melamede Architects & Ram Karmi, 1991
FF: The building features a mosaic pavement from the 5th century, recovered from a synagogue at the Hamat Gader hot springs.

L: Via Dolorosa at St Stephen's (Lion) Gate
A: Unknown, 1131–8
FF: Saint Anne's acoustics were designed for Gregorian chanting, and all visitors are allowed to sing here – as long as the piece is a religious one.

Mecca

'The holy precincts around the Ka'aba contain stories stretching back to the very beginning of time.'
Ziauddin Sardar, *Mecca: The Sacred City*

Stanley Kubrick's *2001: A Space Odyssey* opens at the beginning of time, with a black monolith that reappears, later in the film, on the moon. The presence of the monolith is unexplained, mysterious, but clearly significant, and its meaning has been the subject of much speculation, including that of a 15-year-old New Jersey student called Margaret Stackhouse. Upon reading her analysis, Kubrick suggested that her thoughts were 'perhaps the most intelligent that I've read anywhere… What a first-rate intelligence'. Stackhouse described the monolith as the 'source of infinite knowledge and intelligence, perfection represented in its shape; and its colour – perfect black – as incomprehensible to man who, with his limited senses, cannot comprehend the absence of colour or light'. Stackhouse suggests that perfect knowledge, represented by the monolith, is always present, but our understanding of it will always be imperfect.

It is thought that the **Ka'aba**, a black, cube-shaped building housed within the **Al-Masjid al-Haram** mosque in Mecca, was Kubrick's inspiration for his monolith. The sacred Ka'aba, believed to have been originally built by Ibrahim (Abraham), is the focus of all Muslims and the direction in which they pray.

Mecca is the birthplace of the Prophet Muhammad and the place where the sacred text of Islam, the Koran, was first revealed to him so, in AD 630, he declared that every Muslim should make the Hajj (pilgrimage) here at least once in their lifetime as one of the five Pillars of Islam – the five obligations that every able-bodied Muslim must satisfy in order to live a good and responsible life according to Islam.

While the 'forbidden city' of Mecca is off limits for non-Muslims, there have been intrepid travellers who have risked incurring the penalty – death – in order to reveal the secrets of the most sacred of all Islamic sites. One such traveller was the 19th-century British explorer Sir Richard Burton who, in 1853, stained his face with walnut juice and entered the holy city disguised as an Afghan pilgrim.

Burton's story of his journey was a sensation. In his *Personal Narrative of a Pilgrimage to Al-Madinah And Meccah*, Burton described in great detail the ceremonies that were performed, including that of El Ihram, meaning 'to assume the pilgrim garb', followed by the Tawaf, which involves seven circuits, anti-clockwise, around the Ka'aba.

'First I did the circumambulation of the Haram. Early next morning I was admitted to the house of our Lord; and we went to the holy well Zemzem [sic], the holy water of Mecca, and then the Ka'abah, in which is inserted the famous black stone, where they say a prayer for the Unity of Allah.'

Ibrahim built the temple in thanks for the spring of water that God provided when his son Ishmael was thirsty; Hajira (Hagar), Ibrahim's second wife, desperately ran between the two small hills of **Al Safa and Al Marwah** in search of water and a small spring opened up in the ground. Today the hills are located within the Al-Masjid al-Haram – the largest mosque in the world – approximately 450m (1,480ft) apart. Pilgrims perform the Sa'i, which means 'ritual walking', between the two hills in commemoration of Hajira's search, travelling back and forth seven times within a covered gallery. The **Zamzam Well** was built up around the spring, taking its name from Hajira's command *'Zomë Zomë'* ('stop') as the water poured out.

When the temple was completed, it is believed that Gabriel brought the 'Black Stone' (Hajarul Aswad) that Burton refers to. The stone, originally set into the Ka'aba's wall by Muhammad in AD 605, is variously thought to be a meteorite or even a great white sapphire from the Garden of Eden, and perhaps to have magical properties.

Today, the Zamzam Well is about 20m (65.5ft) away from the Ka'aba. It was moved from its original spot so that pilgrims could circumambulate the Ka'aba more easily, and it is this popularity of the Hajj that, ironically, is contributing to the site's gradual deterioration.

In order to accommodate more worshippers, the mosque itself is being extended, at a cost of many billions, but the cost to the city will be much higher as Mecca's oldest neighbourhoods are destroyed in the process.

It's also rumoured that the oldest surviving part of the mosque itself, including exquisite marble columns with carved Islamic calligraphy dating back to the 16th and 17th centuries, are likely to be destroyed in order to create prayer halls. Currently a temporary elevated roundabout above the Ka'aba – built 13m (42.6ft) in the air to accommodate wheelchairs – blocks the view of the Ka'aba itself. And such wanton destruction isn't new… the house of Khadija, the wife of the Prophet Muhammad, has already been demolished and built over with a toilet block.

Another important site in the Hajj is **Mount Arafat**, where Muhammad gave his farewell sermon to those who had accompanied him on his Hajj. Today's pilgrims spend the day on the hill.

On the last day of the Hajj, pilgrims perform the 'Stoning of the Devil' ritual at the **Jamarat Bridge** in Mina. Originally the pilgrims would throw pebbles at three pillars, known as *jamarāt*, but for safety reasons, these were replaced by walls in 2004. Following hundreds of deaths as a result of overcrowding, the single-tiered bridge, originally built in 1963, has also since been replaced with a multi-level bridge.

In his book *Mecca: The Sacred City*, Ziauddin Sardar argues that Mecca has become a place of consumerism, and he suggests that the Abraj Al-Bait or **Makkah Royal Clock Tower** is a fine example of it; towering over the Ka'aba, the world's second tallest building has the biggest clock face in the world and was described by Oliver Wainwright as 'Big Ben on steroids'. Housing luxury hotels and apartments, the tower was built on the site of a now-demolished Ottoman fortress.

Zamzam Well

Ka'aba

Al Safa and Al Marwah

Al-Masjid al-Haram

L: Mecca, Al-Hejaz
A: Unknown, possibly
Abraham (Ibrahim)
FF: The well was
moved and rebuilt
to accommodate
more pilgrims to
circumambulate the
Ka'aba.

L: Mecca, Al-Hejaz
A: Unknown
FF: Thought to be the
inspiration for Stanley
Kubrick's monolith in
2001: A Space Odyssey.

L: Masjid al-Haram
A: N/A
FF: Mount Safa is thought to be the mountain referred
to in the proverb: 'If the mountain will not come to
Muhammad, Muhammad must go to the mountain.'

L: Masjid al-Haram Road
A: Unknown, 1955–2011
FF: The indoor and outdoor praying spaces can
accommodate two million pilgrims during the Hajj.

L: Oum Al Qura Street
A: Dar Al-Handasah Architects, 2012
FF: The destruction of an Ottoman fort sparked an international outcry.

L: Mina, Mecca
A: Unknown, 1963; Dar Al-Handasah, Bin Laden Group, 2007
FF: It's the largest pedestrian bridge in the world.

L: East of Mecca
A: N/A
FF: Each year over two million pilgrims climb Mount Arafat as the final part of their Hajj.

Lhasa

'There is no need for temples, no need for complicated philosophies.
My brain and my heart are my temples; my philosophy is kindness.'
Tenzin Gyatso, recognised since 1950 as the 14th and current Dalai Lama, 2014

The Dalai Lama, the most sacred monk of the Gelug school of Tibetan Buddhism, offers a daily quotation online, and in May 2014 added the one above to his thoughts on kindness, peace, understanding and tolerance that are the touchstones of his faith. The quotation may have perplexed the millions of visitors to temples in a city whose literal translation is 'place of the gods'. And the Tibetan Heritage Fund may have felt a frisson of anxiety, given its members' ongoing attempts to preserve and restore vernacular Tibetan architecture in the fast-changing landscape of Lhasa.

But with the city a popular destination for Chinese tourists, and the obvious focus of more than a million Buddhists who make a pilgrimage here annually, the temples of Lhasa must, for now, be as well protected as any UNESCO World Heritage Site. Top of the tree, literally and metaphorically, the **Potala Palace** actually is a UNESCO site, along with the **Jokhang** and Norbulingka temples. This trio is the holy trinity of Tibetan Buddhism, with the Potala the most imposing of the three. Built as the centre of the Tibetan government by the fifth Dalai Lama, and home to the country's political and religious leaders until the Chinese invasion of 1951 and the departure into exile of the 14th Dalai Lama in 1959, its imposing red and white structure of stone and wood can be seen for miles around. It comprises two palaces, the White Palace, which is the ancient seat of Tibetan government, and the Red

Palace, which has been the winter estate of the Dalai Lama since 1755.

South of them, at 3,725m (12,220ft) above sea level, **Chakpori Hill** is a challenging hike for pilgrims and visitors, and affords great views of the cityscape – as well as of the Potala. It's not uncommon to see pilgrims labouring up both on their knees, but for Tibetan Buddhist pilgrims, the more low-key Jokhang is far more important and the holiest destination in Tibet. This is in part due to its age – founded around AD 639, it was one of the first Buddhist temples erected in Tibet, and marks not just the beginning of the Tibetan state but also of Tibetan Buddhism. But it's also about the actual building, which is thought to be one of the world's oldest timber-frame buildings, and a fine example of traditional Tibetan construction and its basis in the Indian Buddhist monastery style called *vihara*. Around its outer walls, devout pilgrims follow one of the three devotional routes around Barkhor, the area radiating from Barkhor square.

Across town, the **Norbulingka Palace**, built in 1755 and the so-called summer residence of the Dalai Lama, forms the third part of the UNESCO site, and is revered as the last palace occupied by the current Dalai Lama. To get to it from the Potala Palace, pilgrims pass the **Lhasa Zhol Pillar**, an 8th-century stone pillar inscribed with what may be the oldest known example of Tibetan writing, and a very different edifice, the **Tibet Peaceful**

Liberation Monument. Celebrating what the Chinese euphemistically refer to as 'the "Peaceful Liberation of Tibet" by the People's Liberation Army', it is shaped as an abstract Mount Qomolangma (Mount Everest), and is, according to the Tibetan government in exile, 'a daily reminder of the humiliation of the Tibetan people'.

Further afield, **Pabonka Monastery** adds another unusual dimension to Lhasa's skyline. Built on a flat-topped granite boulder, Pabonka is one of the most ancient Buddhist sites in the region, possibly predating both the Jokhang and Ramoche temples. The current version dates from the 11th century, after the nine-storey original by Songtsän Gampo, reputed to be the founder of the Tibetan Empire, was destroyed and totally rebuilt – albeit with just three storeys. Three miles from Lhasa, **Drepung Monastery** was once the largest monastery in the world, housing between 8,000 and 10,000 monks. It was shut by the Chinese authorities in 2008, but by then was a shadow of its former self, some 40 per cent of the old monastic town having been destroyed after the Chinese arrived in 1951.

It's back in the old town that what remains of Lhasa's traditional Tibetan architecture can be seen at its best. The style, dating back 1,300 years, is remarkable for its mix of manmade and natural materials suited to the local climate and geography, and for its sound ecological basis; every part of a Tibetan building can be reused, and if left to decay simply reverts to being a natural part of the landscape. The Tibetan Heritage Fund is doing its best to preserve the 50 remaining examples, having begun with saving and restoring the three-storey stone and mudbrick **Trapchishar House** when it was founded in 1996. It bears many traditional motifs, including a flat roof and interior courtyard, an intricately carved interior timber frame, and beautiful religious carvings and decorative paintings on corner stones and interior walls.

The restoration of a far more significant building in 1986 was part of the thrust that led to the saving of the Trapchishar; the **Ramoche Monastery and Temple**. Large sections of the 7th-century temple, founded at the same time as the Jokhang and considered to be Lhasa's second most important temple after it, are reconstructions from the late 20th century, but it still offers a great mix of Han and Tibetan architectural styles. A far more modern building, the **Tibet Museum**, also draws on traditional Tibetan and Han architectural styles with Tibetan doors, beam-decoration and patterns, and a central courtyard designed using traditional monastic conventions showing the achievements of Tibet's past.

But it's the buildings that have nothing to do with religion or culture that offer a glimpse into the future of troubled Tibet – the Lhasa City Police Headquarters, for example, a towering monster that symbolises the recent history of Lhasa and the wider 'Tibetan Autonomous Region'. And the elegant low-slung **Qingzang Railway Station**, which even more insidiously reflects the current state of relations between Tibet and China. While supposedly referencing historic Tibetan palace architecture with a series of halls based on 'interpreted' traditional design, and laudably addressing and exploiting local problems and opportunities – among them low levels of oxygen, bright sunshine and sandstorms – the building is a prime example of architecture by committee, an overblown affair that handles just five trains a day, and has numerous soldiers from the People's Liberation Army dotted around its vast courtyard to keep undesirables from entering the station. Maybe they anticipate a future where millions more visitors will arrive in Lhasa, which may be what the Dalai Lama was obliquely asking us not to do in his quotation.

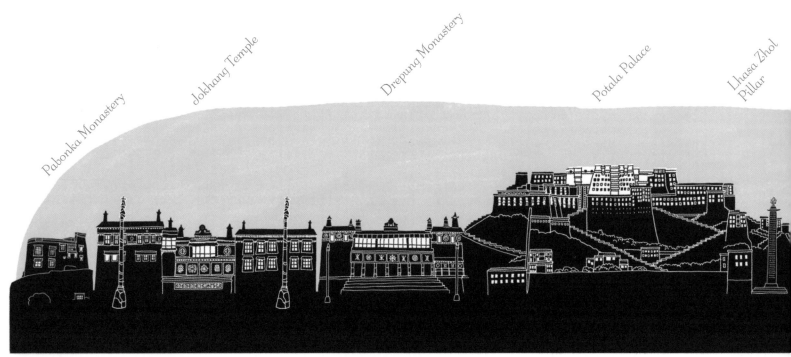

Pabonka Monastery

Jokhang Temple

Drepung Monastery

Potala Palace

Lhasa Zhol Pillar

L: Mount Parasol, Nyang Bran Valley
A: King Songtsen Gampo, 7th century
FF: The monastery is said to be the birthplace of the Tibetan alphabet.

L: Barkhor Square
A: Unknown, 7th–18th centuries
FF: The temple's gilded canopy roofs have historically constituted the height limit within the central city area. In the central hall is the Jokhang's oldest and most precious object, a life-sized sitting statue of Sakyamuni when he was 12 years old. This was carried to Tibet by Princess Wencheng from her home in Chang'an in AD 700. It is the most sacred statue in the eyes of the Tibetan people.

L: Mount Gephel
A: Unknown, 1416
FF: Seen from afar, the grand white construction gives the monastery the appearance of a heap of rice. In the Tibetan language, its name literally means 'rice heap'.

L: Moburi ('Red Hill'), central Lhasa
A: Unknown, 1645 onwards
FF: The Potala is the highest ancient palace in the world. Its highest point is 3,750m (12,300ft) above sea level, it has more than a thousand rooms set over 13 storeys and its stone walls are 3m (10ft) thick on average.

L: Zhol Village (foot of the Potala)
A: Unknown, 8th century
FF: The script on the pillar is thought to be the earliest example of Tibetan script, reputedly adapted from elements of Indian script by Thonmi Sambhota at the request of Songstän Gampo.

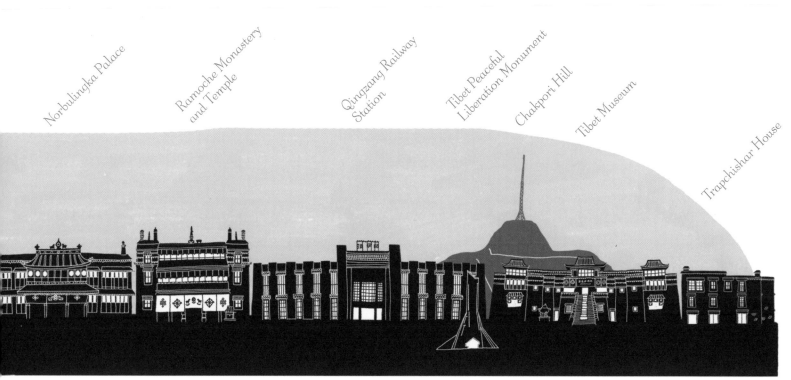

Norbulingka Palace

Ramoche Monastery and Temple

Qingzang Railway Station

Tibet Peaceful Liberation Monument

Chakpori Hill

Tibet Museum

Trapchishar House

L: 21 Luobulinka Road, Chengguan District
A: Unknown, 1755
FF: Norbulingka is the largest manmade garden in Tibet, covering an area of 19 hectares.

L: North of Jokhang Temple, Chengguan District
A: Han Chinese architects, 7th century
FF: It's thought the temple faces east to manifest the homesickness of Han Princess Wencheng, who was in charge of the project.

L: Liu Wu, Stod Lung Bde, Chen Rdzong
A: Cui Kai, leading the China Architecture Design & Research Group, 2006
FF: The huge station has several tracks – and just five arrivals each day.

L: Potala Palace Square
A: Unknown, 2002
FF: The 37m (121ft)-high monument has an inscription stating that the People's Liberation Army expelled the imperialist forces from Tibet in 1951, which led Tibet to advancement, prosperity and democracy, and opened a new era.

L: Chakpori Hill
A: Unknown
FF: There are 69 stone statues engraved on the rock, along with figures of Buddha and Buddhist scripture in Tibetan characters engraved on the cliff.

L: 19 Luobu Linka Road, Chengguan
A: Unknown, 1999
FF: The museum, covering an area of nearly two and a half hectares, was opened to coincide with the 50th anniversary of the Founding of the People's Republic of China and the 40th anniversary of Tibet's 'Democratic Reform'.

L: Barkhor Street
A: Unknown, 17th century
FF: Trapchishar was the first historic building in Lhasa to be saved from demolition by the Tibetan Heritage Fund.

Santiago de Compostela

'There was never a pilgrim that did not come back to his own village with one less prejudice and one more idea.'
Chateaubriand

Whether you view pilgrimages as lengthy acts of religious mania or life-changing journeys of self-discovery, most people who've done the Camino de Santiago agree that it is one of the best experiences of their lives. It would be trite to say this is in part due to what they find at the end of their journey, but it's certainly true that if they're hoping to find something mind-expanding and unforgettable, Santiago de Compostela doesn't disappoint.

With its grandiloquent Gothic, Baroque and Renaissance buildings set on and among vast squares, Santiago is an arrestingly beautiful city, and the sight of arriving or prostrate pilgrims, with their distinctive walking sticks and scallop shells, is genuinely moving. They've been coming here, to the shrine of St James the apostle, for more than a thousand years, nowadays taking one of the dedicated pilgrims' routes through France and Spain that range from 750km (467 miles) to just 115km (72 miles), the minimum pilgrims must walk before they can earn their certificate, the *compostela*. They do this in the suitably magnificent edifice that is **St James' Cathedral**, whose origins are as humble as many of the modern-day pilgrims visiting it.

Back in the 9th century, the building housing what Bishop Teodomiro of Iria Flavia established as the tomb of the apostle Saint James – after a hermit was led to it by 'celestial' lights – was just a small Roman temple, one which King Alfonso II promptly encased in a small, but crucially, non-pagan church. With the apostle's resting place officially identified came huge numbers of pilgrims – their arrival coinciding neatly with the need to reconnect the region with the rest of Europe after the expulsion of the Moors, and with Turkish invasions interrupting the popular pilgrimage to Jerusalem. And so a more appropriate edifice was begun, in 1075, with royalty and archbishops falling over themselves to enlarge and embellish the work of predecessors. What began as a granite Romanesque structure would expand to take in Baroque through to neoclassical additions, in time becoming the most notable piece of Romanesque art in Spain. Around it all would grow lavish royal palaces, monasteries, pilgrims' hospitals and hospices, and even colleges and schools.

Clustered around the Plaza de Obradoiro, or radiating out from it, the **Colexio de San Xerome**, the entrance to the **Pazo de Raxoi** and the **Hostal dos Reis Católicos** are three fine examples. The first of these was established by the Archbishop Fonseca III in 1501 as an art school for the poor; it was moved here to the square in the 17th century, but still bears many Gothic motifs across the two floors of its elegantly symmetrical facade. Adjacent to it, it's hard to imagine that the imposing colonnaded granite of the huge Pazo de Raxoi was once a seminary for confessors. Far more discreet on the square is the entrance to the Hostal dos Reis Católicos, founded in 1492 by Catholic monarchs Isabella of Castille and Ferdinand II of Aragon as a pilgrims' hospice – and now a luxury parador. Its facade features some beautiful details, including a central door flanked by a memorable religious frieze designed by Martín de Blas and Guillén de Colás. Nearby on Praza da Inmaculada, the **Monasterio de San Martiño Piñario**, its 20,000sq m (215,280sq ft) housing a hotel, museum and church, is a grand affair of Renaissance and Baroque styling that can't fail to impress, not least for its late 17th-century main facade, designed by Fray Gabriel de las Casas.

West of here, the **Monasterio de San Paio de Antealtares** closes one side of Praza da Quintana with a wall punctuated by 48 symmetrical iron-grilled windows. The flanks' harmony is arresting, and belies its relative youth; the Benedictine monastery was founded in the 11th century, but this replacement is just 300 or so years old. Some lovely examples of Gothic architecture do still remain though. The 12th-century **Colegiata Santa María a Real do Sar** features nine arcades from a 13th-century cloister and a Gothic baptismal font, but it's the visibly inclined inner walls and columns, and the notable buttresses built between

the 17th and 18th centuries to keep the whole thing from toppling over, that are the big draw. The **Convento de San Francisco**, founded by St Francis of Assisi on his visit to the city in 1214, also features some Gothic remains in a rectangular cut-granite church that sets it apart from other 16th-century religious buildings, particularly with its facade in a Baroque style on the lower part and neoclassical on the upper. It's unusual, but not as unusual as the facade of the church of the **Convento de Santa Clara**,

whose peculiar 18th-century curtain facade offers a great example of Compostela's Baroque style.

A third, late Gothic church and monastery stand apart from these two for a very distinct look. The Convent and Church of **San Domingos de Bonaval** feature a range of different styles, from their founding in 1228 to the 14th century, with modifications in the 18th. The church, one of the largest in the city, has a winning simplicity that contrasts nicely with its monumental stature, making it feel accessible and of the people. Like many of the city's former monasteries, it is now literally very much of the people; the convent is the headquarters of the Galician People's Museum. The number of similarly imposing religious and secular buildings in Santiago is mind-boggling, attesting to the importance of the city not just in medieval times, but even now, and not only to its religious communities.

As the symbolic centre of Galicia, modern Santiago has unsurprisingly attracted architects of world renown, commissioned by public institutions keen to use the wealth of its visitors in much the manner of their medieval predecessors. Norman Foster, Álvaro Siza, Giorgio Grassi, John Hejduk, Josef Paul Kleihues, Jean Nouvel and Arata Isozaki have all designed buildings here. Peter Eisenman's City of Culture of Galicia and Antón García Abril's Escuela de Altos Estudios Musicales and SGAE headquarters stand out, the latter's use of granite nicely drawing on the past to fashion the future. Álvaro Siza's **Centro Galego de Arte Contemporánea** does this eloquently too, housing challenging contemporary artworks in an equally challenging structure that, one hopes, Archbishop Fonseca, in founding his 16th-century art school, might have viewed with the kind of open mind Chateaubriand attributed to returning pilgrims.

Colegiata Santa María a Real do Sar

Colexio de San Xerome

Monasterio de San Paio de Antealtares

Pazo de Raxoi

St James' Cathedral

L: Rúa do Sar
A: Unknown, 12th, 17th–18th centuries
FF: The barrel-vault ceiling of the basilica had to be rebuilt in the 16th century to stop it falling in.

L: Praza do Obradoiro
A: Unknown, 17th century
FF: The ornate Gothic doorway shows images of St Lawrence, St John and St Francis on the left, and St Peter, St Paul and St Mauro on the right.

L: Antealtares, 23
A: Fray Gabriel de Casas (church), 17th–18th centuries
FF: In the centre of the wall that closes one side of Plaza de la Quintana, a plaque commemorates the Literary Battalion, formed by the city's university students and staff to defend Galicia against Napoleon's troops.

L: Praza do Obradoiro
A: Carlos Lemaur, 1766
FF: The palace was built as a seminary for confessors, but today it is the site of Santiago's City Hall.

L: Praza do Obradoiro
A: Maestro Esteban, Bernard the Elder, Robertus Galperinus, Bernard the Younger, and others, 11th–18th centuries
FF: The roof of the cathedral houses the Cruz dos Farrapos, under which medieval pilgrims burned their old walking clothes in a purification ritual.

Monasterio de
San Martiño Piñario

Convento de San Francisco

San Domingos de Bonaval

Hostal dos Reis Católicos

Convento de Santa Clara

Centro Galego de Arte
Contemporánea

L: Praza da Inmaculada, 5
A: Various architects, including
Mateo López, Bartolomé
Fernández Lechuga, Peña y Toro,
Fray Tomás Alonso and Fray
Gabriel Casas (all worked on the
church), and Fernando de Casas
(monastery), 16th–17th centuries
FF: This former Benedictine
convent is the largest in Galicia.

L: Campiño de San Francisco, 3
A: Church, Simón Rodríguez,
1742; cloister, Ginés Martínez,
1607
FF: The land for the original
convent and church was bought
from the monks of San Mariño
for the symbolic annual rent of a
basket of trout.

L: Calle Bonaval
A: Various architects, including
Domingo de Andrade, 13th–14th
and 17th centuries
FF: Galician novelist Rosalia de
Castro is buried in the interior of
the convent temple.

L: Costa do Cristo
A: Enrique Egás, 1501
FF: The hostal is thought to be
one of the oldest continuously
operating hotels in the world.

L: Rúa Santa Clara
A: Unknown, 17th century
FF: Simón Rodriguez's 1719
facade leads not into the
church, as you might expect,
but into a small garden, at
the end of which is a much
smaller door into the actual
convent and church.

L: Rúa Valle Inclán, 2
A: Álvaro Siza, 1988–93
FF: Siza originally designed
the CGAC with a white marble
exterior, but complied with the
authorities who were keen to
conserve Galicia's monumental
heritage with the use of granite.
The interior, however, is clad in
white marble.

Kyoto

*'The peace within and flowing from sacred spaces and architecture places
is clothed in forgiveness, renunciation, and reconciliation.'*
Norris Brock Johnson, *Tenryu-ji: Life and Spirit of a Kyoto Garden*

To wander the ancient streets of Kyoto, Japan's capital city for over 1,000 years, is to be transported to the world of Sei Shōnagon, 10th-century author of *The Pillow Book*. A profusion of ancient shrines and temples, quiet Zen gardens with carefully raked pebbles and public parks filled with late March pink cherry blossom all hark back to a time long past. But there's a modern Kyoto that sits, not always comfortably, by its side, providing a skyline that is an irresistible fusion of ancient and modern.

Shōnagon was a well-educated middle-ranking aristocrat who became court lady-in-waiting to Empress Sadako and lived during the Heian era (794–1192). She would have been familiar with many of the 17 World Heritage Sites that still exist, despite there being just two official Buddhist temples until the 13th century, when a rush of prosperity and religiosity saw the construction of hundreds of unofficial temples. The roots of this strong religious culture survived and thrived so that today the city boasts more than 1,600 Buddhist temples and over 400 Shinto shrines.

But spirituality isn't the first thing visitors are likely to associate Kyoto with. Arrivals to the city emerge from a bullet train at the futuristic glass and steel **Kyoto Railway Station**, and immediately encounter the **Kyoto Tower**, built for the 1964 Tokyo Olympics. The tallest structure in the city, while not beautiful to look at, offers spectacular views of Kyoto as far as the mountains of Higashiyama and Arashiyama and, on a clear day, to Osaka, 35 miles away.

Many of the city's original buildings, constructed from trees in all their guises, were destroyed through war and fire, but Kyoto was saved thanks to Henry L. Stimson, creator of the atomic bomb. It was Stimson who discounted the city from the list of those to be targeted during the Second World War, saying: '…there was one city that they must not bomb without my permission, and that was Kyoto.'

One of the city's oldest and best examples of Heian-era architecture is the **Byōdō-in Temple**. The Fujiwara clan, a powerful family of regents who feature prominently in Shōnagon's writings, had dominated Japanese politics throughout the Heian era through a skilful strategy of marrying their daughters to emperors. The clan moved their seat of governance to Heian-kyō (one of several early names for Kyoto) because of its good river access to the sea, and one of their more spectacular villas, Phoenix Hall, was converted into a temple in 1052. Its main hall was designed to emulate the Buddha's palace in paradise and resembles a majestic bird spreading its wings, especially when reflected in the pond before it.

Of no less historical importance is the 17th-century **Imperial Palace**, the residence of the Japanese Imperial family until the capital moved to Tokyo in 1868. As an early Edo-period building (though rebuilt later in 1855), it reflects the architectural style of the Heian era, with a number of buildings with gently sloping roofs, and floor spaces that could be manipulated with sliding doors to break rooms down to human dimensions or expand them to create spaces for important ceremonies. In this early approach to harmony and versatility of space, Japanese building design would influence not just centuries of architecture in Japan, but centuries of architectural practice around the globe.

But set against this clean, understated expression of power was a much more traditionally dominant style of building, for while the Emperor was the legitimate ruler of Japan, it was the shoguns who had the real control, and they needed buildings that showed it. The 17th-century **Nijō-jo Castle**, surrounded by a moat with enormous stone walls, elaborately decorated gates and beautiful gardens, was a very visible sign of the power of the Tokugawa shoguns, who ruled Japan for more than 260 years. But illustrations of the shoguns' power could be subtler too; the shimmering lacquer and gold **Kinkaju-ji Temple** nearby was originally bought by retired shogun Yoshimitsu as a guesthouse for the Emperor. Luxurious parties were held here, and it was described as 'almost like heaven… There are some very tall structures, a fascinating pavilion, and splendid buildings with beautiful paintings and carvings. They are scattered in the precincts, as if they were stars in the sky'. Yoshimitsu's son converted it into a temple, though its roof of gold leaf was a replacement of the 14th-century original, destroyed by a schizophrenic temple monk.

So admired was the temple that it acted as inspiration for the enormous conservatory at the Kyoto Botanical Garden, where around 250,000 plant specimens are set in a glass- and iron-framed complex built to resemble the temple and Kyoto's northern mountains. Close by is a building that couldn't be more different in visual style, but takes some of the cornerstones of Japanese aesthetics and qualities to create an arresting and mesmerising building. The thoroughly modern **Kyoto Concert Hall**, designed by Arata Isozaki using ceramic panels and limestone, was built as part of the 1,200th anniversary celebrations of the foundation of Heian-kyō and brings aspects of centuries-old temple design into the 20th century as elegantly and expressively as another modernist architect, Tadao Ando.

Inspired by the likes of Ludwig Mies van der Rohe and Frank Lloyd Wright, this truck driver and boxer-turned-self-taught-architect achieves a combination of Japanese sensibilities – creating harmonious spaces with walls that fold like origami – with modern materials like glass, stone and concrete. His **Times Building**, located alongside a canal, manages to resemble a boat despite a boxy, concrete construction in gunmetal grey that resembles something from a Tarkovsky film. It looks modern, yet as though it's been there forever. Past and future are interwoven together in this way everywhere in Kyoto. Another of Japan's leading modern architects, Shin Takamatsu, has created some intensely futuristic buildings, but his Wood Architecture Project seems to hark back to Kyoto's past, creating a large urban structure from wood.

Perhaps one of the most modern of them all is the **Katsura Imperial Villa**. Though built in the 17th century, the combination of *Sukiya-zukuri*, a refined style of Japanese architecture, and the Japanese aesthetic principle of *Ma*, referring to the empty or open space, was much admired by the most famous modernist architects of the 20th century. The removal of all unnecessary internal walls and the opening up of the space between interior and exterior can be seen in work by Le Corbusier, Frank Lloyd Wright and Walter Gropius.

Gropius' desire to 'create the purely organic building, boldly emanating its inner laws, free of untruths or ornamentation' was so clearly influenced by his visit to Japan that he wrote in his *Architecture in Japan* (1955): 'You cannot imagine what it meant to me to come suddenly face to face with these houses, with a culture still alive, which in the past had already found the answer to many of our modern requirements of simplicity, of outdoor-indoor relations, of modular coordination, and at the same time, variety of expression, resulting in a common form of language uniting all individual efforts.' Gropius' paean to the architecture of Japan comes to life in Kyoto, perhaps more than in any other city in the country.

Kyoto Railway Station

Byōdō-in Temple

Kinkaju-ji Temple

L: Shimogyu Ward
A: Hiroshi Hara, 1997
FF: The 15-floor building houses shops, restaurants, a theatre and a hotel, as well as an art museum.

L: Uji
A: Unknown, AD 998
FF: The Phoenix Hall contains a statue of Amida covered in gold leaf that has been positioned to catch the morning sun's rays on its face.

L: Ikinkakuji-Chō, Kita-ku
A: Unknown, 1397
FF: Each floor represents a different style of architecture: first floor Shinden, second floor Bukke and third floor Chinese Zen.

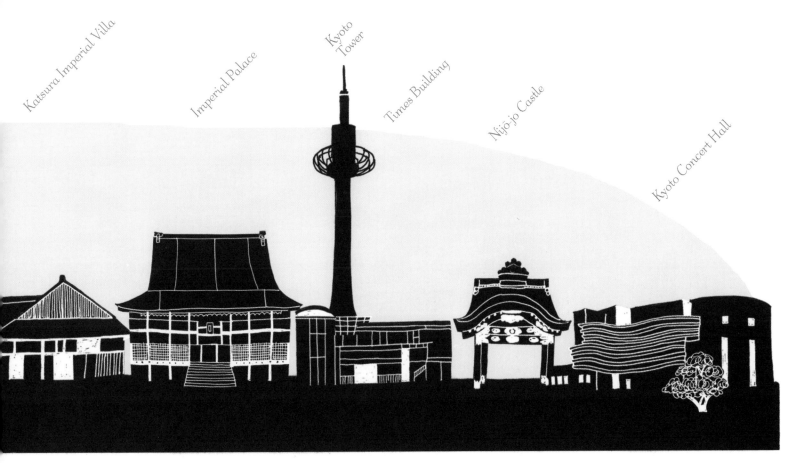

Katsura Imperial Villa

Imperial Palace

Kyoto Tower

Times Building

Nijō-jo Castle

Kyoto Concert Hall

L: Katsuramisono, Nishikyo-ku
A: Kobori Ehshu, mid-17th century
FF: The gardens are a masterpiece of Japanese garden design.

L: 3 Kyoto-Gyoen, Kamigyo-Ku
A: Unknown, AD 750–855
FF: Emperor Hirohito announced Japan's capitulation on 15 June 1945, ending the Second World War, from the basement of a concrete library here.

L: 721-Ikarasuma-Don, Higashi Shiohoji-Cho
A: Makoto Tanahashi, 1963
FF: A viewing platform offers panoramas of the entire city.

L: Nr Sanjokobashi Bridge, along Tasake River
A: Tadao Ando, 1986–91
FF: Sitting on the river terrace, the overhead bridge is meant to offer protection from the rain, but because it's separated from the wall water pours down through the gap.

L: 541 Nijojocho, Nakagyo Ward
A: Unknown, 1603–1626
FF: The painted screens in the main chamber were made by artists of the Kano school using gilt to depict flowers, trees, birds and tigers.

L: 1-26 Hangi-Chō
A: Arata Isozaki, 1995
FF: The design of the floor creates an optical illusion, reminiscent of Escher.

Varanasi

'Older than history, older than tradition, older even than legend and looks twice as old as all of them put together.'
Mark Twain's impression of Varanasi

When Lord Shiva carried Mata Sati's burned body to rest in Himalaya, her earring fell down at Manikarnika Ghat, the riverfront steps that lead down to the river Ganges. It's one of the oldest ghats in Varanasi and considered one of the most auspicious places to perform *puja* (prayer) or to be cremated.

Hinduism is rich in such stories of love, war, creation and destruction, and Varanasi, one of the oldest living cities in the world, is its most important city – the city of Shiva – where even the river is worshipped as a deity; the goddess Ganga. The Ganges, with its source in the Himalayas, flows 2,500km (1,550 miles) through four states. Its sacred waters are said to cleanse bathers of sin, and millions of Hindu pilgrims come to the ghats that line the river to pray and purify themselves, or bring the ashes of their loved ones to sprinkle on the Ganges, believing that this will bring them closer to *moksha* (liberation from the cycle of life and death).

The cycle of life is fundamental to the Hindu religion, which posits that death feeds life, which in turn feeds death, which feeds life, and on and on, and this is most obvious along the river Ganges, where the living are literally mingling with the dead. The ghats, where it all takes place, are architecturally interesting in their own right; stretching along the river's edge, on the west side only, the immense stone steps lead down from the river's bank, allowing pilgrims easy access to the water for washing, praying and, at the 'burning ghats', for public cremations. The ghats have been referred to as far back as the 2nd century and the Dashashwamedh Ghat (which literally means 'ten-horse sacrifice') is one of the most significant; it's reputedly where Lord Brahma, the creator of life, sacrificed ten horses to welcome the Lord Shiva who, along with Vishnu and Brahma, is the third god in the Hindu triumvirate. By the 17th century, the areas around the ghats had become the centre of economic activity where the city's wealthiest citizens built their palaces. Ashrams, temples and Sanskrit schools all followed.

Close to the Dashashwamedh Ghat is the **Kashi Vishwanath Temple**, the holiest of all the Shiva temples. This incarnation of the Vishwanath, built around 1780 by the Maratha queen, Ahilyabai Holkar, is also known as the Golden Temple, owing to two magnificent domes plated in gold donated by Maharaja Ranjit Singh of Punjab in 1835. The original Vishwanath was located close by and, over its lifetime, was destroyed and reconstructed many times, the final time by Mughal emperor Aurangzeb. The son of Shan Jahan wanted to show the ruling Hindu elite his power by destroying much of their sacred temple, using its columns in the construction of his own **Gyanvapi Mosque** and the old temple wall to form the mosque's *qibla* wall. The facade of the Gyanvapi has been compared with the Taj Mahal that his father built in tribute to Aurangzeb's mother, Mumtaz. The mosque's octagonal minarets are a dizzying 71m (232ft) high.

Mughal architecture is drawn from several different cultures, including Persian, Islamic, Turkish and Hindu, and another example of it can be found in the exquisite tomb of **Lal Khan**, a Mughal nobleman. Built in 1733, the mausoleum features a coloured tiled dome that rests on a rectangular court with decorated 'kiosks' in each corner, each featuring handcarved stone depicting ancient Mughal art.

Typical of north Indian (Nagara) architecture is the 18th-century **Durga Mandir**, a Hindu temple dedicated to the goddess Durga, protectress of the city and manifestation of Parvati, the consort of Lord Shiva. In Hinduism, Durga is the embodiment of *shakti*, or female power, and she's usually represented, clad in red, on the back of a tiger and armed with Shiva's trident, Vishnu's discus and a sword. The temple, decorated in red ochre, has a multi-tiered spire (*shikhara*) made up of many separate spires that appear fused together, and square columns and stonework that feature finely carved deities and elephants. It's thought that the goddess Durga herself appeared in the form of a statue (*murti*) that can still be found in the inner sanctum.

When the British made Varanasi an Indian state in 1910, they took up residence in the **Ramnagar Fort** on the eastern bank of the Ganges, once home to the kings of the city. The majestic building is typical of the Mughal style – a creamy sandstone structure that features beautiful carved balconies, pretty pavilions and open courtyards.

Bringing their own architectural expertise to the city, British engineers built the **Malviya Bridge** in 1887 to connect the Raj Ghat to the railway station on the other side of the river. The Raj Ghat Bridge, as it has become known, was the first of its kind to be built on the Indian subcontinent; resting on 15 pillars are seven spans of 106m (350ft), and nine of 33m (110ft). It has two levels, one for trains and one for vehicles, and it can be seen from the site of the tomb of Lal Khan.

Varanasi is also an important site for Buddhists, and the **Dhamek Stupa** is one of the most significant of all the Buddhist structures in India as it's believed to enshrine the relics of the Buddha himself. The giant stupa was built in AD 500 and replaced a much earlier one that was commissioned in 249 BC by Mauryan King Ashoka, who commissioned several such stupas for the purpose of housing relics.

But in spite of the city's spiritual importance, not all of Varanasi's temples are dedicated to formal religions. The **Bharat Mata**, or 'Mother India', is dedicated to the entire country; built by a Gandhian follower, the temple is a pentagonal cone standing on five pillars, each representing the five elements of earth, wind, fire, water and sky. It also houses a scaled relief map of India, carved out of marble, and offers beautiful views of the river Ganges and the nearby ghats.

Bharat Mata

Dhamek Stupa

Durga Mandir

Gyanvapi Mosque

L: Mahatma Gandhi Kashi
Vidyapeeth Campus
A: Babu Shiv Prasad Gupt, 1936
FF: The temple was inaugurated by
Mahatma Gandhi in 1936.

L: Saranatu
A: Unknown, AD 500
FF: The stupa, rising to 139m
(456ft), has a diameter of 28m
(93ft).

L: Ramnagar Road
A: Unknown, 18th century
FF: The temple is also known as the Monkey Temple, owing to
the vast number of monkeys that live in the nearby trees.

L: Lahori Tola
A: Beni Madhav Rao Scindhia, 1669
FF: 'Gyanvapi' refers to the 'well of
knowledge', located between the
mosque and the rebuilt Hindu temple.

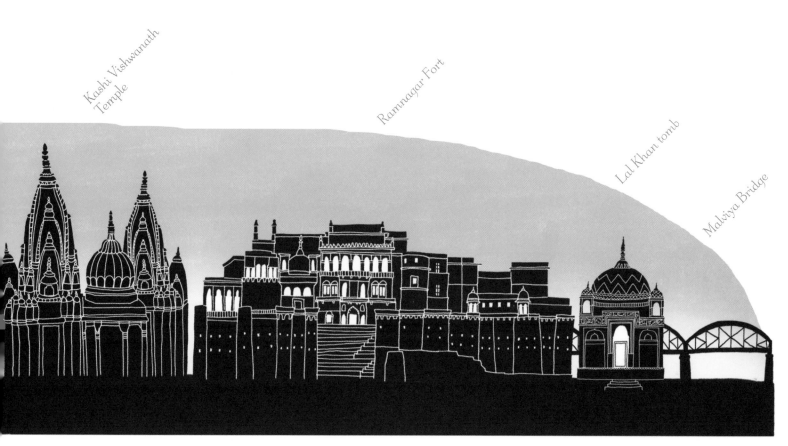

Kashi Vishwanath Temple

Ramnagar Fort

Lal Khan tomb

Malviya Bridge

L: Varanasi
A: Unknown, 1780
FF: Two domes are gold-plated, with a third dome due to be gold-plated once the money has been raised.

L: Kila Road, Crossing, Ram nagar
A: Kashi Naresh Raja Balwant Singh, 1750
FF: A favourite spot for films, the fort also houses the Veda Vyasa temple and a museum.

L: Tomb Road, Near Adikeshav Mandir, Rajghat
A: Unknown, 1773
FF: The building is protected by the Archaeological Survey of India.

L: Crossing the Ganges
A: Unknown British engineers, 1887
FF: The bridge's deterioration has led to the barring of heavy vehicles.

Cusco (including Machu Picchu)

'And so, just a dozen years after Cortés had been forced to destroy Montezuma's Tenochtitlán,
Pizarro massacred Atahualpa and his six thousand unarmed followers under a flag of truce and ravaged Cusco.
The city was too rich, the temptation too great, the loss incomparable.'
John Julius Norwich, *Great Architecture of the World*

The Incan empire, which grew to include much of Ecuador, Peru and Bolivia, and extend as far as Chile and Argentina, began at Cusco, the oldest continuously inhabited city in South America. The city was believed to have been laid out in the shape of a sacred puma, outlined by the rivers Tulumayo and Huatanay that then join to make the puma's tail. When Spanish conquistador, Francisco Pizarro, arrived in the 16th century, he described it as the 'very noble and great city of Cusco', before he destroyed most of its sacred temples and palaces to build Spanish-style buildings in their stead.

In *Great Architecture of the World*, John Julius Norwich suggests that the Incas were the 'best stone-masons the world has ever known'. They built sophisticated, well-drained road networks that stretched for thousands of miles across their empire, revolutionised agriculture by building terraces on steep mountainsides, and created entire cities at altitudes never even reached by others. They cut rock – some weighing as much as 50 tons – without explosives, transported it without wheels or draught animals, and shaped it without chisels, to create exquisite temples and palaces, curved walls and buildings so stable that they survived earthquakes, unlike many of the Spanish ones that followed, such as the Baroque **Church of Santo Domingo**.

The Incas believed they were the children of the Sun and Moon and that their supreme ruler – the Sapa Inca (the 'Only Inca') – was a direct descendant of Inti, the Sun God. Gold was the sweat of the Sun, and silver the tears of the Moon, and so both were used in abundance to decorate everything they valued, especially the **Qurikancha** (Gold Enclosure), the temple dedicated to Inti, the Sun God and situated at the heart of the puma.

The temple was stripped and then destroyed, before the Spanish colonists built the Church of Santo Domingo on its foundations. Following an earthquake in 1950 the church collapsed but the Incan foundations remained solid and more of Qurikancha was revealed, including the spectacular curved granite wall made with tightly interlocking stones, once entirely covered in gold. It is thought that, when an earthquake occurs, the stones, which have been cut with a technique known as *ashlar*, are able to 'bounce' through the tremors and slip back into place, the reason why the Incan buildings have survived many earthquakes.

Each successive Sapa Inca built his own palace; on the Plaza de Armas (Square of the Warrior), the Spanish-built **Cathedral Basilica of the Assumption of the Virgin** stands on the foundations of the palace of Viracocha Inca (Creator God Ruler). The Gothic Renaissance structure reveals little of Incan culture save for a carved jaguar head (an important religious motif) on the cathedral door. The nearby Iglesia de la Compañía de Jesus (**Church of the Society of Jesus**) was built in colonial Baroque style on the foundations of the Amara Cancha (Palace of Serpents) of Inca ruler Huayna Capac. It too was badly damaged in an earthquake in 1650 and completely rebuilt almost 20 years later.

One of the best examples of the masonry skills of the Inca is the '12-angle' stone of green diorite that can be found on the palace wall of Inca Roca. Perfectly assembled with the stones that surround it, the huge rock has been honed flawlessly.

Pachacútec Inca (He who Remakes the World), the son of Viracocha, was the most charismatic of all the Inca Sapa and responsible for the enrichment of the Qurikancha. Much of the gold that was amassed when the Spanish ransomed Atahualpa, Huayna Capac's son, was taken from here.

Pachacútec was also responsible for building **Machu Picchu** (Old Mountain), high above the Urubamba gorge. After the Spanish defeated the Incas, the city was thought to be 'lost' and wasn't 'rediscovered' until Hiram Bingham found it in 1911.

Of all the Incan cities, Machu Picchu is the best preserved and something of Incan society can be seen by the hierarchy of the houses: the more elaborate were for the priests; those with fewer designs were for soldiers and the most basic were reserved for the craftsmen themselves.

The site itself was chosen for its auspicious position between four mountains and is thought to have had astronomical, as well as agricultural, merits. Machu Picchu was built as an observatory and as a place for rituals, as well as to provide Cusco with food that was grown

on the terraces around the city. The most important building was the **Temple of the Sun**, a semi-circular observatory made from smoothly joined stonework. Its two windows corresponded with the summer and winter solstice because the Inca observed the sun's movements and the position of the stars as a guide to planting and harvesting crops.

The **Temple of the Moon**, a ceremonial temple set in a cave, was created for sacrifices and offerings, and also reveals exceptional masonry – beautifully shaped stones fitted together with no mortar – and five niches cut into the wall where coca leaves, tobacco and maize would be offered.

Italian Giulio Magli, an astrophysicist and archaeoastronomer making connections between the importance of the stars to ancient cultures, has suggested that even the journey from Cusco to Machu Picchu may have served a ceremonial purpose: he believed that the Inca Trail, though visually stunning, is far less practical than simply following the Urubamba River and may have been designed to prepare pilgrims for their entry into Machu Picchu. The last leg of the journey was climbing the steps to the **Intihuatana** (Hitching Post of the Sun) stone, the highest spot in the ruins, and an important astronomical site. The stone was a type of astronomical and agricultural clock and important ceremonies would have been held on 21 March and 21 September at midday, when the Sun would be directly above the stone and, leaving no shadow, would appear to be 'tied' to it.

The 'lost' city of Machu Picchu was more likely to have been abandoned following an outbreak of smallpox, but today it's the largest tourist attraction in South America.

Temple of the Moon

Cathedral Basilica of the Assumption of the Virgin

Machu Picchu

L: Machu Picchu
A: Unknown, 15th century
FF: A throne, carved out of rock, can be found in the centre of the cave.

L: Plaza de Armas
A: Juan Miguel de Veramendi, 1559–1654
FF: The Black Christ (from years of dust and candle smoke) crucifix is taken outdoors during Holy Week in commemoration of the 1650 earthquake.

L: Peru
A: N/A
FF: One of the most important archaeological sites in the world, Machu Picchu lies in the middle of a tropical forest 2,430m (7,972ft) above sea level.

Church of the
Society of Jesus

Qurikancha
(foundations) and
Church of Santo Domingo

Temple of the Sun

Intihuatana

L: Plaza de Armas
A: Unknown, 1576
FF: The painting of *El Matrimonio de Martín García de Loyola con Beatriz Clara Coya* shows the marriage of a conquistador with an Inca woman.

L: Avenida El Sol/Calle Santo Domingo
A: Unknown, 1534 and rebuilt in 1680
FF: The garden below the temple would once have been embellished with gold and silver flowers and animals encrusted with gems.

L: Machu Picchu
A: Unknown, 15th century
FF: The stone inside the temple was for rituals and sacrifices.

L: Machu Picchu
A: N/A
FF: It is said that sensitive people can see into the spirit world when they rub their forehead against the stone.

Visionary Cities

* Minsk

Chandigarh
*

Dubai

Utopia
*

Brasilia

'There is no other place like it. It is monumental. The curves of those buildings are those of a beautiful woman.'

Oscar Niemeyer

Back in 1833 an Italian priest call Dom João Bosco dreamt of a city that rose up around a lake. He thought it was Utopia, and believed it to be in Latin America and located between the 15th and 20th parallels. In the late 1950s, more than 100 years later, President Juscelino Kubitschek made a decision to move Brazil's centre of government to a brand new, as yet un-built, city and invited the finest architects in the country to present their plans.

The 1950s were the age of glamorous air travel and urbanist Lúcio Costa's Plano Piloto (Pilot Plan) laid out the new city, with separate zones, in the shape of a giant aeroplane: residential sectors in the 'wings', commercial and cultural centres housed in the 'fuselage', and the power of the city – the palace and supreme court – in the plane's 'cockpit'. It was a masterpiece of vision and engineering, with chief architect, Oscar Niemeyer, designing more than 20 buildings, 15 of them between 1956 and 1962. And there are some incredible statistics: it took 60,000 workers just three years to build the entire city using one million cubic metres of concrete and 100,000 metric tons of steel. The cement and sand had to be airlifted in, as the location, in an uninhabited area in the centre of the country – between the 15th and 20th parallels – had no roads yet.

Costa and his designers, who had worked with modernist Le Corbusier, were keen to move away from the traditional neoclassical style. Le Corbusier had just finished his Unité d'Habitation in Marseilles so, when the opportunity arose to build a new capital, Costa and his team could consider Le Corbusier's ideas about building for the people, but on a much grander scale.

The first permanent building was Niemeyer's **Alvorada Palace** – the official residence of the President of Brazil – built on the side of a man made lake, just as Dom Bosco had envisaged. Looking like an inverted Roman colonnade, the marble-faced curved columns support a roof that extends beyond glass walls in order to protect them from the sun.

On the 'Ministries Esplanade', Niemeyer's **Palace of the National Congress** comprises a double tower, a convex and a concave structure – the Secretariat, Senate Chamber and House of Representatives – set on a long base block. The shape of the Senate's convex dome was intended to signify the members' openness to all ideologies. Further to the east is Niemeyer's **Itamaraty Palace**, the Foreign Ministry, low-rise with concrete arches that tower over a reflecting pool, and surrounded by beautiful landscaped gardens by Roberto Burle Marx. The marble and granite **Palácio do Planalto** also has a pool that reflects the building's simple fine lines and sequence of columns that mirror those of the Alvorada Palace.

Though he was an atheist, Niemeyer built over 23 churches in his lifetime but his modernist **Catedral Metropolitana Nossa Senhora Aparecida** was his most spectacular. Built to resemble a crown of thorns, 16 curved 90-ton concrete supporting pillars house an exquisite stained glass interior that earned him the 1988 Pritzker Prize. Another stained glass masterpiece is the **Santuário Dom Bosco** shrine dedicated to the man who inspired the Brasilia dream. From the outside it's a concrete box but the interior is bathed in a heavenly blue light, thanks to Cláudio Naves' floor-to-ceiling stained glass windows – 2,200sq m (23,680sq ft) of glass squares in 12 different shades of blue. A central chandelier, designed by Alvimar Moreira, is made up of 7,400 pieces of Murano glass and weighs 2.5 tons; it symbolises Jesus, the 'Light of the World'.

Brasilia's earliest residents were housed in *Superquadra*, or 'super-squares' of 280m (918ft) and six storeys high, that were surrounded by Roberto Burle Marx's landscaped parkland. The squares were intended to be autonomous, with everything a resident would need nearby: school, church, clubs and sports facilities.

Niemeyer's communist leanings were never far from his work and, in his **Memorial for Juscelino Kubitschek**, Niemeyer placed a statue of the former president inside a sickle. But in spite of the social aspect of their work, there were critics. In the late 1960s, the 'Arquitetura Nova' group, established by Sérgio Ferro, Vilanova Artigas and Rodrigo Lefèvre, believed that the modernists excluded ordinary people; Sérgio Ferro was particularly critical of Niemeyer's showcase buildings that, due their technical complexity, had resulted in some work-related accidents. Arquitetura Nova wanted to democratise design but, in spite of their apparent desire for a group construction process, Lefèvre was still considered to be the architect behind Brasilia's National Department of Highways (DNIT), noteworthy for its concrete 'sun-visors' – an interesting

update of Le Corbusier's 'brise-soleil' which, in turn, had been inspired by the Arabian moucharabieh, designed to allow light in but cut the sun's rays out.

Alexandre Chan was determined to design with the community in mind when he created his triple-arched **Juscelino Kubitschek Bridge**. Structurally complex and visually spectacular – three asymmetrical arches diagonally criss-cross the deck, which is suspended by interlaced steel cables – the bridge has a sidewalk for pedestrians and cyclists. It was awarded the Gustav Lindenthal Medal for 'a single, recent outstanding achievement showing harmony with the environment, aesthetic merit and successful community participation'.

To celebrate the 50th anniversary of the city, Niemeyer designed the **Digital TV Tower**, known as the Cerrado Flower. It was his last work for Brasilia.

Costa and Niemeyer's utopian city was the antithesis of colonial – every design and structure was new, built along rational lines – but as the population expanded, from an original 500,000 to over two million, the city sprawled, with wide roads traversing vast distances, and the needs of pedestrians getting lost along the away. Even Niemeyer himself expressed disappointment: 'the way Brasilia has evolved, it has problems. It should have stopped growing some time ago. Traffic is becoming more difficult, the number of inhabitants has surpassed the target, limits are being exceeded.' In *Trouble in Utopia* Robert Hughes is less kind, suggesting that, in less than 20 years, Brasilia 'ceased to be the City of Tomorrow and turned into yesterday's science fiction… an expensive and ugly testimony to the fact that, when men think in terms of abstract space rather than real place, they tend to produce miles of jerry-built nowhere, infested with Volkswagens.'

Alvorada Palace

Itamaraty Palace

Palácio do Planalto

Digital TV Tower

L: Via Palácio Presidencial
A: Oscar Niemeyer, 1958
FF: The entrance hall has a golden wall inscribed with 'From this central plateau, this vast loneliness that will soon become the center of national decisions, I look once more at the future of my country and foresee this dawn with an unshakeable faith in its great destiny – Juscelino Kubitschek, October 2, 1956'.

L: Esplanada dos Ministérios
A: Oscar Niemeyer, 1970
FF: The 'Palace of the Arches' houses works by Brazilian sculptors Maria Martins and Franz Weissmann.

L: Praça dos Três Poderes
A: Oscar Niemeyer, 1960
FF: A Changing of the Guard ceremony takes place outside the gates every hour at weekends and every two hours during the week.

L: Sobradinho
A: Oscar Niemeyer, 2012
FF: The observation deck offers a 360-degree panorama of the city with a view of the horizon.

Palace of the National Congress

Catedral Metropolitana Nossa Senhora Aparecida

Santuário Dom Bosco

Memorial for Juscelino Kubitschek

Juscelino Kubitschek Bridge

L: Esplanada dos Ministérios
A: Oscar Niemeyer, 1958
FF: The chambers are colour-coded, blue for the Senate and green for the House of Representatives.

L: East Monumental Axis
A: Oscar Niemeyer, 1958
FF: The cathedral has a significant collection of artworks, and outside there are sculptures of the four evangelists by Alfredo Ceschiatti.

L: W-3 Sul, Quadro 702, Bloco B
A: Carlos Alberto Naves, 1958
FF: Inside are Carrara marble statues of Dom Bosco and Our Lady of Help, a 10-ton square marble altar and Gotfredo Tralli's crucifix carved from a single cedar tree.

L: Lado Oeste Praça do Cruzeiro
A: Oscar Niemeyer, 1981
FF: A granite tomb within the memorial holds the former president's remains.

L: Brasilia
A: Alexandre Chan, Mário Vila Verde, 2002
FF: It's one of Brasilia's favourite landmarks, especially at night when it's lit up.

Las Vegas

'A little bit of this town goes a very long way.'
Hunter S. Thompson, *Fear and Loathing in Las Vegas*

Las Vegas exists as the accumulated vision of a succession of people and a combination of their dreams and visions, from farmers and panhandlers to gamblers and, perhaps more than anyone, gangsters. Even before its founding just 110 years ago, the valley settlement – named in 1821 by Mexican scout Rafael Rivera as 'Las Vegas', or 'the meadows', for its spring-watered grasses – had already established itself as one built on hopes and dreams. Between Rivera's visit and the 1905 arrival of the Salt Lake City to Los Angeles railroad, the valley moved from Mexican to US rule, and farmers and ranchers trickled in before the valley was deluged with miners. But it was the catalyst of the railroad that brought the real estate speculators, who saw the potential for vast wealth. Within months lots were changing hands at ten times their original asking price, and the seeds for modern Las Vegas were sown – with all the requisites in place for today's city; prostitution, gambling and drinking dens were rife, and mushroomed in the 1930s to service the desires of the thousands of workers building the nearby Hoover Dam. Freemont Street, the city's sole paved road, was the focus of the men's attentions, but when in 1941 LA hotelier Thomas Hull opened the city's first casino hotel, El Rancho Vegas, south of the city limits on US 91, the Strip was born.

Most of the Strip's casino hotels from that period are long gone, but the game-changing **Flamingo**, the oldest on the Strip, remains – though with none of the original structure. Financed in part by gangster Bugsy Siegel, and the drug money of famed gangster Meyer Lansky, original owner Billy Wilkerson wisely picked up on El Rancho's appeal and built on it. When it opened on 26 December 1946, the $6 million Flamingo, complete with 105 rooms, flashing neon signage and Art Deco styling, did so with some of America's best stars performing on stage and some of its biggest screen stars in attendance. But, of course, the likes of Siegel weren't in the business solely for the cachet or glamour; the casino resorts were perfect places in which to launder money, sell drugs, secrets and sex, and make big deals and even bigger money, and if Siegel didn't have much time to enjoy what he'd created – he was murdered the next year – it didn't stop other organised-crime syndicates quickly moving in where he'd left off.

Links with legitimate investors, Frank Sinatra's Rat Pack and topless showgirls helped pull in millions of visitors to places like the Sahara (demolished in 2014 to make way for Philippe Starck's boutique hotel SLS), the Riviera, the Sands and the Desert Inn – the latter two bought by Howard Hughes in the late 1960s. By 1954, eight million tourists a year were pouring in to see some of the biggest stars in the world, get fast weddings or quickie divorces (or both), and gamble on everything from racing and boxing to cards and slot machines. As the Strip turned into a neon wonderland, Betty Willis' iconic Googie-style **Welcome to Fabulous Las Vegas sign**, installed on Las Vegas Boulevard in 1959, seemed the perfect symbol for the city, and a fitting end to the fabulous decade.

With the 1960s came a new style of building in the city, influenced by, of all things, the nearby Nevada Test Site, where more than 100 nuclear bombs were detonated between 1951 and 1963. Rather than worry about radiation fallout, brash Las Vegas embraced the mushroom clouds on the horizon with a slogan – the 'Up and Atom City' – and Jetsons-style mid-century modern architecture like the **La Concha Motel**. In a wonderfully inventive piece of preservation, the motel's elegant reception area, a concrete conch shell canopy, was moved piece by piece to the Neon Museum, where it now acts as the visitor centre. Such funky wonders didn't last long, soon giving way to lucrative resorts like the MGM Grand and the hugely influential **Las Vegas Hilton**, originally The International. This nicely realised example of the International Style by prolific Las Vegas architect Martin Stern Jr sported a unique tri-form Y-shape that would provide the model for so many others, including the Mirage, Treasure Island, the Venetian, Mandalay Bay and the Bellagio.

If Stern's Y-shape physically shaped modern Las Vegas, it would be a different kind of hotel that determined its feel. In 1966, gambler and bon viveur Jay Sarno and landowner Kirk Kerkorian, with funding provided from a pension fund loan by Teamsters Union boss Jimmy Hoffa, opened a European-style Roman-Grecian resort on the Strip that transported guests to another world; in this case, to ancient Egypt and **Caesar's Palace**. Showgirl Cleopatras and goddess waitresses working in a showroom modelled on Rome's Colosseum and statuary carved from Italian Carrara marble combined to offer pure escapism via themed environments. Fronting the *porte cochère*, 18 huge fountains would predate and influence those of the Bellagio's dancing fountains by decades, and interior design innovations were to have far-reaching consequences too; Sarno put the casino bang in the middle of the resort, with everything radiating off it.

Others were quick to follow. By 1989, when casino developer Steve Wynn opened the first megacasino, the Mirage, it was a standard feature, as was the idea of themed resorts, which took their aesthetic cues from fiction (*Treasure Island*), the tropics (the Polynesian-themed Mirage and upscale Mandalay Bay), and exotic and historic cities (The Rio, Venetian and Palazzo), coming full circle in 1993 with the **Luxor Pyramid**. With its laserbeam shooting up into the nighttime sky, it perhaps sums up the forward thrust of modern Las Vegas better than any other resort, but occasionally, other modern resorts have taken different routes. The 350m (1,150ft) **Stratosphere**, for example, offers an endearingly different throwback to an earlier era.

Beyond the Strip, the city's architecture is evolving. Downtown, the Container Park incorporates nearly 40 shipping containers into an arresting shopping complex, and the **Veer Towers** and **Crystals Retail Centre**, both part of the 2009 CityCenter complex, offer contemporary architecture at its best, with Helmut Jahn's irregular residential towers propped up by Daniel Libeskind's stack of cubes at odd angles creating fittingly innovative spaces for tenants like Prada and Jimmy Choo.

These may well offer a vision of the city's future, but one can't help thinking that if the likes of Bugsy Siegel and Jay Sarno were around, instead of these, or even the mighty scale of the **LINQ Complex High Roller**, what they'd be admiring is the chutzpah and architecture-as-ego of the **Cleveland Clinic** Lou Ruvo Center for Brain Health designed for Las Vegas entrepreneur Lou Ruvo at a whopping $1,311 per square foot. Ruvo wisely figured that spending big would reap big rewards via glitzy fundraisers, and so far he's been proved right; one gala event held in the centre's white sculptural interior raised $20 million. Proving perhaps that in a city of high-rollers, thinking – and gambling – big will always pay off.

La Concha Motel

Cleveland Clinic

LINQ Complex
High Roller

Las Vegas Hilton

Stratosphere

L: Neon Museum, 770 Las
Vegas Boulevard North
A: Paul Revere Williams, 1961
FF: Two of the motel's original
signs – the mosaic lobby sign
and a section of the main
roadside sign – have been
restored and illuminated
as part of the museum's
collection.

L: 88 West Bonneville Avenue
A: Frank Gehry, 2007–10
FF: The undulating centre is the focal
point of the new 61-acre Symphony
Park arts and science development.

L: 3545 South Las Vegas Boulevard
A: Unknown, 2014
FF: The High Roller is the world's tallest
observation wheel, and accommodates up to
40 passengers in 28 spherical cabins, taking
them up to a height of 167.6m (550ft).

L: 3000 Paradise Road
A: Martin Stern Jr, 1969
FF: Stern's first major Las Vegas commission
introduced the Y-shape triform structure to
the city because, given a roughly square plot
of land to work with, it meant each room
would have a nice view.

L: 2000 South Las Vegas
Boulevard
A: Ned Baldwin, 1996
FF: The Stratosphere is
the tallest freestanding
observation tower in the US,
and contains SkyJump, a
bungee jump ride that drops
people 261m (855 feet).

Flamingo

Las Vegas sign

Luxor Pyramid

Caesar's Palace

Veer Towers

Crystals Retail Centre

L: 3555 South Las Vegas Boulevard
A: Various, inc. George Vernon Russell and Richard R. Stadelman, 1946, Martin Stern Jr, 1968 (remodel of original motel), and various others, 1970–90
FF: None of the original Flamingo hotel remains, but four of its towers date back to the 1980s, with a fifth and final tower added in 1990.

L: 5100 South Las Vegas Boulevard
A: Betty Willis, 1959
FF: The white circles enclosing the letters that spell the word 'welcome' are meant to represent silver dollars, referencing Nevada's nickname as 'the Silver State'. There are two replicas of Willis' original sign, one at Las Vegas Boulevard and 4th Street, and one on Boulder Highway.

L: 3930 South Las Vegas Boulevard
A: Veldon Simpson, 1993
FF: On a clear night, the Pyramid's Sky Beam can be seen up to 443km (275 miles) away by aircraft at cruising altitude, and is the strongest beam of light in the world.

L: 3570 South Las Vegas Boulevard
A: Various architects, 1966–2011
FF: The original 1966 Caesar's Palace contained 700 rooms in a 14-storey tower and three-storey wings, and cost $24 million on completion – selling three years later for $60 million. It now has 3,998 rooms and is the tenth largest hotel in the world.

L: 3722 South Las Vegas Boulevard
A: Helmut Jahn, 2007–10
FF: The foyers of both leaning towers feature site-specific artworks in mud by British artist Richard Long. Works by other artists, including Claes Oldenburg, Henry Moore and Jenny Holzer, feature through the complex.

L: 3720 South Las Vegas Boulevard
A: Daniel Libeskind, 2009
FF: The centre utilises a range of eco-friendly features, including FSC certified wood, radiant floor cooling which targets air conditioning to areas being used, skylights for natural illumination and preferential parking for alternative fuel vehicles.

Dubai

'I want to go to – what's that hot country with a lot of money?'
Grandmaster Flash, *Dubai*

Little more than 50 years ago, Dubai was a small fishing village, and what took other cities centuries to build, Dubai has achieved in decades. Today, described as a 'skyline on crack', with up to a quarter of the world's cranes, it's a super-skyscraper capital of superlatives… the world's largest waterfront development, the largest manmade artificial islands in the world, the tallest hotel in the world, the world's tallest completely twisted tower, the world's first underwater hotel – well, that hasn't actually happened yet, but in Dubai, it's probably just a matter of time and, of course, money.

Once a stopping-off point for caravans, the city grew up around a 15km (9 mile) creek that runs into the Arabian Gulf. Thanks to natural sandbars and an abundance of pearl oysters, a burgeoning industry developed, but everything changed when oil was discovered in 1966. An explosion of industrial buildings and infrastructure was further fuelled (sorry) by the oil crisis of 1973 and, with petrodollars pouring in, Dubai became one of the world's most popular destinations for tourists looking for high-end luxury hotels, designer shops and Michelin-starred dining.

Dominating the Jumeirah coastline, the high-tech **Burj Al Arab** is the perfect example of what they come for: the seven-star hotel shaped like a *dhow* – a traditional Arabian sailing boat – houses the first Armani hotel and has its own helipad. A double skin of translucent white cloth stretched across the structure reflects much of the light energy back outside. The membrane is illuminated, creating a spectacle inside and out. Designer Tom Wright of W. S. Atkins described it as 'futuristic… Arabian and super-luxurious'.

Just over a decade later, the visually spectacular **Cayan Tower** was completed, twisted 90 degrees, by creating a hexagonal floor plate on a circular core and slightly twisting each of the exterior columns, floor by floor. The structural design reduces wind and creates more stability. And apparently, if it weren't for that pesky wind, it would be possible to build a structure 20km (12.5 miles) high – even use it as a launch pad for a space rocket. Or so physicist-turned-sci-fi author Neal Stephenson and civil engineer Professor Keith Hjelmstad calculated: 'In a windless environment making a structure that tall would almost be trivial, but when you build something that is going… to get hit by the jet stream from time to time, then it becomes shockingly much more difficult.'

Which makes the neo-Futurist **Burj Khalifa** – currently the tallest artificial tower in the world – a real feat of construction technology and engineering. The floor plan, in a 'Y' shape, ensures maximum outside views from each tower, and the central core provides stress resistance. The reinforced concrete base is topped by a steel spire, and according to structural engineer Bill Baker, aspects of the design, such as the spiral minaret, incorporate cultural and historical elements. The Burj contains, among other things, the world's highest restaurant, highest nightclub and highest observation tower.

One of the most outlandish projects was the creation of a totally man-made archipelago, the Palm Jumeirah, by land reclamation in 2001. The opulent ocean-themed **Atlantis** was the first resort to be built there and, along with its distinct Arabian elements, it has a six-lane underwater vehicle tunnel, 17 hectares of water park amusement and one of the largest open-air marine habitats in the world.

The iconic twin towers of the Emirates Tower Complex are over a decade old, but the sleek, modernist **Jumeirah Emirates Towers Hotel** is still the world's third tallest all-hotel building. Together with the 54-floor Emirates Tower they are two of the most iconic Dubai buildings. Some critics, however, have suggested that the 'up, up and away' approach has diminished design, but there is much about Dubai's architecture that is worthy of mention: the airplane-shaped **Emirates Aviation University** was one of the quirkier designs, and the sweep of the **Jumeirah Beach Hotel**, resembling a wave and reflecting the city's seafaring history, is visually stunning. The *dhow*-inspired **National Bank of Dubai** was designed by Uruguayan architect Carlos Ott, often considered to be the true designer of the Burj Al Arab. The **One&Only Royal Mirage** also looks to Dubai's cultural past, with its Arabian fort design set in a landscape of fountains and lush gardens; refreshingly low-rise, the fort style bears comparison with one of Dubai's oldest buildings, the **Al Fahidi Fort**, which dates back to 1787 and is now the site of Dubai's National Museum. The square-shaped fort, built from coral rock, contains an Arish (palm hut built by the Bedouins) with a traditional wind tower that creates a

siphoning effect, drawing cool clean air in and pushing stale air out.

Dubai is the biggest air conditioning user in the world, and that's bad news for the environment, so some newer constructions are not just referencing earlier styles, but also early 'technology', such as that of the wind tower. Dr Ben Hughes, Professor of Building Physics at Leeds University, understands that the higher up you go, the faster the wind speed. Hughes has patented a contemporary version of the wind tower, which has successfully reduced inside temperature by as much as 12 per cent.

Following the global credit crisis of 2008, many construction projects were put on hold, including the Burj Khalifa, which was only finished with the help of neighbouring Emirates. Others still on hold are the Dynamic Tower, with revolving floors and powered by wind turbines and enough solar energy sufficient to fuel five similar buildings. The Nakheel Tower, set to become the tallest building in the world, is also on hold, as is the flower-shaped Burj Al Alam ('World Tower') – a proposed 108-storey, 510m (1,670ft) hyperboloid. Zaha Hadid's Dancing Towers look set to stay at the project stage, too, as well as the Opus Dubai, which was set to become the first opera house in the Middle East.

After a late entry, Dubai will host Expo 2020, and its theme will be 'Connecting Minds, Creating the Future', with sub-themes of sustainability, mobility and opportunity, so we expect to see a few more sustainable buildings popping up before then. The Water Discus – Dubai's underwater hotel – doesn't, at the time of writing, have a completion date, but designers say that its modular design will mean that it can be moved in case of an environmental disaster, with buoyant upper pods that could be launched as lifeboats – but hopefully it won't come to that…

Al Fahidi

Burj Al Arab

Emirates Aviation University

One&Only Royal Mirage

Cayan Tower

Burj Khalifa

L: Opposite Grand Mosque, near Arabian Court Hotel – Al Fahidi Street
A: Unknown, 1787
FF: Life-size dioramas of the pre-oil era include an archaeological site in the Al Qusais area that dates back to 3000 BC.

L: Jumeirah Beach Road, Jumeirah 3
A: Tom Wright of W. S. Atkins & Partners, 1999
FF: The Burj lies on an artificial island 280m (306ft) from Jumeirah beach, and is connected by a private curving bridge.

L: Al Garhoud, Casablanca Street
A: Unknown, 20th century
FF: The Emirates Aviation University (EAU) has had official university status since 2010.

L: Al Sufouh Road
A: WATG, 1999
FF: Set in 26 hectares of palm tree gardens with fountains, peacocks and a cascading swimming pool.

L: Dubai Marina
A: Khatib & Alami, Skidmore, Owings & Merrill, 2013
FF: Titanium panels and staggered screens help restrict direct sunlight falling on the apartments.

L: 1 Sheikh Mohammed Bin Rashid Boulevard
A: Adrian Smith, Marshall Strabala, George J. Efstathiou, William F. Baker, 2010
FF: At its tallest point, the tower sways a total of 1.5m (4.9ft).

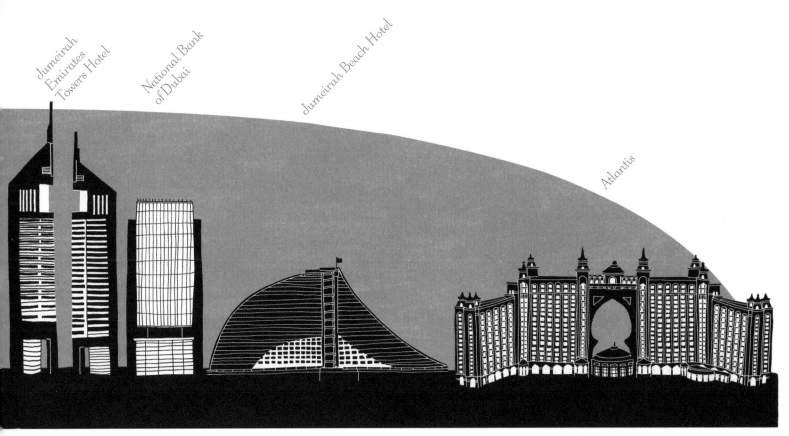

Jumeirah
Emirates
Towers Hotel

National Bank
of Dubai

Jumeirah Beach Hotel

Atlantis

L: Sheikh Zayed Road
A: Hazel W. S. Wong Norr,
Norr Group Consultants
International Ltd, 2000
FF: A ride in the glass lift
almost makes it worth
booking a room.

L: Rigga Al Buteen
A: Dubarch Architects in
association with Carlos
Ott, 1998
FF: When it was built,
it was the fifth tallest
building in Dubai.

L: Jumeirah Road
A: W. S. Atkins & Partners,
1997
FF: The hotel's dive centre
uses its own manmade reef.

L: The Palm
A: Wimberly, Allison, Tong & Goo (WATG), 2008–9
FF: The 2009 opening saw the world's biggest firework
display and a performance by Kylie Minogue.

Chandigarh

'Chandigarh is . . . unfettered by the traditions of the past, a symbol of the nation's faith in the future.'

Jawaharlal Nehru, Indian Prime Minister 1947–64

When newly independent India's first Prime Minister, Jawaharlal Nehru, made his comment about the northern Indian city of Chandigarh in 1947, he wasn't talking just about its architecture and design, but its creation as a new, purpose-built city, a state capital for the divided Punjab after the bloody partition of India and Pakistan. The creation of a city from scratch offered a wealth of possibilities for developing the chosen site – 114sq km (44sq miles) in the foothills of the Shivalik mountains – and Nehru himself spearheaded a modern, radical approach to it. He effectively commissioned Le Corbusier to build the city, but not before a tragic incident that could have resulted in a very different one. The original master plan for Chandigarh was developed by American architect/planner Albert Mayer and Polish-born architect Matthew Nowicki; when the latter died in a plane crash, Mayer resigned, and in 1951 Le Corbusier called on three architects – his cousin Pierre Jeanneret, and husband-and-wife team Edwin Maxwell Fry and Jane Drew – to join him in overseeing the task of designing Chandigarh.

The group began by modifying Mayer's original fan-shaped design for the city, which drew on the ideas of Sir Ebenezer Howard's English Garden Cities, to a grid structure comprised of a series of 1sq km sectors numbered 1–46 (with no unlucky 13), bisected by a pedestrian-only belt of green land accommodating schools, sports and recreational facilities.

Each sector would feature tree-lined avenues and leafy squares, and be separated from its neighbours by a broad 'V3' road, part of a hierarchical transport system that went from the V1 national highway to V7 pedestrian paths and, later, V8 paths for cyclists.

Functionality lay at the heart of Le Corbusier's proposal, but a functionality built around human needs that was to some extent literally laid out along the idea of the human body, with the whole presided over by a clearly defined head – the Capitol Complex, Sector 1. It's here that Le Corbusier has left his biggest mark on the city, with his **Secretariat Building**, **Punjab and Haryana High Court** and the Legislative Assembly (**Vidhan Sabha**) separated by large piazzas and surrounded by a 25m (82ft)-wide, 5km (3 mile)-long woodland grove bordering the serene manmade Sukhna Lake. The imposing concrete trio exhibit classic brutalist tropes, with swooping lines and bright colours offsetting the concrete blocks that form their core. The Vidhan Sabha stands out for its swooshing curved roof on the south facade – vaguely reminiscent of an elaborate nun's wimple – held aloft over a small lake by slim full-height concrete piloti and slab partitions; but the High Court is equally compelling, its three brightly coloured partition screens soaring up the full height of the building and its wide concrete screen dotted with coloured panels.

Facing the Vidhan Sabha across its ornamental pool, the **Tower**

of Shadows is a nicely judged counterpoint to the functionality of the complex's civic buildings. A light-filled pavilion of shadows and sunbeams, it's a space for contemplation, and a great spot from which to appreciate the **Open Hand Monument**. As the official emblem of Chandigarh, this metallic birdlike sculpture symbolises the city's motto of being 'open to give, open to receive'. The rotating sculpture looks like something Picasso might have designed, unlike the city's other key sculpture, the **Chandigarh War Memorial**, whose arresting design symbolises the three wings of the armed forces coming together, and was inspired by its garden setting in the 8km (5 mile) long Leisure Valley Park.

Unsurprisingly, Le Corbusier's Chandigarh plan was not universally acclaimed, resulting in far fewer of his buildings in sectors outside Sector 1 – though the central area features some distinctly Corbusian landscaping and ornamental fountains, and in Sector 10, the **City Museum** is the most arresting part of his Government Museum and Art Gallery complex. Inside, a fascinating mix of documents and plans show how similar Le Corbusier's plans were to Mayer and Nowicki's original, but it's in the fabric of the

building that Le Corbusier made his real mark, with a solid concrete structure whose cubed piloti and slabbed geometric roof are trademark motifs.

More unusual is a building he designed in Sector 14. The circular, three-storey **Panjab University Students' Center** – known to all as the 'Stu-C' – remains a favourite meeting point for students and university alumni and ex-faculty members, and amid the hubbub of surrounding shops and cafés, manages to impose its elegant bulk on the campus. Another campus building, the **Gandhi Bhawan**, does the same but with even greater panache. The lotus-shaped building was designed to evoke the image of a floating flower and is just one of the structures on the campus designed by Pierre Jeanneret, who also designed much of the

city's housing. Modern Chandigarh perhaps reflects Jeanneret's feelings for the city more than Le Corbusier; his belief in Le Corbusier's plan and his love of the city led him to become its senior architect, a role he maintained with passion and enthusiasm until 1965, when he had to leave for health reasons. On his death five years later, his ashes were scattered in Sukhna Lake, following his wishes.

While Le Corbusier's designs faltered, it's interesting that they've not been joined by many noteworthy companions or competitors. A popular exception is the **Nek Chand Rock Garden**, the most visited attraction in the city and possibly one of the most surreal in the country. Built on old waste ground, this 25-acre sprawl of manmade rock gardens and waterfalls criss-crossed with pathways is filled with thousands of figurative sculptures made of recycled materials – including broken crockery, bottle fragments and colourful tile pieces. It's all the work of one roads inspector/folk artist, Nek Chand Saini, who secretly began building the illegal garden in the early 1960s, and it wouldn't have existed but for the part played by concrete in creating the city, a material that forms the basis for the garden and its sculptures.

In its short life, Chandigarh has been beset by the problems most cities face at some time in their existence, including overcrowding and poverty, but it is one of India's more arresting and pleasing cities, and, perhaps more importantly, is one of its most successful. It has the highest per-capita income and literacy rate in India and one of the lowest crime rates. In 2007 it became the first smoke-free city in the country, and its residents are proud of a city they feel is progressive, modern, cultured and educated. As Nehru said of it: 'It is the biggest example in India of experimental architecture. It hits you on the head and makes you think. You may squirm at the impact but it has made you think and imbibe new ideas.'

Chandigarh
War Memorial

Nek Chand Rock Garden

Gandhi Bhawan

Open Hand Monument

Punjab and Haryana
High Court

Tower of Shadows

L: Bougainvillea Garden,
Sector 3
A: Nanki Singh and Shivani
Guglani, 2006
FF: The Chandigarh War
Memorial is not an official
war monument, but was built
through a people's initiative
led by The Indian Express
newspaper group, in memory
of 8,500 people who died from
the Punjab, Haryan, Himachal
Pradesh and Chandigarh. The
names of the martyrs are etched
onto its black granite form.

L: Sector 1
A: Nek Chand Saini,
1960s–70s
FF: There are more than
5,000 pottery-encrusted
concrete human figures in
the garden, some sporting
human hair the artist
collected from barber
shops. They're joined by
numerous animals, including
monkeys, peacocks,
elephants and bears, often
set in complex tableaux.

L: Panjab University, Sector 14
A: Pierre Jeanneret, 1950s
FF: Pierre Jeanneret designed not just
some of Chandigarh's buildings, but
lots of its objects too, including cast-
iron manhole covers featuring Le
Corbusier's city plan on them, lamp
posts, furniture and the pedal boats
sailing on the lake his ashes were
scattered into when he died.

L: Sector 1
A: Le Corbusier, 1950s
FF: The 12.50m (41ft)
wide and 8.86m (29ft)
high hand is sculpted out
of beaten iron sheets. A
metal structure, designed
to turn gently with the
wind, holds it 27.80m
(91ft) above the 'Trench of
Consideration' at its base.

L: Sector 1
A: Le Corbusier, 1955
FF: The High Court houses nine courts
of law, and along with designing the
building, Le Corbusier also undertook
the design of furniture, light fittings,
and nine large tapestries, one for
each court.

L: Sector 1
A: Le Corbusier, 1950s
FF: In 2007, a cedar model
of the Tower of Shadows
made by Giani Rattan
Singh, Le Corbusier's model
maker, sold at Christie's for
$US33,600.

Vidhan Sabha

Secretariat Building

City Museum

Panjab University Students' Center

L: Sector 1
A: Le Corbusier, 1950s
FF: The recessed windows on the office side of the building not only ensure shading in the interior, but great views framed within the concrete shades.

L: Sector 1
A: Le Corbusier, 1952
FF: The eight-storey, 244m (800ft) long Secretariat is made of rough-cast concrete, and was one of the first buildings designed as a 'healthy building', with careful attention paid to natural lighting, ventilation and efficiency.

L: Part of the Government Museum and Art Gallery, Sector 10-C
A: Le Corbusier, 1968
FF: Confusingly also referred to as the Chandigarh Architecture Museum and Le Corbusier's City Museum, the building was established as a city museum in 1997 to mark the 50th anniversary of India's independence.

L: Panjab University, Sector 14
A: Le Corbusier
FF: As well as one of the city's oldest coffee houses, the 'Stu-C', as it's known to locals, houses a recreation room, the Students' Council offices and the Dean-students welfare (DSW) office.

191

Minsk

'I am starting to reconsider my desire about staying. The work is drab, the money I get has nowhere to be spent. No nightclubs or bowling alleys, no places of recreation except the trade union dances. I have had enough.'

Lee Harvey Oswald, in his diary, on living in Minsk, January 1961

As Moscow becomes a collection of ever-taller towers piercing the sky, and other Russian cities follow suit, finding examples of Stalinist architecture and social planning in the former USSR is becoming harder and harder. But the capital city of Belarus, Minsk, is like a city preserved in a kind of architectural aspic – perhaps because, beyond being known by a few history buffs as the place that Lee Harvey Oswald defected to in 1959, when the city was the capital of the Soviet Republic of Byelorussia, it's one of those places most people would struggle to locate in modern geography. But if they did, what they'd find is an astonishing collection of buildings, built in the past 80 or so years, that offer a fine insight into the vision of Joseph Stalin to create cities that not only symbolised, but physically embodied, the tenets of communism and the might of post-war USSR, following strict socialist realist principles.

That Stalin chose Minsk in which to offer the world this dubious vision was no accident, but a strategy determined by the turbulence of the First World War and the Russian Revolution, and the virtual wholesale destruction of the city in the three years after the Nazis marched into it in the summer of 1941. With 90 per cent of the old city gone, Stalin had carte blanche to plan and create a new city, one with avenues nearly 50m (16.5ft) wide, subway stations that celebrated the achievements of

Soviet leaders, and monumental buildings that employed all the modern materials and techniques available through then-emerging industrialisation and mass production.

Unsurprisingly, Stalinist architecture drew its aesthetic from the utilitarianism and austerity of brutalism, and nowhere is this best seen than along Independence Avenue (formerly Lenin Avenue). Along and around its central length from Independence Square to Victory Square, planned by Soviet architects Mikhail Parusnikov and Mikhail Barshch, are a plethora of key civic and government-sanctioned buildings predominantly constructed between the 1940s and 1960s, including Minsk City Hall, the Central Post Office, the GUM Department Store, the KGB headquarters, and the Trade Union Palace of Culture (these last two being anachronistic sprawling cream neoclassical buildings with Corinthian columns). But the **House of Government** and the **Palace of the Republic**, despite sharing a streamlined vertical facade, surprisingly span five decades; the former, fronted by its statue of Lenin, is one of the few buildings to survive the Second World War, and the latter a very recent addition to the city's landscape, having been opened on New Year's Eve 2001. If its style looks older, that's because it was designed in the 1980s at the behest of Piotr Mironovich Masherov, first secretary of the central committee of the Communist Party of Belarus, and embodies many old socialist realist tropes, albeit imbued with a lighter, elegant facade more in keeping with the later International Style.

But there are plenty of buildings in the area that do exhibit more traditional socialist realist touches, including the **House of Officers**, whose recessed central section flanked by imposing wings and columns is a perfect example of the style, right down to the stars above the two entrances and the angular balconies. Angularity is taken to the extreme in the constructivist **Faculty of Architecture** at the Belarusian National Technical University (BNTU). With its succession of overhanging lecture theatres, this late 20th-century concrete block, described by photographer Frédéric Chaubin in his book *Cosmic Communist Constructions Photographed* as an example of the 'fourth age' of Soviet architecture, shows an imaginative, lyrical styling that's a long way from the blocky structuralism of the 1930s. North-west of here, between the Dreamland and Pieramohi parks, the **BelExpo Exhibition Centre** exhibits similarly outlandish flights of fancy, its floating parabolic petal roof offering another and very different take on late Soviet architecture.

These, and similarly diverse, unschooled Soviet buildings of the era, Chaubin describes as representing a chaotic impulse brought about by a decaying system, their diversity signalling the end of the Soviet Union. But if they did, they've left behind a legacy of imaginative design, particularly in the area of Vostok. Here, old and new are merged with panache in a winning mix that spans the gamut from a typically austere Soviet residential block, undermined by a full-height, gaily decorated communist wall painting, through to an underground station whose architecture was inspired by the Vostok space programme, and a flying saucer-shaped bus station that looks equally space age.

Opposite the apartment block with the Soviet mural, the area's latest addition is arguably its most arresting: the **National Library of Belarus**, which sports a fetching rhombicuboctahedron completed less than a decade ago. In its spherical form, this sci-fi, futuristic work seems a natural progression from Soviet pieces like the much earlier **October Cinema** and **Opera and Ballet Theatre**, albeit with a perhaps more upbeat, hopeful aspect than its forebears, which could be straight out of an Andrei Tarkovsky film. Still, in their imaginative detailing and inventive use of concrete, they are a lot more appealing to look at than the dominant construction of the time; as the serried ranks of tower blocks around the city's perimeter testify. Most of the city's high-rise blocks conform to the grimly stereotypical Soviet accommodation, but the sleek Hotel Orbita and the state-owned **Hotel Belarus**, with its triform Y-shape and curved roof, show how tower blocks can be both functional and elegant.

As Minsk moves into the 21st century, it remains to be seen how much the architectural vision of Stalin will shape it; will iconic aspects of the city accommodate newer styles – as they do near the Nemiga Street metro, where the hulking, brooding *Solidarity* workers' relief sculpture has managed to survive despite its incongruous setting above the **House of Fashion**? Certainly there are moves to create some more characterful tower blocks and civic buildings, such as the Gazprom building due to be completed in 2018, and the projected Crystalline Fertilizer Company HQ, as well as low-rise buildings like a hockey arena and sports facilities. But it's the mixed-use Magnet Minsk complex that perhaps points the best way forward, in a development that clearly references the inventiveness and imagination of late Soviet architecture, while leaving behind the rest of a vision that proved to be inhuman both physically and ideologically.

L: Nezavisimosti Avenue, 65
A: V. Anikin and I. Yesman, 1983
FF: The futuristic building has been described as a ski slope and passenger ferry. The right-hand stepped side of the building contains a series of lecture halls with raked seating.

L: 14 Peramozhtsau Avenue
A: Leonard Moskalevich, 1988
FF: The flower shape of the exhibition centre was created using five elegant hyperbolic parabolids, and required engineering feats that make it a standout example of late Soviet design.

L: Starazhowskaya Vulitsa, 15
A: Unknown, 20th century
FF: The basement of this 22-storey tower block features a large swimming pool whose walls are decorated with a huge nautically themed Soviet realist fresco.

L: Parizhskaya Kommuna Square, 1
A: Losif Langbard, 1938
FF: The reliefs on the exterior of the building were designed by Zair Azgur in the 1930s, but the sculptures were only added in 2009, when the theatre underwent extensive renovations.

L: Independence Square
A: Losif Langbard, 1929–34
FF: Government House was built without the use of mechanical construction equipment, and on its completion was the tallest building in the city.

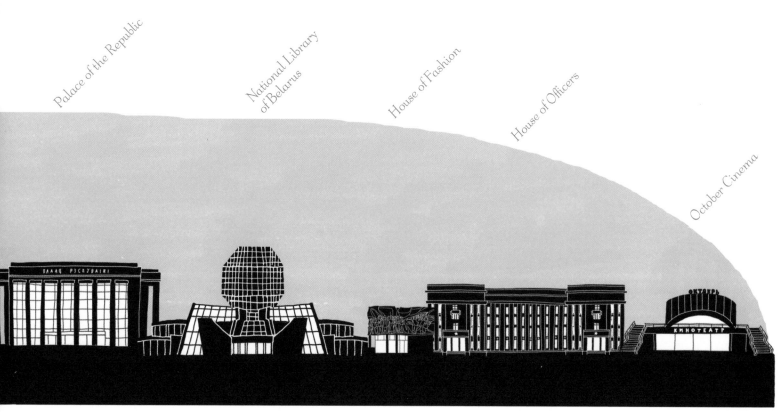

Palace of the Republic

National Library of Belarus

House of Fashion

House of Officers

October Cinema

L: Oktyabrskaya Square 1
A: Belgosproek Institute (M. Pirogov, V. Danilov, L. Zdanevich, L. Moskalevich, V. Novikov, M. Turliuk, V. Usimov, A. Shabalin), 1984–2001
FF: The lengthy build of the Palace was down to the collapse of the Soviet Union, when the project was shelved for five years. It's now the city's pre-eminent concert hall and conference centre.

L: Nezavisimosti Avenue, 116
A: Mihail Vinogradov and Viktor Kramarenko, 2006
FF: This impressive library has 22 floors, a book museum and an observation point reached via an external glass lift. Membership is open to everyone with a valid passport, regardless of nationality.

L: Nemiga Street
A: Anatol Artimovich, 1979
FF: When the relief was unveiled, it's said that local people hated it for its depressing, imposing nature, and its cynical attempt to please an ideological authority in decline.

L: Krasnoarmeiskaya Street, 3
A: Losif Langbard, 1934–9
FF: This building was the first in Minsk to contain a swimming pool. It also housed a 1,000-seat theatre, a 500-seat cinema, a conference room, a gym, basketball and tennis courts and a lavishly inlaid chess room.

L: Nezavisimosti Avenue, 73
A: V. Malyshev, 1975
FF: Screenings are still held daily in the cinema; unfortunately for non-Russian speakers, they're usually dubbed rather than subtitled.

Venice

'If you died and in your will you asked for your ashes to be spread gently on the Grand Canal at midnight with a full moon, everyone would know this about you – you loved and understood beauty.'
William Goldman (under the pseudonym of Simon Morgenstern), *The Silent Gondoliers*

As high streets go, the Grand Canal must surely be one of the grandest in the world. Along its length lie some 170 sumptuous buildings, any handful of which would make a stunning standalone skyline. But the skyline that tells the story of this city is a very different one, and much more far-reaching. It doesn't begin here at all, but on the island of Torcello, at the northern end of the lagoon. Founded in the 5th century by residents of the mainland Roman town of Altino fleeing invaders after the fall of the Roman Empire, the settlement quickly thrived, thanks in no small part to the discovery of deep channels through the lagoon. These offered access to large sailing ships, and a maritime trading powerhouse was born.

Of the numerous palazzi and churches built on Torcello, two still dominate the island. The 11th- and 12th-century cathedral and campanile of **Santa Maria Assunta**, founded in AD 639 and the oldest building on the lagoon, is the one that is most visible as you approach the now near-deserted island, but it's the contemporaneous Church of Santa Fosca that in some ways is more interesting, its squat, rounded form reflecting eastern Byzantine influences rather than western European ones.

By the 12th century mosquitoes and malaria seemed a bigger threat than invaders for the Torcello settlers, and wealthy families headed instead for Venice, Murano and Burano, quickly establishing themselves so that,

by the 13th century, the city controlled some 70 per cent of the spices brokered from the Far East into Europe. From these vastly different cultural influences, Islamic Cairo and Byzantine Constantinople created an aesthetic that would continue for centuries. It's seen clearly in the city's most famous church, the 11th-century **St Mark's Basilica**, modelled on Constantinople's Church of the Holy Apostles. From its Greek cross floorplan to its five onion domes, the predominant architecture of the church is clearly Byzantine, but it also bears Italian Gothic motifs and Islamic references, not least in the canopies over the domes, which aren't dissimilar to those on minarets. And on the canal, the later **Ca' d'Oro** shows clear Islamic influences in the inflected arches of its windows and the framing around its main floor windows and roof. This 15th-century townhouse beautifully illustrates Venice's unique Arab take on Gothic styling, which is seen to even better effect at the **Palazzo Ducale**, the city's seat of ducal power from the 9th century to the late 18th century. Its eastern-influenced open ground floor, a first-floor arcade of Gothic arches bearing the trademark cusped design, and above them a wall punctuated by more traditional Gothic windows, create a masterly whole.

As Gothic gave way to Renaissance, the Venetian style of arch still played a large part in the architecture; not least because, in a city built on a petrified forest of wooden columns set in a layer of compacted clay, its load-bearing design was perfect. And it looked lovely, too, particularly in townhouses like the **Palazzo Contarini del Bovolo**, a beautiful example of early Renaissance architecture featuring an external staircase with arches rivalling those of both the Ca' d'Oro and the Palazzo Ducale. Nearby, the Renaissance **Rialto Bridge** is the only one of the four footbridges crossing the Grand Canal to sport its own arches. The oldest bridge across the canal, it replaced a 13th-century wooden one and won out over designs by Palladio, Vignola and Sansovino. Palladio, though, did get to design two standout churches in Venice; the striking **Redentore**, generally thought to be one of his finest churches, and the church of **San Giorgio Maggiore**. Facing the piazzetta across the lagoon on the island of San Giorgio Maggiore, this shines like a beacon, its brilliant white marble Renaissance facade a perfect adaptation of his classical style.

While imposing, Palladio's church bears little of the Venetian style's whimsy and eclecticism. For that, one could start on the cemetery island of San Michele, where Venice's first Renaissance church sits in isolated splendour. Built in white Istrian stone in the 1460s, it has beautiful cloisters hidden behind its unusually plain facade, and a dome over the adjoining hexagonal Cappella Emiliani that has a distinct touch of the Orient about it. And Pietro Lombardo's slightly later Santa Maria dei Miracoli is another fine example of the style. But the charm of Venice's churches was not confined to this style, or century. The huge brick Basilica di San Giovanni e Paolo, completed just three decades earlier in the 1430s, offers something very different but equally alluring,

its symmetrical Italian Gothic style fronted by a harmonious facade behind which 25 doges are buried. Similarly harmonious is **I Frari**, an earlier brick Italian Gothic church that took almost a century to build but still stands as a glorious example of this style. And Santa Maria della Salute offers an equally glorious example of late Baroque, its eight Palladian facades and huge buttresses supporting a bombastic dome decorated with angels quickly becoming a much-loved feature of the city's skyline.

Churches weren't the only buildings to plunder different styles and techniques. From the 13th to the 15th centuries, some of the best architects in the city were employed in building *scuole*, a development unique to the independent state. Like grand guild houses, the city's hundreds of *scuole* were prestigious places in which the city's professional classes could congregate, confabulate – and show off their wealth. This was particularly true of the six *scuole grande*, which were literally very grand affairs, from the Scuola Grande di San Giovanni Evangelista, founded in 1261 and the oldest of the six schools, to the late 15th-century **Scuola Grande di San Marco**, whose lovely Mauro Codussi facade is decorated with *trompe l'oeil* panels. As grand as the schools are, and in a city likened by Truman Capote to 'eating an entire box of chocolate liqueurs in one go', choosing one symbolic structure is tricky, but judging by height alone, the accolade would have to go to **St Mark's Campanile**, at 99m (325ft) Venice's tallest structure. It's by no means its loveliest, but a distinct architectural presence in a city that has so many. And, having fallen and risen again on numerous occasions, perhaps, in the slowly sinking city, it's the most potent beacon of hope there is.

San Giorgio Maggiore

Palazzo Ducale

Redentore

St Mark's Campanile

St Mark's Basilica

L: Isola San Giorgio
A: Andrea Palladio and Simeone Sorella, 1565–97
FF: The church's campanile was a much later addition; first built in 1467, it fell down in 1774 and was rebuilt in 1791.

L: San Marco 1, Piazzetta San Marco
A: Filippo Calendario, Bartolomeo Bon, Andrea Bregno, Antonio Abbondi, Giovanni Bon, 1309–1424
FF: As well as being the home of Venice's Doges, the building was home to political institutions and a prison. In one of the cells a *trompe l'oeil* window drawn by a prisoner is visible above a doorway.

L: Guidecca, Campo del Redentore
A: Andrea Palladio/Antonio Da Ponte, 1577–92
FF: The Festival of the Redentore, giving thanks for the end of a 1575–7 bout of plague, takes place each year on the third Sunday in July, when a bridge on barges is built from the Zattere across the Giudecca so that Venetians can make the pilgrimage previously led by the city's Doge and the Signoria.

L: Piazza San Marco
A: Various, incl. Giorgio Sparento, Bartolomeo Bon and Baldasarre Congleva, 1912
FF: The current 99m (325ft)-high bell tower is an exact replica of its predecessor, which was built in 1514 but collapsed in 1902. But that replaced an even earlier tower, built between AD 888 and AD 912.

L: Piazza San Marco
A: Domenico I Contarini, 1063–94
FF: The remains of St Mark, brought here by two Venetian merchants who stole them from Alexandria in AD 828, are thought by some historians to be the remains of Alexander the Great.

I Frari

Scuola Grande di San Marco

Ca' d'Oro

Rialto Bridge

Palazzo Contarini del Bovolo

Santa Maria Assunta

L: San Polo, Campo dei Frari
A: Baldassare Longhena, Jacopo Sansovino, Marco Cozzi, 1340–1492
FF: The church's 1396 campanile, designed by Jacopo Celaga and completed by his son Pietro Paolo in 1396, is the second highest in the city after that of San Marco. The interior features works by Titian, Bellini, Pesaro, Donatello and Sansovino.

L: Castello, Campo Santi Giovanni e Paolo
A: Various, incl. Pietro Lombardo, Giovanni Buora and Mauro Codussi, 15th century
FF: The *scuola* is now occupied by the city hospital, having been converted into a military hospital in 1819.

L: Cannaregio 3932, Calle Ca' d'Oro
A: Bartolomeo Bon, Giovanni Bon, 1421–31
FF: While the Ca' d'Oro's exterior looks positively elegant nowadays, in the 15th century its ultramarine blue and burgundy facade, with 24-carat gold highlights, would have looked a lot more lurid.

L: Grand Canal
A: Antonio da Ponte, Antonio Contin, 1588–91
FF: The Rialto is the city's oldest bridge, and replaced a wooden one that had a movable central section allowing tall ships to pass through. The shops were a later addition to the bridge.

L: Calle Locande, 4299
A: Giovanni Candi, 1499
FF: The building and its staircase feature prominently in Orson Welles' 1952 screen version of *Othello*, in which it was the house of Brabantio. The staircase is thought to be a later addition to the house, designed by Giorgio Spavento.

L: Torcello
A: 7th–12th centuries
FF: The interior of the church features a range of mosaics from the 9th to the end of the 12th centuries, including an 11th-century mosaic floor and a colourful 13th-century mosaic of the *Madonna and Child* in a field of gold on the semi-dome of the apse.

Barcelona

*'There are no straight lines or sharp corners in nature.
Therefore, buildings must have no straight lines or sharp corners.'*
Antoni Gaudí

I f any one European city can be said to have been shaped by a single man, that city is Barcelona, and the man Antoni Gaudí. Most of the city's finest buildings were designed by Gaudí, and a handful of fellow practitioners, and architects have since clearly been inspired by their remarkable work. Gaudí crafted a city that, 30 years after his death in 1926, led Le Corbusier to exclaim: 'What I saw was the work of such strength, such faith, of an extraordinary technical capacity, manifested during a whole life of genius; of a man who carved the stones before his eyes in a well-thought-out pattern. Gaudí is the "builder" of the turn of the century.' Or, as P. Diddy put it on visiting the city in 2003, 'I don't think it gets sexier than this.'

Gaudí's shaping of Barcelona was rooted in Gothic architecture, but a much more fantastical version than that of the medieval buildings of Barcelona's Barri Gòtic. For Gaudí, the vaulted ceilings, gargoyles and grandeur of the Middle Ages were seen through a prism of Moorish and Oriental influences, using a brilliant colour palette. And fluid, organic shapes developed not through the manmade environment around him, but from shapes and forms drawn from nature.

For his inspiration, Gaudí headed for the mountains of Montserrat and caves at Mallorca, where undulating shapes and organic forms chimed neatly with his take on a form of Art Nouveau that was emerging in the city; Barcelona's architects were rushing to embrace the fin-de-siècle modernity sweeping the continent with their own form of *modernisme*, and Gaudí was an enthusiastic champion of this revolutionary art movement.

His first important building, Casa Vicens, exhibited many *modernisme* themes, including decorative ceramics and Mudéjar tiling and colours, but it was with the 1886 commission of Palau Güell that Gaudí's style emerged fully. He rewarded the keen patronage of industrial tycoon Eusebi Güell with a six-floor family mansion decorated with honeybbly tiles, ornate columns and pillars, and intricate wooden ceilings featuring mosaic chimneys and huge parabolic arches.

The Gaudí themes illustrated in the mansion would develop further with more private commissions, in particular with **Casa Batlló** and **Casa Milà**. On the first of these, Gaudí's strong Catalan patriotism is believed to have led him to design a building as an allegory of the legend of Sant Jordi, Barcelona's patron saint, complete with a dragon (the roof with its knobbly spine) and skulls and bones of its victims (the balconies). Whatever it represents, the facade is one of Gaudí's finest and most widely admired.

Casa Milà, or La Pedrera, meaning 'the Quarry', has an even more arresting facade, and a rooftop sculpture park featuring Moorish warriors as chimneys that have stood in for Barcelona on countless book covers. Every aspect of this undulating stone building illustrates something about Gaudí's vision and genius, from innovative technical feats with construction to a unique artistic approach to styling and decoration.

Through the building of Casa Milà, two Gaudí projects continued to develop that would show very different sides to the man whose twin passions of nature and God informed all his work: **Park Güell**, and his magnum opus, the **Sagrada Família**. The former is a delightfully playful affair that exhibits every aspect of Gaudí's arts and love of natural forms in a huge fairy-tale park inspired by patron Eusebi Güell's love of English garden cities. Featuring sculptures, fountains, Gothic archways, stairways, twisted columns and wavy benches all decorated in brightly coloured broken tiles, the park is a magical space. In marked contrast, the majestic Sagrada Família is as muted in colour as it is fanciful in form, with Baroque strokes and abstraction embellishing a facade that will eventually feature 18 towers. When the church is finished in 2026, it's debatable how much of Gaudí's design it will retain, but its bold, visionary design, construction and decoration undoubtedly harness the spirit of Gaudí, and wider *Catalan modernisme*.

The style lent itself to wide personal interpretation. An enthusiastic adherence to the pioneering and experimental spirit of the new age was all that was needed, and many of Barcelona's architects took to it with gusto – among them Lluís Domènech i Montaner. His **Fundació Antoni Tàpies** is one of the first *modernisme* buildings to combine exposed brick and iron, and its sturdy but highly decorative facade, topped with a Tàpies sculpture looking like a wispy mass of spun metal and piping, remains a standout Barcelona building.

With the **Hospital de la Santa Creu I de Sant Pau**, Domènech i Montaner would create a complex of even greater beauty to stand alongside his award-winning Casa Lleó Morera and the **Palau de Música Catalana**. This majestic concert hall features interior displays of bright mosaics and stained glass ceilings, and a red-brick facade studded with the richly decorated pillars and arches so beloved of many of his peers – though not fellow *modernista* Josep Puig i Cadafalch. His **Casa Amatller**, built for the chocolatier Antoni Amatller, is famous for its geometric stepped roof, which contrasts strikingly with the more usual motifs of abstract stained glass and mosaics, and intricate ironwork, tiling and woodwork.

The breadth of imaginative design and invention exhibited by Gaudí and his peers left an unusual legacy in the city, one of bold innovation that has continued through to the 21st century. Towers such as Santiago Calatrava's 119m (391ft) high Torre de Comunicacions on Montjuïc, Norman Foster's Torre de Collserola and Emba Estudi Massip-Bosch's Torre Diagonal ZeroZero all share the spirit of innovation of their forebears, as do low-rise but equally striking designs such as Herzog & de Meuron's Forum, Frank Gehry's La Sagrera train station and tower, and Richard Rogers' renovation of the **Las Arenas** bullring.

Built for the Barcelona Exhibition of 1929, this lovely Moorish arena fell into a sorry state as the popularity of bullfighting in the region dwindled, but the beauty of the facade, topped with Rogers' clever and sympathetic walkway ceiling, has seen it become a new city landmark. But the most distinctive addition to Barcelona's skyline is **Torre Agbar** – which was, according to its designer Jean Nouvel, influenced by two key Catalan structures; the bell towers of the Sagrada Família and the distinctive peaks of the Montserrat mountains.

For many, the structure that most channels the spirit of Gaudí is not a building at all, but Frank Gehry's beautiful **Peix**, the huge fish sculpture that has become the symbol of post-Olympic Barcelona. With the sun glinting off its elegant form, it looks like it might jump right off the waterfront of the Olympic Marina and into the sparkling waters of the Mediterranean. Gehry intertwined gilded stainless steel strips supported by a metal structure to create the sinuous, shimmering form, one whose artistic inspiration is clear. Gehry often cites other art forms as influences in his work, but has also said: 'Architecture should speak of its time and place, but yearn for timelessness.' In Barcelona, Antoni Gaudí has surely achieved just that.

Peix

Casa Milà

Las Arenas

Palau de Música Catalana

Torre Agbar

Hospital de la Santa Creu I de Sant Pau

L: Passeig Marítim de la Barceloneta, Port Olímpic
A: Frank Gehry, 1992
FF: Built for the 1992 summer Olympics. Its copper-coloured metal plates sparkle in the sun and it can be seen from several of Barcelona's beaches.

L: Provença, 261–265
A: Antoni Gaudí, 1910
FF: The top floor, attic and roof are open to visitors.

L: Gran Via de les Corts Catalanes, 373–385
A: August Font I Carreras, then Richard Rogers, 1889–1900, then 2011
FF: Built for the Barcelona Exhibition of 1929, and the Beatles played there in 1966.

L: C/ Palau de la Música, 4–6
A: Lluís Domènech i Montaner, refurbished by Roser Amadó & Lluís Domènach Girbau, 1905
FF: Concert tickets sell out quickly but there are popular guided tours.

L: Avinguda Diagonal, 211
A: Jean Nouvel, 2005
FF: The tower's facade has 4,500 LED luminous devices that allow different images to appear on its facade.

L: Carrer de San Quintí
A: Guillem d'Abriell, 1401, then Domènech i Montaner, 1901–30
FF: Gaudí died here three days after being hit by a tram.

Park Güell

Casa Amatller

Sagrada Familia

Fundació Antoni Tàpies

Casa Batlló

L: El Carmel
A: Antoni Gaudí, 1900–14
FF: In spite of its popularity today, the project was a failure and Güell failed to sell a single house in the park.

L: Passeig de Gràcia, 41
A: Josep Puig i Cadafalch, 1900
FF: The shape of the buildings and the windows have been stylised to look like an 'A', the initials of Antoni Amatller.

L: Carrer de Mallorca, 401
A: Francisco de Paula del Villar, then Antoni Gaudí, 1882–2026 (estimated)
FF: Gaudí is buried in the crypt and a museum tells his story as well as the history of the church.

L: Carrer d'Aragó, 255
A: Lluís Domènech i Montaner, 1990
FF: The building's facade shows Muslim influences, such as the use of unpolished brick, Mozarabic elements and Arabesque-like geometrical compositions.

L: 92 Passeig de Gràcia
A: Antoni Gaudí, 1904–6
FF: The scaled roof represents a dragon with a small turret and a cross symbolising the sword of St George.

Timbuktu

'The rich king of Timbuktu has many plates and sceptres of gold . . . he keeps a magnificent and well-furnished court... There are numerous doctors, judges, scholars, priests – and here are brought manuscript books from Barbary which are sold at greater profit than any other merchandise.'

Leo Africanus, 16th-century traveller

On the last day of Mali's national assembly elections, the only female candidate, Aziza Mint Mohamed, called on a desert blues singer to perform. Known as 'Nightingale of the North', Khaira Arby was a cousin of one of Mali's most famous musicians, the late Ali Farka Touré. She made the 900km (560 mile)-trip from Bamako to attend a final rally outside the 14th-century **Sankoré Masjid**. A crowd had gathered to hear one of Mint Mohamed's male opponents speak, but once Arby began to sing, his supporters moved closer to listen… and Mint Mohamed went on to win the election. Music has always been a vital aspect of the culture of nomadic tribes and, until very recently, Mali's Festival au Désert has been a great celebration of its diversity.

But as well as having a rich oral and music tradition, Mali, and especially Timbuktu, had a long literary history and, by the 14th century, was a destination for scholars, particularly of Islamic studies.

As far back as 1100 Timbuktu was little more than a caravan site that had grown up around a well. A woman, known as Buktu, stayed by the water supply while the nomadic Tuaregs took their animals out to pasture, and she gave her name to the city. Today the well is housed within an **Ethnological Museum**.

Gold traders followed, travelling north to meet salt traders coming down through the desert. Timbuktu became a trading post, but by the mid-1400s an event happened to put it firmly on the map. Emperor Mansa Musa, a devout Muslim, made a holy pilgrimage from Cairo to Mecca with a caravan of more than 60,000 people and 13 tons of gold. It's reported that he spent so much gold in Cairo, the price crashed for many years.

When Mansa Musa returned to Timbuktu he brought with him a Muslim Andalusian architect called El-Saheli. Intending to make Timbuktu a major centre of Islamic scholarship, he embarked on a campaign of building mosques and madrasas. Commerce and education were not incompatible at this time; it was vital that merchants could read the constellations to navigate their way across the desert, for instance, and there was also a trade in manuscripts that had come from Cairo, Baghdad, Morocco and Andalusian Spain.

Traditional constructions were made with mud and straw, such as the extant **bakers' ovens** where the women still take their dough to be baked, but they're fragile and, following the rainy season, require constant maintenance. The sticks that extend from the sides of many such buildings are, rather than decorative, a form of 'ladder' for engineers to climb up to repair any damage. El-Saheli was credited with the creation of the mud brick, giving buildings more solidity. He also added Islamic spires, starting with the adobe-walled **Djinguereber Mosque**, the largest in the city, whose minaret dominates the town. The Sankoré Mosque, where Khaira Arby drew a crowd with her singing, was originally financed by, and took its name from, a wealthy Mandinka woman. By the end of Mansa Musa's reign, it held more books than the Library of Alexandria.

The Sankoré became the town's main teaching venue, along with the Djinguereber and **Sidi Yahya Mosque**, and, at its height, Timbuktu had 25,000 students. The manuscripts of many of these students, as well as their teachers, now form part of the city's treasures. Whether it was the reputation of the Timbuktu scholars, or the rumours of great wealth, the city drew many explorers, including Alexander Gordon Laing. The first European to venture here, Laing arrived in 1826 in poor health, having been attacked

by Tuareg tribesmen. He stayed for just over a month, was booted out of town and was eventually murdered. Frenchman René Caillié, who studied Islam and Arabic, was the first European to reach Timbuktu and return home alive; and German explorer Heinrich Barth, who spoke seven African languages and developed relationships with Islamic scholars and rulers in the regions, arrived in 1853. His Timbuktu house is now a small museum.

The simple houses of travelling merchants also tell a story: built from quarried limestone, many possess square pilasters that might have been inspired by Egyptian architecture; others have doors with geometric designs that look typically Moorish. It's thought that El-Saheli had a hand in designing far more than the mosques.

Timbuktu's Golden Age ended following an invasion by Morocco, in alliance with England, which provided the firearms. Gold and even people, including Timbuktu's most famous 16th-century scholar, Ahmed Baba, were taken back to Morocco. Ahmed Baba eventually returned to Timbuktu to continue his classes.

The **Ahmed Baba Institute of Higher Learning and Islamic Research** opened in 1970, holding up to 100,000 priceless manuscripts dating as far back as the 13th century, many in local languages and on subjects as diverse as medicine, astronomy, poetry and Islamic law, as well as family history. The library was attacked in 2013 and many of the manuscripts were moved to a new site designed by South African architects. The project architect purchased mud bricks from local craftsmen, but also employed a local mason who mixed mud with concrete to make the exterior rain-repellent. In spite of using some traditional methods, there have been criticisms that the building is too modern for such a low-tech society.

Timbuktu has seen more than its fair share of violence, often between nomadic tribes and successive ruling governments. On the outskirts of town, the **Flamme de la Paix** peace monument was built on the spot where more than 3,000 weapons were burned at the end of the Tuareg rebellion. The burnt-out remains were integrated into the steps that lead up to the white stone peace monument. Today the town's historians fear for the safety of their precious manuscripts again – whether from the elements or from those who would destroy them – even though at least one of the manuscripts may be a biography of the Prophet Mohammed dating back to the 13th century.

bakers' ovens

Sidi Yahya Mosque

Flamme de la Paix

Sankoré Masjid

L: All over
A: Unknown
FF: Specialities include *widjilaas*, fritters that accompany fish, and *toukassou*, spicy steam-cooked wheat flour.

L: Timbuktu
A: Mohamed Naddah, 1441
FF: Groups who believed it to be un-Islamic recently attacked the richly decorated door of the Sidi Yahya mosque.

L: Timbuktu
A: Unknown, 1996
FF: Close by is the tree-filled Jardin de Paix.

L: Timbuktu
A: Abu Ishap Es-Saheli Altouwaidjin, 14th century
FF: The Qadi of Timbuktu, the Imam Al Aqib, demolished the sanctuary in order to rebuild it to the exact dimensions as Mecca's Ka'aba (having taken the measurements with a piece of rope on his last pilgrimage).

Djinguereber Mosque

Ethnological Museum

Ahmed Baba Institute
of Higher Learning and
Islamic Research

L: Askia Mohamed Boulevard
A: Abu Ishap Es-Saheli Altouwaidjin, 1325–27
FF: The mosque has three inner courts, two
minarets, 25 rows of pillars and space for 2,000
people.

L: Timbuktu
A: Unknown, 20th century
FF: Exhibits include clothing,
musical instruments, colonial
photographs and jewellery.

L: Sankoré precinct, Timbuktu
A: Andre Spies, DHK Architects, 2009
FF: The centre holds around 20,000 manuscripts.

Utopia

'The modern Utopia must not be static but kinetic, must shape not as a permanent state but as a hopeful stage, leading to a long ascent of stages.'

H. G. Wells

Can a utopian city exist, or is it an oxymoron to expect one place to be all things to all people for all of their lives? For centuries planners have strived to create the perfect settlement, and again and again they fail. From Victorian ideals of new towns to the City Beautiful movement taken up so enthusiastically in the US, and on through the UK's Garden City movement inspired by Ebenezer Howard, utopian models of cities have broken down. Perhaps it's because the ideal utopian city isn't about structure at all, but about relationships; housing programmes integrated with work opportunities and effective transport networks, good public spaces, the promotion of social citizenship, and flexibility of tenure and structures, all populated by buildings trying to be the best they can be. Playing with that idea, it seemed to us that we should be able to draw the types of structures that could form the ideal city from the 49 cities we chose to include in *Skylines*.

In terms of recreation and public spaces, we were struck by the beauty of Genoa's Biosphere and the way in which Barcelona immediately took Frank Gehry's *Peix* to its heart as a symbol of the city's post-Olympics prosperity and reinvention, but its psychedelic **Park Güell** is still in many ways the apotheosis of a recreational space, one that inspires, delights, intrigues and relaxes. The city also houses one of the world's most forward-thinking and holistic approaches to healthcare in its **Hospital de la Santa Creu I de Sant Pau**, built by Lluís Domènech i Montaner as a series of isolated, beautifully decorated pavilions and airy wards connected by underground tunnels, which ensured that patients could be transported safely and comfortably around the site while also enjoying outdoor spaces integral to their well-being and recuperation.

While healthcare requirements have evolved over years to make the best of emerging technologies and space planning, residential design has often stumbled. Tower blocks like Ernö Goldfinger's Trellick Tower in London, developed as an ideal 'machine for living' with all the amenities residents would require, instead turned into the Tower of Terror. But the modular, open apartments weren't the problem, their style a descendant of the Japanese aesthetic principle of *Ma*, referring to the empty or open space. The principle is applied beautifully at Kyoto's 17th-century **Katsura Imperial Villa**, where the removal of all unnecessary internal walls and the opening up of the space between interior and exterior has influenced architects to this day. A fine contemporary example lies in Herzog & de Meuron's **Beirut Terraces**, a vertical village of irregularly stacked apartments which reference the city's tumultuous history through their layering, and break down the borders between interior and exterior via garden terraces that take advantage of the city's views.

Herzog & de Meuron's work in cultural institutions often reference a city's social fabric and history, but for our utopian ideal we've chosen Jean Nouvel's **Arab World Institute** in Paris, famed for a responsive metallic south-facing *brise soleil* which reacts to sunlight and regulates the amount of light in the building. The building's genius lies not just in its engineering, but in the way its design and decoration clearly reference Islamic art, creating a thoughtfully interpreted space that ensures accessibility and encourages understanding of Arab culture in anyone who visits it.

In both these buildings, engineering and technology play a large part in helping to integrate a space in its surroundings while also making it an engaging space to enter and experience, a trend that's driving cultural spaces as diverse as the Museum of Anthropology in Vancouver, the Museum of Tomorrow in Rio de Janeiro and the Museo Soumaya in Mexico City. In education institutions too, the idea of being in an inspirational space is behind the likes of Zaha Hadid's **Jockey Club Innovation Tower** (part of the Hong Kong Polytechnic) and the Orthodox School in Remle, Jerusalem. But the idea of a building inspiring students and reflecting their activities is nothing new; Fidel Castro's vision of five national arts schools was eloquently realised at the School of Ballet, where graceful domes and open piazzas reflected freedom and openness outside, and vaulted ceilings and ceramic decoration featured in curved buildings that would reflect the dancers' movements.

The spiritual needs of humans are integral to a city's make-up, and Helsinki's **Kamppi Chapel** stands out as a much-loved feature of the city, due in no small part to its diminutive simplicity; a gentle, warm space for quiet contemplation rather than vocal veneration. Atheists who follow Marx's belief that '…religion is the opium of the people…' might prefer the alternative opiate of sports. Here, many Olympic stadiums have turned out to be superlative buildings, among them Rome's Palazzetto dello Sport, made from 1,620 prefabricated concrete pieces and put together in just 40 days, and Beijing's **National Stadium**, based on Chinese ceramics and designed like a bowl or a 'public vessel' using steel beams that hide supports for a retractable roof. The real opiate of the masses is arguably neither religion nor sport, but shopping, and perhaps unsurprisingly, little surprised or thrilled us in this area, with one exception in, of all places, Las Vegas. Here, the stacked cubes of Daniel Libeskind's **Crystals Retail Centre** create fittingly innovative spaces for tenants such as Prada while utilising a range of eco-friendly features.

Finally, no city can function without leadership, and there have been many exciting and exemplary examples of civic architecture through the centuries. From the Doges' Palace in Venice to Brasilia's convex-domed Senate, many have worked around the idea of the building somehow signifying or reflecting the openness and transparency of its workings – literally in the case of the post-reunification **Reichstag** in Berlin, whose renovation Norman Foster conceived as a 'dialogue between old and new', with angled mirrors in the dome reflecting the workings of democracy below. Other government buildings go further to incorporate eco-friendly and sustainable features, and even address the mental and physical well-being of its workers. Le Corbusier's **Secretariat Building** in Chandigarh for example was one of the first buildings to be designed as a 'healthy building', with careful attention paid to natural lighting, ventilation, and efficiency.

Le Corbusier's Chandigarh still stands as a great example of city planning, and if any one city could be said to be near-ideal, it's a strong contender; it has the highest per capita income and literacy rate in India, and one of the lowest crime rates. In 2007 it became the first smoke-free city in the country, and its residents are proud of a city they feel is progressive, modern, cultured and educated. As Nehru said of it: 'It is the biggest example in India of experimental architecture. It hits you on the head, and makes you think. You may squirm at the impact but it has made you think and imbibe new ideas.' And surely, that's the most we can ask of our cities?

National Stadium
(Beijing)

Katsura Imperial Villa
(Kyoto)

Kamppi Chapel
(Helsinki)

Secretariat Building
(Chandigarh)

Hospital de la Santa
Creu I de Sant Pau
(Barcelona)

Beirut
Terraces
(Beirut)

L: Olympic Green Chaoyang, Houhai
A: Herzog & de Meuron, 2008
FF: Now staging national and international sports events and concerts.

L: Katsuramisono, Nishikyo-ku
A: Kobori Ehshu, mid-17th century
FF: The gardens are a masterpiece of Japanese garden design.

L: Simonsgatan
A: Kimmo Lintula, Niko Sirola and Mikko Summanen, 2012
FF: Light enters via a void in the ceiling as the chapel has no windows.

L: Sector 1
A: Le Corbusier, 1952
FF: The eight-storey, 244m (800ft)-long Secretariat is made of rough-cast concrete, and was one of the first buildings designed as a 'healthy building', with careful attention paid to natural lighting, ventilation and efficiency.

L: Carrer de San Quintí
A: Guillem d'Abriell, 1401, then Domènech i Montaner, 1901–30
FF: Gaudí died here three days after being hit by a tram.

L: Minet El Hosn
A: Herzog & de Meuron, 2015
FF: The site is close to a bombsite beside the Saint-George Hotel.

Reichstag
(Berlin)

Jockey Club
Innovation Tower
(Hong Kong)

Park Güell
(Barcelona)

Arab World Institute
(Paris)

Crystals Retail Centre
(Las Vegas)

L: Platz der Republik 1
A: Paul Wallot, 1884–94
FF: The bronze letters of *Dem Deutschen Volke* (to the German People) were added in 1916 by Wilhelm II and cast from seized French cannons.

L: The Hong Kong Polytechnic University,
Hung Hom, Kowloon
A: Zaha Hadid, 2014
FF: Public spaces in the college include a design museum, permanent and temporary exhibition galleries and a communal viewing lounge.

L: El Carmel
A: Antoni Gaudí, 1900–14
FF: In spite of its popularity today, the project was a failure and Güell failed to sell a single house in the park.

L: 1 Rue des Fosses
A: Jean Nouvel, 1987
FF: Big names in the Arab music world perform in the auditorium, and the roof terrace once offered fabulous views but closed in 2010 following elevator problems.

L: 3720 South Las Vegas Boulevard
A: Daniel Libeskind, 2009
FF: The centre utilises a range of eco-friendly features, including FSC certified wood, radiant floor cooling which targets air conditioning to areas being used, skylights for natural illumination and preferential parking for alternative fuel vehicles.

Index